RACE AGAINST TERROR

ALSO BY JAKE TAPPER

Nonfiction
Body Slam: The Jesse Ventura Story
Down & Dirty: The Plot to Steal the Presidency
The Outpost: An Untold Story of American Valor

with Alex Thompson
Original Sin: President Biden's Decline, Its Cover-up, and His Disastrous Choice to Run for Reelection

Fiction
The Hellfire Club
The Devil May Dance
All the Demons Are Here

RACE AGAINST TERROR

CHASING AN AL QAEDA KILLER AT THE DAWN OF THE FOREVER WAR

JAKE TAPPER

ATRIA BOOKS
New York   Amsterdam/Antwerp   London
Toronto   Sydney/Melbourne   New Delhi

An Imprint of Simon & Schuster, LLC
1230 Avenue of the Americas
New York, NY 10020

For more than 100 years, Simon & Schuster has championed authors and the stories they create. By respecting the copyright of an author's intellectual property, you enable Simon & Schuster and the author to continue publishing exceptional books for years to come. We thank you for supporting the author's copyright by purchasing an authorized edition of this book.

No amount of this book may be reproduced or stored in any format, nor may it be uploaded to any website, database, language-learning model, or other repository, retrieval, or artificial intelligence system without express permission. All rights reserved. Inquiries may be directed to Simon & Schuster, 1230 Avenue of the Americas, New York, NY 10020 or permissions@simonandschuster.com.

Copyright © 2025 by The Hellfire Corporation

All rights reserved, including the right to reproduce this book or portions thereof in any form whatsoever. For information, address Atria Books Subsidiary Rights Department, 1230 Avenue of the Americas, New York, NY 10020.

First Atria Books hardcover edition October 2025

ATRIA B O O K S and colophon are trademarks of Simon & Schuster, LLC

Simon & Schuster strongly believes in freedom of expression and stands against censorship in all its forms. For more information, visit BooksBelong.com.

For information about special discounts for bulk purchases, please contact Simon & Schuster Special Sales at 1-866-506-1949 or business@simonandschuster.com.

The Simon & Schuster Speakers Bureau can bring authors to your live event. For more information or to book an event, contact the Simon & Schuster Speakers Bureau at 1-866-248-3049 or visit our website at www.simonspeakers.com.

Interior design by Davina Mock-Maniscalco

Manufactured in the United States of America

1 3 5 7 9 10 8 6 4 2

Library of Congress Control Number

ISBN 978-1-6680-7944-7
ISBN 978-1-6680-7946-1 (ebook)

To Tony Auth;
To James Wright;
To David Carr and Peter Jennings;
To Joan Walsh and Kerry Lauerman;
To Amy Entelis and Virginia Moseley;
To Diane Sawyer, Ted Koppel, and Charlie Gibson;
To Jeff Zucker.

Thank you for the lessons.

Justice, justice shall you pursue.

Deuteronomy 16:20

CHAPTER ONE

THE DETECTIVES

Brooklyn, New York

"I just got this crazy call from Italy," said the man on the other end of the phone.

Dave Bitkower, assistant US attorney for the Eastern District of New York, had just been contacted by the FBI. It was a steamy Brooklyn summer day as Bitkower listened to Joint Terrorism Task Force Supervisor Ari Mahairas describe some wild scenes on a boat in the Mediterranean Sea. Just shy of thirty-six, wiry and intense, Bitkower was the type of attorney built for the extreme pressures of the Eastern District's Violent Crimes and Terrorism Section—a runner, studious, even a former *Jeopardy!* champion. After graduating Harvard Law School, he had decided to serve his country, opting for downtown Brooklyn over a white-shoe law firm across the East River. It was a spartan life with long hours. And although he had a new wife and baby boy at home—a dumpy, unrenovated, third-floor walk-up in Brooklyn Heights—he rarely saw any of the three.

Mahairas explained that the Italian authorities had a man in custody who claimed to be a member of al Qaeda who had killed American soldiers. The man had been detained immediately, in June 2011, for relatively minor infractions and couldn't be held for very long. If they didn't act soon, this potential deadly terrorist would be dispatched to a low-security camp among the general refugee population hoping to emigrate to Europe. And Bitkower and Mahairas knew all too well how easy it was to sneak out of one of these camps and slip into Europe without a trace.

"What's the name?" Bitkower asked.

"Spin Ghul."

Bitkower knew the name. Ten years after the September 11 terrorist attacks, al Qaeda and its affiliates were more active than ever in plotting against Americans, including on US soil. The FBI, CIA, NSA, military, and even assistant US attorneys had to be on top of their game 24/7. Detainees at Gitmo were talking about Spin Ghul. His name had come up in an investigation into terrorism in Africa. Spin Ghul was one of the terrorists the nation's counterterrorism investigators had been trying desperately to locate.

Despite the steady threat of terrorism since 9/11, President Barack Obama, in the third year of his first term, was busy trying to shift the tenor of US foreign policy. Giving a speech in Cairo, Obama had talked of "a new beginning between the United States and Muslims around the world, one based on mutual interest and mutual respect, and one based upon the truth that America and Islam are not exclusive and need not be in competition." This stood in stark contrast to the uneasy reality on the ground—terrorists didn't care about President Obama's desire to reset America's standing in the world. Extremists showed little interest in reconciliation.

If anything, the war on terror, including the ongoing wars in Iraq and Afghanistan, had acted as a tool of recruitment. The new face of terrorism was not extremists coming from abroad, but Americans and green card holders who had become radicalized. In 2009, a Colorado man and two friends had plotted to blow themselves up on three New York City subways, packed during the rush hour. In 2010, an attempt to detonate a car bomb in Times Square was foiled only by chance and the alertness of a souvenir vendor. And earlier in 2011, the Michigan-born Colleen LaRose aka "Jihad Jane" pleaded guilty to terrorism-related charges for plotting to kill a Swedish artist who had drawn an image of the prophet Mohammed.

While law enforcement was supposed to maintain the public face of confidence and composure, the reality was that they, and the American public they protected, often got lucky. Pretty much everyone familiar with these cases admitted as much privately. Bitkower had worked the New York City subway bombing plot and had seen firsthand how close the city had come to disaster. A young man from Queens living in Denver, Najibullah Zazi, and his two friends had planned to blow themselves up on the subway trains as they arrived at the Grand Central and Times Square Stations, potentially taking out hundreds of innocent commuters during rush hour. Law enforcement had known he was planning something and tracked his movements from Colorado to the George Washington Bridge, where he was stopped by Port Authority cops. But somehow Zazi was able to get onto the island of Manhattan and vanish. The only reason no one was hurt was because Zazi panicked and fled back to Colorado before he could do any harm. Bitkower was brought in to help interview Zazi in one of his first jobs running the Violent Crimes and Terrorism Section of the Eastern District.

Bitkower's primary lesson from his experiences prosecuting and investigating terrorists was therefore far from reassuring. The terrorist threat was unrelenting. Determined young zealots came out of nowhere and focused on the softest targets throughout the world. It was impossible to stop all of them. But it was their job to try.

Upon hearing this latest FBI tip, Bitkower immediately grasped the urgency of the situation. If Italian authorities were holding the real Spin

Ghul and ultimately let him go, his intention to commit mass murder would be directed at American and other Western targets. In just the previous few weeks, a suicide bomber on a motorbike had attacked a US consulate vehicle in Peshawar, Pakistan, killing one and wounding ten others; husband and wife suicide bombers had killed ten people at a Kolachi, Pakistan, police station; a bomber with al Qaeda–inspired Boko Haram had killed six in an attack on Nigerian police headquarters; and al Qaeda had announced that Ayman al-Zawahiri would lead al Qaeda, replacing Osama bin Laden, whom Navy SEALs had killed on May 2.

Bitkower walked down to the office of his fellow assistant US attorney Shreve Ariail. Shreve was a tousled-haired, friendly Virginian who had somehow remained buoyant even during what was a terrible year personally: a pipe explosion had destroyed his apartment, a basement walkout on Warren Street near the Brooklyn courthouse, and both his father and father-in-law had died within two months of each other. But Shreve's generosity and diligent work ethic remained infectious.

Bitkower told Shreve about the case. The men knew each other well. They had worked together in Washington, DC, on Obama's Guantánamo Review Task Force, where they were charged with the seemingly impossible task of figuring out what to do with the 240 accused terrorists being kept in extralegal detention.

Now they had another terrorist on their hands. They wondered about the circumstances under which Spin Ghul had been detained, why he would have admitted any wrongdoing. They would need to find that out. Bitkower wasn't surprised that a member of al Qaeda would brag about killing Americans, having worked on a case where an aspiring terrorist, postarrest, kept boasting about his importance to al Qaeda. He couldn't shut up about it, frankly. It was a theme.

Shreve understood right away what was at stake with Spin Ghul. The obstacles they would face just to get him under US authority would be considerable. First, they would have to fly to Italy and hear the suspect's claims about having killed American soldiers, assess his credibility, cut through a ton of bureaucratic red tape, and come up with evidence for a possible crime that happened on some remote battlefield. All the while, the clock would be ticking. If they didn't accomplish this task, and quickly, Spin Ghul would be released, free to plan his next attack of terror on innocent civilians. If they were successful in bringing Spin Ghul in, the job would only get more difficult. Bitkower and Shreve would have to expeditiously build a case tight enough to withstand the toughest New York City court-appointed US defense attorney. They would have to track down clues and evidence that cut across the most dangerous parts of the world, including war zones, and in the darkest corners of the terrorist underworld. They wouldn't be just lawyers shuffling papers, filing motions and appealing to judges and juries. They would have to sleuth. They would have to become counterterrorism detectives.

CHAPTER TWO

WATER

Lampedusa, Italy

In reality, Bitkower and Shreve were already playing catch-up. The countdown to lock up Spin Ghul had truly started days before on the morning of June 24, when Francesco Morgese, an officer with a special Anti-Terrorism and Rapid Response Unit of the Italian police, boarded *The Excelsior*, a commandeered cruise ship en route from Lampedusa Island to Taranto, Italy.

Historically, Lampedusa, one of Italy's southern Pelagie Islands, had been known as a gorgeous, roughly eight-square-mile haven of tourism and fishing. But the once-tranquil destination was becoming the focal point of an unprecedented refugee crisis. Closer to Tripoli than to Rome, Lampedusa had become a lifeline for tens of thousands of people fleeing the turmoil of the Arab Spring.

What had started in 2010 with one oppressed Tunisian street vendor setting himself on fire in protest had sparked revolution throughout North Africa and the Middle East. From Tunisia to Libya to Egypt to Syria to Bahrain, what came to be known as the Arab Spring constituted a series of antigovernment uprisings. Repressive regimes met these revolutionaries with force and slaughter. Among these conflicts was the bloody civil war in Libya, where Muammar Gaddafi, the flamboyant and narcissistic dictator of the country since 1969, was barely clinging to power. His forces had been committing horrific atrocities since February. By June, after just a few short months of chaos, hundreds of people fleeing Libya had drowned in the Mediterranean trying to escape the violence. Those who survived entered a different kind of crisis, as more than ten thousand refugees fleeing Libya and twenty thousand fleeing Tunisia arrived on Lampedusa, quickly overwhelming the small island, population just over six thousand.

Morgese, thirty-nine, had been on the island for just over two weeks. Along with other Green Berets, his task was to provide some kind of security framework for these migrants. He and his fellow soldiers also tried to cheer up the children with sweets and toys. One of the children's favorite pastimes was playing with latex gloves, inflated to look like balloons.

The highlight so far for Morgese, however, had been Angelina Jolie. She had visited a few days before as a United Nations Goodwill Ambassador for refugees, thanking aid workers, hearing the stories of migrants at a refugee holding center, and participating in a ceremony memorializing refugees who had been lost at sea. Morgese had been impressed not

An aerial view of Lampedusa

just by her beauty, but by how genuinely interested she seemed to be in the conditions of the migrants, especially the children. Her emotional reaction, her teary eyes, stayed with him. It was, after all, how he felt as well.

Morgese and his team had been assigned to *The Excelsior*, a twelve-year-old, ten-deck ship capable of holding 2,250 tourists and commuters. On one side of the ship, in giant blue letters, was the name of the shipping company, *Grimaldi Lines*. On the other: *Grandi Navi Veloci* (Big Fast Ships). *The Excelsior* had been repurposed for the migrant crisis, and on board that day were roughly 1,180 migrants, along with forty or so law enforcement officers tasked with preserving order. Families and women were accommodated in a first section of the ship, while unaccompanied men were housed in a second section. They left Lampedusa and were due at their first stop, Taranto harbor—on the inner heel of Italy's "boot"—the next day.

All was proceeding well. Morgese's officers were on the case, and the migrants were behaving in an orderly manner. It was peaceful. A nice cruise in the Mediterranean. No signs of any of the Libyan fighters who Gaddafi threatened would arrive in Europe "like a swarm of locusts or bees."

At around 11 a.m., a short, middle-aged man—from sub-Saharan Africa, Morgese guessed—approached the Italian Green Beret. Morgese looked like an obvious authority figure—muscular, tan, in camouflage combat fatigues with a green beret and a black holster with a gun.

"Water," the man said. Part request, part demand.

Morgese had noticed the man before. He had been isolating himself from the others, pacing nervously along a corridor, reading a liturgical book of some sort. He gave the man a bottle of water and a serious look.

The man was thin and short, maybe five feet six inches tall, with heavy-lidded eyes, nostrils that flared, full lips, and a scraggly beard. He had a scar on his arm, one that Morgese recognized as consistent with a gunshot entry wound. In 1998, during an antidrug operation, Morgese had engaged in a firefight with a suspect whose leg was struck by a round from another officer's Beretta pistol. He was familiar with scars caused by bullets.

Morgese gently grabbed the man's arm and looked at the other side of it, seeing what looked like a larger, scarred-up exit hole.

"What happened?" Morgese asked him. "How did you get that?"

The man looked away, pretending he hadn't heard him.

"What happened?" Morgese asked again.

Nervously, the man began uttering phrases in Arabic and shaking his book.

Morgese told him to calm down and take a seat. He called for Ismail, a Somali interpreter who spoke Arabic and Hausa, a language used in parts of West Africa.

"Why are you so agitated?" Morgese asked, through Ismail. "How did you get those wounds?"

The odd and vaguely threatening little man explained: his name was Ibrahim Adnan Harun. He was Nigerien. He had recently arrived at Lampedusa aboard a boat.

And the scar?

That was from a gunshot. "American soldiers," he said.

"Do you have any other wounds?" Morgese asked. "Where did this happen?"

The man who called himself Ibrahim Adnan Harun motioned for Morgese to follow him through a door to another part of the ship. There he lifted his shirt and turned around, displaying even more bullet scars on his back. Harun and Ismail began conversing in Hausa as Morgese watched. With each sentence Harun uttered, Ismail's face grew more shocked, even horrified.

"What is he saying?" Morgese asked Ismail.

"He says he's not a refugee, he's an al Qaeda fighter," Ismail said. "He fought American soldiers."

Morgese's mind instantly went to the threats Gaddafi would make to export the war in Libya to Europe by sending jihadis there.[1] "Hundreds of Libyans will martyr in Europe," the dictator warned. "I told you it is eye for an eye and tooth for a tooth."

Why was this man confessing to crimes? Perhaps out of pride, or fear, or for lack of ability to keep silent. Regardless, this little man had chosen this moment to come clean, to admit he fired upon American troops. And Harun's story wasn't far-fetched. For years, Gaddafi had been packing his prisons with jihadis, worried they would turn their fury from the West to him. And now, as Gaddafi's regime crumbled, those prisons were being emptied—some intentionally, some by circumstance. Hundreds of guards had left their posts to help control the streets. Others simply fled for fear of reprisals by a population furious after four decades of oppression at the hands of a vicious dictator. It was certainly possible that Harun was one of those escapees.

Other passengers—migrants—began gathering and listening to the conversation. With the help of another officer, Morgese, wary of upsetting the peace, escorted Harun to a private room.

Harun sat down and began talking. He revealed that he had been arrested in Libya in 2005, six years before. He had been in prison up until the moment Libyan police came into his cell, hooded him, and delivered him to a large boat crammed with refugees bound for Lampedusa. But he insisted he was not a refugee and did not belong there among the refugees. He was an al Qaeda fighter, he said proudly, one who had fought against the American military. One who had killed American soldiers.

---

[1] "Jihad" literally means fight, battle, or holy war. In Islam, the greater jihad is the battle within oneself, while lesser jihad is physical war against others. Contemporary Islamist extremists mean it as holy war against nonbelievers, which is how this book uses the term.

Morgese left the room and went to another part of the ship, to the makeshift office of state police officer Dr. Guglielmo Battisti. He brought Battisti up to speed, and they agreed to follow law enforcement protocol. They walked to the room where Harun was sitting and Battisti engaged with him.

"I'm not afraid of you," Harun spat, which Ismail translated. "I'm not afraid of ending up in Guantánamo."

Battisti and Morgese looked at each other, confused.

"I'm an important person!" Harun said. "I was in a prison!"

"Where were you in prison?" Battisti asked.

"In Libya," Harun said.

"Why?"

"Because I was in al Qaeda."

"How did you get out?"

"One night the jailers came to my cell and took me out," Harun said. There was so much chaos in Libya, so many competing strategies, that somehow the insanity of this explanation made sense.

Battisti asked him to formally write, in his own hand, in Arabic, all that he had told them about who he was and where he'd come from, thinking that the process might calm him. The policeman also wanted a clean record, fearing an oral history translated from the several languages being spoken might not be effective evidence. He also wanted to buy precious time.

Harun began, using a ballpoint pen on a blank piece of copy paper, his Arabic handwriting loose: "I, the so called, Adnan Ibrahim Harun Adam."

He revealed his nom de guerre, the only word he wrote using the English alphabet: *Espingol*, or "Spin Ghul." A bastardization of the Pashto for "the White Rose."

In writing, Harun, a.k.a. Spin Ghul, acknowledged being "a member of al Qaeda organization in West Africa." And then came a frantic outline of his background and preposterous demands of the Italian authorities.

"I am demanding to be either handed over to the INTERPOL, or to the International Court of Justice in Scotland, or to call the Embassy of Niger or the Niger Intelligence to do what is appropriate," Spin Ghul wrote. "I didn't voluntarily come to Italy; I was forced to be on the Italian soil in an illegal way. The procedures governing the illegal immigrants do not apply to me because I am not an illegal immigrant. I have been detained for 6 years, from 2005 to 2011.

"I entered Libya with an official passport and an official visa through Jagboub/Katroun land port of entry under the name of ADNAN IBRAHIM HARUN ADAM."

Harun stopped writing. Something clicked inside him, though it was difficult for Morgese to figure out what it was. A bizarre combination of pride and mania seemed to overwhelm him.

"Now I'm done and now I'm getting off," he said.

He stood defiantly. Morgese and Battisti stood too.

"I'm getting off no matter what," Harun said. "I'm jumping off the ship and I will swim back to Libya."

Harun scowled.

"I want to speak to the ambassador from Niger," Harun said. "I want to speak to Ban Ki-moon! I want to speak to President Obama! I'm not a refugee, I'm a fighter. I want to go back to Libya to fight. I will swim back if I need to," he shouted at the officers.

Things escalated quickly. Harun rushed to the exit door, having apparently meant literally that he was intending on jumping ship. But before he could escape, Morgese put himself between Harun and the door, trying to block his exit. Two other Italian soldiers in the room also tried to restrain him. Harun panicked, elbowing the officers and trying to grab a painting off the wall to use as a weapon. He used a handrail on the wall for balance and began kicking the officers working to subdue him.

Harun managed to force his way out of the room. Morgese called for back-up and ultimately applied a special maneuver on Harun, a Krav Maga technique. He pinned the suspect to the deck with control of one arm and both legs, blocking his shoulder blades with a knee and then, keeping his arm in hyperextension, bending one arm to be handcuffed behind his back. Then he cuffed the other arm. Harun continued to fight back, violently.

"Allahu Akbar!" Harun shouted, an Islamic expression praising God as the greatest, one that Islamist terrorists have co-opted to justify religious violence. "Allahu Akbar! Allahu Akbar!" And then, as if his purpose were not already clear: "Osama bin Laden Akbar!" Osama bin Laden is the greatest, he said.

A soldier was dispatched to retrieve the doctor on board, Pellegrini Valentino, to help get Harun under control. Morgese knew that the mood was combustible among the hundreds of refugees on board. He worried that this wild little desperate man might provoke a riot if not contained. Moments later, Valentino arrived with his kit.

"Sedate this man!" Morgese said.

Harun was injected with a sedative and quickly passed out.

Guards then carried Harun to the infirmary, where he was shackled to a bed and monitored. Battisti set up watch shifts. They wouldn't reach port until late the next morning.

Morgese went to the wheelhouse and asked the captain to check their current coordinates. He needed to know precisely which jurisdiction they were in at that moment—Harun had committed assault and resisted arrest. The coordinates dictated that Harun would need to be brought to the public prosecutor's office of the city of Agrigento, in Sicily.

Harun would need to be tried for his disorderly conduct on *The*

Excelsior. But those would be minor violations in Italy, and detention would be relatively short, maybe a month or two. It seemed clear to Morgese that Harun was likely guilty of far worse. For all Morgese knew, this little man was one of the most dangerous terrorists in the world. They would do what they could to make sure he was tried, imprisoned, and put somewhere he couldn't hurt any innocents.

They would need to call the Americans.

CHAPTER THREE

LA MAFIA

Agrigento, Italy

The courtroom had high ceilings and was about the size of a basketball arena, but Dave Bitkower could feel Spin Ghul's intensity from across the room. Shackled and scowling, Spin Ghul sat near Judge Stefano Zammuto surrounded by heavily armed guards, as if he were the head of a drug cartel. A dozen interrogators were arranged at the heavy oak tables behind him. It was September 2011.

The Americans were jet-lagged and a little rough around the edges. Bitkower, Shreve, and others from the US Justice Department and FBI's Joint Terrorism Task Force had flown on the red-eye, coach, from JFK Airport to Rome, then to Palermo, the capital of Sicily. Fifteen hours of travel. Upon landing, they changed into their suits and ties in the airport bathroom and got to work.

At the airport they were met by US Justice Department attaché Bill Nardini, who had worked at the US attorney's office in Connecticut for ten years before being posted in Italy. Nardini was six one, though he seemed even taller somehow. With neatly parted thick brown hair and glasses, he projected the image of an American diplomat from the 1960s. He spoke Italian fluently and was the type of man who would work in the occasional Chaucer quote if you let him. But backing up this erudition was the more important fact that Nardini could work the levers of power in Rome better than most native Italians.

Nardini picked up the Justice Department team in a clunky white passenger van for the two-hour drive south. The van had a manual transmission, which all three men felt as Nardini inexpertly shifted through the hills of Sicily. They would make a quick stop at the Palazzo di Giustizia, the Palermo Justice Building, on their way to the courtroom in Agrigento, Sicily. It was a curious place to begin the process of investigating a man from Saudi Arabia with Nigerien roots who said he had killed Americans in Afghanistan.

Palermo had its own nasty history, of course. As they made their way from the airport to the city center, Shreve knew they were driving on the very road on which the Sicilian mafia had assassinated Judge Giovanni Falcone with a bomb on May 23, 1992. Judge Falcone was famous throughout Italy for his crusade to rid the country of organized crime. For his efforts, the judge was targeted by the Corleonesis—a faction of the Italian mafia—who blew up a tunnel underneath highway A29 with thirteen drums of Semtex and TNT, killing him, his wife, and three police escorts. Then the mobsters celebrated their successful terrorist attack with a champagne toast. Francesco Morgese, the man who would one day apprehend Spin Ghul on *The Excelsior*, was in his first year of university at the time of Falcone's assassination. Morgese was so deeply impacted by the assassination that he decided to become a member of law enforcement and signed up for the Financial Guard, inspired by Falcone's advice to all investigators: *seguite i soldi e troverete la mafia*—follow the money and you will find the mafia.

Much of the criminal justice infrastructure in Italy had been built to go after members of organized crime. The specific courthouse in which they would interview Spin Ghul was adjacent to a prison, the entire building originally constructed for the mass prosecution of mafiosi. The foundation of the building was erected to withstand rockets and explosions. The walls inside were lined on the left and right sides of the room with yellow steel bars so that dozens of prisoners could stand and be tried at the same time. In the cavernous space between, there was room for potentially dozens of attorneys to sit at desks if multiple defendants were tried as, well, a mob.

On their way to the courthouse, Nardini was gushing about how quickly and smoothly the Italian government paved a way for Bitkower and Shreve's visit. Normally, arranging a US law enforcement interview in Italy dictated through an "MLAT" process—a mutual legal assistance treaty in criminal matters—is about as complicated and bureaucratic as its name suggests. The MLAT process is famously so inefficient, it's often likened to sixteenth-century correspondence. Often DOJ officials would just shrug and say, "Don't bother."

It was a system seemingly designed to prevent the effort from even beginning. After Bitkower and Shreve drafted the formal request in Brooklyn, in consultation with Alamdar S. Hamdani at the Justice Department's National Security Division, it went to Nardini, who then got sign-off from a supervisor at the Office of International Affairs of the US Justice Department in Washington, DC. Nardini then submitted his request to interview Spin Ghul to the Italian Ministry of Justice's office of international affairs, which then forwarded it to the Prosecutor General's Office at the Court of Appeals in Palermo, which then filed a motion with the regional Palermo Court of Appeals asking for authorization, which then had to grant the motion and appoint a lower-court judge in the local Agrigento court to provide the requested assistance. Dates then had to be coordinated for the interviews with all involved—the lower-court judge in Agrigento, Bitkower and Shreve, FBI legal attaché in Rome Stew Roberts, the prosecutor in Palermo

Emanuele Ravaglioli, the prison warden, the Italian cops, plus interpreters conversant in Italian, English, and Hausa. And of course due to the nature of the threat they needed police escorts. Theoretically this could have involved *years* of red tape. To get in front of an Italian judge a month after an MLAT request was a miracle that would have impressed the pope.

Nardini and Roberts, the attachés for the Justice Department and the FBI, knew that the Italians weren't being so efficient just to be kind. They wanted Spin Ghul, a terrorist potentially capable of mass murder, out of their custody and off their continent. This wasn't without its difficulties. Europeans were wary of the Americans waging their war on terror. The war in Iraq was widely perceived by European leaders to have been an unnecessary battle built on lies, resulting, by the end of 2011, in more than four thousand Americans killed and more than thirty thousand wounded, with the direct price climbing northward of half a trillion dollars and unfathomably greater costs to the Iraqi people. President Obama was bringing that war to an end by the end of 2011, however, while the war in Afghanistan—perhaps seen as more justifiable because al Qaeda had launched its deadly plot from within its borders—had become a Vietnam-like quagmire, with more than 1,700 Americans killed and more than fifteen thousand wounded by the end of the year. To Europeans in the streets and legislatures, the Bush years were full of American excesses and wanton human rights violations.

In Italy in particular, the case of Abu Omar had been a notorious scandal that tarnished the reputation of the United States. The CIA abducted the imam, whose full name was Hassan Mustafa Osama Nasr, while he was walking in Milan in February 2003. Then he was flown to Cairo from the joint Italian-US air base via Germany and locked up for four years without trial, beaten, and tortured by the government of Egyptian dictator Hosni Mubarak, whose regime Abu Omar had fled. He was released in 2007 after an Italian newspaper published a letter he wrote describing his kidnapping. Italian authorities eventually pursued the Americans and Italians who abducted Abu Omar. In November 2009, the CIA base chief in Milan, twenty-one suspected or known CIA agents, one Air Force colonel, and Italian intelligence agents had been convicted of kidnapping Abu Omar.

The friction hadn't stopped there. In November 2010, WikiLeaks published US government cables revealing candid, sometimes harsh, assessments of European allies as well as information suggesting the US was spying on its own allies. Working with the Americans on the prosecution of a suspected terrorist could be fraught, to say the least. They certainly weren't going to hand over anyone if there was a chance he might end up at Guantánamo Bay.

The courtroom, cavernous and ominous, was sweltering. For security reasons, presumably, the windows didn't open, and the air-conditioning was weak. Beyond the oppressive, stifling interior, the room was tense as the Americans arrived. The first thing Judge Zammuto told them was that Spin Ghul was refusing to come out of his cell.

FBI agent Greg Paciorek was disappointed to hear this news. Paciorek had been serving in Nigeria and had been sent to Italy as part of a "clean team" of agents with limited information about the Spin Ghul case so that preconceived notions about the accused terrorist did not influence their observations. They had all traveled quite far for this proceeding—Paciorek had been in Abuja when Ari Mahairas had phoned—and what Judge Zammuto was telling them was frustrating. But Paciorek wasn't willing to take the judge's word for it.

Some on the team wondered why the Italians weren't just forcibly bringing him into the courtroom.

After consulting with Bitkower, Shreve, and others, Paciorek grabbed their Hausa translator, Mohommed Hassan,[1] a.k.a. Mo, and asked the

---

[1] Not his real last name.

judge if they could talk to Spin Ghul off the record. He granted their request.

Italian guards guided them through the secured rooms and down the halls to his cell.

Spin Ghul was quiet as Paciorek gave him his name.

"I'm with the FBI," he explained, noting that he was part of a team of officials from law enforcement and the US Justice Department. "We've traveled a long way to hear your story, because what we've heard is intriguing and interesting. We would love to have a conversation with you. But we're told you won't come out of your cell."

Spin Ghul said he was willing to talk to them. The issue was that he was refusing to put on shoes to go into court, and the Italians wouldn't let him leave the cell without them on.

Paciorek was stunned. Were the Italians really going to sandbag this whole hearing just because an accused terrorist wanted to be barefoot?

He and Mo went back to their colleagues and explained what Spin Ghul had told them. They asked Nardini to approach the judge and explain that, in this case, it might be better for everyone if wardrobe protocols were disposed of and Spin Ghul was permitted to address the court.

Judge Zammuto ultimately made an exception, and Spin Ghul was escorted, barefoot, out of his cell and brought in to testify.

Paciorek chalked up the Italians' willingness to delay the entire proceeding to the culture of Southern Italy—adhering to strict protocols and norms, akin to a Southern Italian shunning a cappuccino later in the day because it would be improper; milk and espresso should never be mixed after the breakfast hours. As for Spin Ghul, Paciorek concluded that after years of imprisonment by the Libyans, and now the Italians, this was his one small act of asserting some control over his life.

As the proceedings began, Shreve and Bitkower watched from several tables back. Judge Zammuto asked where and when he was born, and Spin Ghul balked at that. He didn't know his birth date, but it was around 1970, and he was born in Mecca while his parents were on pilgrimage. This wasn't enough information for the judge, who wanted the precise location—in which country? In which region?

"He didn't exactly declare which state Mecca is in," the judge said. "If he can declare exactly which, uh, the name of the town and where it is exactly."

"There's only one Mecca and everybody knows it's in Saudi Arabia," Spin Ghul replied through Mo.

While Bitkower and Shreve fretted that an irritated Spin Ghul might soon stop cooperating and telling his story, FBI attaché Roberts found this reaction funny. Spin Ghul was incredulous that Judge Zammuto didn't know where Mecca was.

"I was tricked into coming here," Spin Ghul said. "I don't know the laws of this land.... I don't know if he's a judge. I don't know if all of you are part of some mafia.... I want you to understand that I'm not refusing to answer, I just don't know who you are."

Bitkower and Shreve were keenly aware that American prosecutors were the only ones who could lock Spin Ghul up for killing American soldiers. As one of his very first acts as president, Barack Obama had ordered the closure of the detainee facility at Guantánamo Bay, so shipping Spin Ghul there for a military commission trial seemed no longer an option. This meant the American criminal system of law and justice would have to suffice. Bitkower and Shreve needed to be able to prove in a US courtroom, before an American judge and jury, beyond a reasonable doubt, that Spin Ghul had committed terrorist acts. Any defense attorney of basic competence would be able to rip apart a confession as the mere rantings of someone with psychological problems. Bitkower and Shreve needed a new credible confession and details they could then investigate for physical evidence, such as where he had killed American soldiers and who these soldiers were. Bitkower and Shreve had the burden of proof, and it was indeed a burden. And they couldn't achieve any of it without the mercurial defendant being able to tell his story.

But Shreve had a hunch that Spin Ghul was desperate to speak to the Americans. He asked FBI agent Paciorek to pass up his official badge so that Shreve could show it to Spin Ghul.

Shreve gave Spin Ghul his Justice Department credential and Bitkower's, but it wasn't until Spin Ghul opened the leather wallet with Paciorek's FBI badge that a glint appeared in his eyes, suggesting recognition of those three letters. MLATs, AUSAs, and DOJ attachés meant nothing to him, but the FBI stamp was a shining symbol Spin Ghul recognized. He looked back to the Americans. Suddenly he seemed more willing to talk. *He loves it*, Bitkower thought, watching the previously difficult witness become animated.

Shreve Ariail's and David Bitkower's credentials

This was the first time in years anyone had treated Spin Ghul with any respect or deference. From the moment he'd been arrested by the

Libyans to being shunted onto a refugee boat to all his time in Italian custody, he had been treated like a common criminal. In a perverse way, Spin Ghul held a special reverence for the country that he hated. The Americans quickly decided their best strategy was to treat him with the respect he believed he deserved. Seasoned terrorist interrogators knew it was often easier to get information from a suspect by playing to their ego rather than trying to intimidate them.

"My name is David Bitkower, and with me is Shreve Ariail," he announced to the court, standing, speaking plainly so his words weren't lost in translation. "We are here from the Department of Justice of the United States. And with us are representatives of the Federal Bureau of Investigation in the United States. And we understand that you are saying you were not brought here voluntarily of your own will. But we learned that you were here. And we are very interested to hear what it is you have to say. And that is why we came from the United States, so we could have a chance to talk to you."

This seemed to please Spin Ghul, who looked at Bitkower and the other Americans with a serious expression. Bitkower and Shreve were hopeful that perhaps the presiding judge might notice Spin Ghul's change in behavior and let the Americans interact with Spin Ghul more freely. After all, it was in everyone's best interest for the Americans to get what they needed in order to extradite Spin Ghul. Bitkower and Shreve currently had no evidence of any crime, and their only witness was the man they hoped to convict.

At this point, they didn't even have any way to figure out which battle in Afghanistan he'd claimed to have fought in. If they didn't get him talking, he would likely be able to return to Afghanistan—or anywhere—to kill more Americans.

Spin Ghul became chattier. He gave his full name, the name that he was known by in Afghanistan, Spin Ghul. And his friends, he said, called him Abu Tamim.

"Abu Tamim." Bitkower made a note. Foreign fighters who went to Afghanistan or Pakistan to fight jihad would assume a *kunya*, a specialized wartime alias or nom de guerre, when they joined jihadi groups. Bitkower had spent hours showing photos to cooperating terrorists, and he found that frequently they knew their former fellow fighters only by their kunyas. They knew that it would be essential to get Spin Ghul to reveal any aliases he had used.

Spin Ghul kept talking. He was born Adnan Ibrahim Harun Adam in Saudia Arabia while his parents were on pilgrimage. He was raised in Saudi Arabia, though his parents were initially undocumented, so the nationality assigned to him was his father's, who was from Olléléwa, Niger. He had moved around, from Saudi Arabia to Niger to Pakistan to Libya, where he was imprisoned. He had never owned property and did not complete high school.

Judge Zammuto asked if Spin Ghul could please answer the question "without going around introducing other facts."

Spin Ghul immediately reverted to being defensive. "I don't want any problems," he said. "If you're not pleased with my answers, we can stop and we can take this to a higher power."

Bitkower winced. Judge Zammuto seemed determined to stick to the customary way of doing things. Spin Ghul was getting increasingly aggravated.

The process was also taking three times as long as normal because of translation issues. Bitkower or his team would ask a question in English. The Italian interpreter would translate it for the judge and Spin Ghul's lawyer into Italian. Then Mo would say it in Hausa. Spin Ghul would respond in Hausa, then Mo would translate that back to English for the Americans. The Italian interpreter would translate it from English to Italian for the court. Spin Ghul was told to remain silent until the judge heard the translated response and asked whether Spin Ghul wanted to respond any further. It took forever.

Shreve then read him his Miranda rights.

"This lawyer," Spin Ghul said, motioning toward Shreve. "Is he an American? Are you FBI or CIA or the police?"

"I'm a lawyer with the Department of Justice, in the United States," Shreve said. "I think you had an opportunity to look at our credentials earlier," he added.

"What I want is to be handed over to the Americans," Spin Ghul declared. "I'm not concerned with the Italian lawyers or the Italian judge. I want to be handed over to the Americans, and when we get to America we can discuss as much as we want."

Judge Zammuto began reading from the Italian procedure book—law code, law article, law number—which Spin Ghul seemed to find utterly incomprehensible, as did Bitkower and Shreve.

Spin Ghul grew increasingly angry and volatile as the proceedings dragged on. Finally, he asked to go to the restroom.

"I can't concentrate," Spin Ghul said. "My mind is not all together right now."

"Shit, this is going downhill," Bitkower whispered to Shreve.

They both saw what was happening: Italian bureaucracy was causing Spin Ghul to pull back and shut down.

"Bill," Bitkower said to Nardini. "This is going south. Can you relay to the judge—in a way that doesn't upset him—they need to allow Spin Ghul to talk?"

Their entire case depended upon Spin Ghul opening up and confessing. They would have no shot at extradition if he didn't talk to them.

Thankfully, Nardini worked his magic, and Judge Zammuto took the note. When Spin Ghul returned from his bathroom break, he was essentially handed the microphone and asked to tell his tale.

"What I want to tell you is: I want to give you a history of how I entered into terrorism," he said.

CHAPTER FOUR

JIHAD

Taif City, Saudi Arabia

Spin Ghul's desire for jihad started when he was a child in Saudi Arabia, where his parents had traveled on holy pilgrimage. From his elementary school days, he was determined to become a religious soldier, especially after learning about the Soviet–Afghan War, and how the Islamist holy warriors—the mujahideen—were helping defeat the USSR in the bloody battle.

After the collapse of the USSR in 1991, many mujahideen joined Chechen rebels to fight for independence, Chechnya being a majority-Muslim autonomous republic. The First Chechen War lasted from 1994 until the Chechens recaptured their capital city of Grozny in August 1996, prompting Russia to agree to a ceasefire. Tens of thousands of Russian soldiers, Chechen fighters, and Chechen civilians were killed. In September 1999, the Second Chechen War broke out after four apartment blocks in Russia were bombed, which Russia blamed on separatist militants. Fueled with money and fighters from Arab countries, backed to a much greater extent than the first time around, this war lasted for a full decade and included Vladimir Putin's bloody siege of Grozny.

This was the battle Spin Ghul had wanted to join.

His life had been bleak. The world of peasants, undocumented, essentially indentured servants, was even worse in Saudi Arabia for Blacks.

In 2000, a friend of his, Amran, who knew Spin Ghul liked military magazines, gave him one he'd picked up. The magazine had photographs of airplanes as well as a picture of the Pentagon.

Spin Ghul took the magazine and asked his friend, "Where can we steal an airplane and go hit the Pentagon with it?"

Amran took the magazine back from Spin Ghul. He didn't give his friend an answer. He didn't say yes or no. This wasn't just a random comment, after all. Amran worked for the Saudi government, in an office run by a man named Suleiman.

Suleiman was something of a neighborhood jihadi legend. He'd fought the Soviets in Afghanistan during the 1980s and claimed to know Osama bin Laden. When Spin Ghul met him, Suleiman was still very much involved in jihad, albeit in a different role. Suleiman recruited and sent would-be fighters to sites of jihadi conflict: Bosnia, Chechnya, Afghanistan, and elsewhere. Not that Spin Ghul had to be recruited for jihad. He was already committed to it. The magazine sparked the moment of action and set the plans into motion, but the desire was already there.

Suleiman introduced Spin Ghul to a man named Mahir in the city of Taif, Saudi Arabia. Using his birth name, Adnan Ibrahim Harun Adam, and a Niger passport, Spin Ghul received a visa in Riyadh, and then he and Mahir, a fixer and coordinator, flew together from Jeddah, Saudi Arabia, to Doha, Qatar, then on to Karachi, Pakistan, and finally Quetta.

From Pakistan, they drove a small car across the Afghanistan border. Mahir served as a liaison between Spin Ghul and members of al Qaeda. They didn't talk much on their trip. Spin Ghul didn't talk about his hopes for jihad or his plans until they arrived in Afghanistan and Spin Ghul joined a group of other wannabe jihadis who were hooked up with al Qaeda operatives. Spin Ghul was shuttled to an al Qaeda safe house near Kandahar, Afghanistan, in August 2001, where he and the new recruits awaited their next assignment.

Day-to-day operations were run by three al Qaeda operatives: Abdul Fida al-Yemeni, Usaid al-Yemeni, and Abu Zubair al-Haleidi. At the safe house, jihadis would communicate with operatives out in the field and with informants from throughout the area.

Of the three, Spin Ghul found Abdul Fida al-Yemeni to be the friendliest. Abdul Fida al-Yemeni had been in Afghanistan for a while already, having trained at the notorious al Farouq training camp.

He told Spin Ghul that he'd met "the Sheikh," the legendary Osama bin Laden, and the Sheikh had discussed a plan to attack America using airplanes. A few days later, they were all sitting around the safe house in September 2001 when they heard their friends happily shouting on the radio. They were celebrating, ululating, crying "Allahu Akbar," because al Qaeda operatives had succeeded in hijacking four US commercial airplanes and flying them into the Twin Towers of the World Trade Center and the Pentagon, killing thousands of innocent American civilians. Spin Ghul's friends and fellow jihadis told them on the radio that they would record the news and bring the videotapes to show them the scenes of carnage.

A few days later, they were loaded into a large truck and driven to a training camp a few hours outside Kandahar. It was the last time Spin Ghul saw Abdul Fida al-Yemeni, who would eventually be arrested by Pakistani security forces after September 11, and sent to Guantánamo Bay. It wasn't clear what the plan was for Spin Ghul, though his impression was that he was going to be training in preparation either for American soldiers coming to Afghanistan or for an al Qaeda attack on an

American ship, similar to the attack on the USS *Cole*, a suicide bombing in Yemen in 2000 that had killed seventeen American sailors.

One day, a Toyota truck pulled into the training camp, driven by a man with a limp who was a top al Qaeda official. Other jihadis came and went. Senior al Qaeda operative Abu Faraj al-Libi was there, as was Osama bin Laden's spiritual adviser Khallad al-Kuwaiti, long before either man was captured and sent to the detainee center at Guantánamo Bay. Spin Ghul had difficulty discerning who was with al Qaeda and who were just run-of-the-mill jihadis.

Making these recruits jihadi warriors was, of course, the plan. The truck, Spin Ghul was pleased to discover, was headed for the infamous al Farouq training camp.

Abdul Bara al-Suri was the al Qaeda operative who initiated the training of new recruits, explaining the rules and laws of the camp. Al-Mohajiri, a Yemeni man, supervised their day-to-day training, taught with new zeal because of the September 11 attack on the US. For a month or so, Spin Ghul and his fellow recruits were instructed on how to use weapons, mostly Soviet ones, Kalashnikov rifles and RPGs. They were also trained in small arms and Uzi submachine guns. They learned how to operate what was called a "Pika," a PK light machine gun. They were shown how to use grenades.

Realizing that his new path could quickly lead to death, Spin Ghul approached an al Qaeda leader named Abdul Hadi al-Iraqi and told him that he wanted to leave a *wasiyya*. For most Muslims, a wasiyya is their last will and testament. To Islamist terrorists, it often takes the form of a video message recorded in the event that they are killed, to be shown to their families and offering one last opportunity to preach their zealotry and damn their enemies from beyond the grave. It was the first time Spin Ghul ever recorded a video, and when he finished, Abdul Hadi al-Iraqi gave it to Abu Faraj al-Libi to send to Spin Ghul's family should he become a "martyr."

By the time Spin Ghul began training at al Farouq in the fall of 2001, alumni of this al Qaeda training ground included Mohammed Saddiq Odeh and Mohamed Rashed Daoud al-'Owhali, both convicted in 2001 for assisting in the 1998 bombing of the US embassies in Nairobi, Kenya, and Dar es Salaam, Tanzania; Saeed al-Ghamdi and Ahmed al-Nami, two of the four men who hijacked United Airlines Flight 93, which took off from Newark Airport and crash-landed in Pennsylvania; Wail al-Shehri and Waleed al-Shehri, two of the four men who hijacked American Airlines Flight 11, which took off from Boston's Logan Airport and was flown into the North Tower of the World Trade Center; "American Taliban" John Walker Lindh; and "Australian Taliban" David Hicks.

Recruits began by learning how to integrate into military life. Then they moved to training in mostly Russian-made weapons, available either because they were relics from the war that had ended in 1989 or were more easily trafficked because of proximity—Kalashnikovs, of course, but also AK-74 assault rifles and other variants, self-loading SKS carbines, RPD and RPK light machine guns, and more.

From there, Spin Ghul and his classmates went to a new camp with more seasoned trained fighters. After passing through Kandahar, they were put into a car and driven to a safe house in Kabul, Afghanistan, then to the Malik training camp, where they were taught to use mines and mortars. Then they were taken to a camp called "Maskar 9" or "Camp Nine," where they were instructed in how to take advantage of terrain and geography, as well as how to detonate TNT and other explosives.

At Maskar 9, Abdul Wakil al-Masri was the commander. Indeed, he was the commander of all al Qaeda forces in the north. It was at Camp Nine where Adnan Harun Adam became "Spin Ghul," or "White Rose." A young Pashto cook gave him the name as an homage to a fallen Black fighter, a Somali killed during the war against the Soviets, to whom they'd given the name as an ironic twist on his dark skin. Al Qaeda was not without racism against non-Arab fighters.

Less than a month after the attacks of September 11, 2001, the US began retaliating against al Qaeda and the Taliban-run government of Afghanistan for sheltering them. The American bombing campaign began on October 7, 2001, in Afghanistan, and that's when al Qaeda leaders divided the jihadis in Camp Nine into two groups. Spin Ghul and his group of jihadis moved into a safe house in a small town called Angoor Ada, the site of a border crossing between Pakistan's Waziristan region and Afghanistan.

Abdul Hadi al-Iraqi would run this safe house. Day-to-day operations were run by an al Qaeda operative named Abdul Faras, who also taught military tactics. Another group of jihadis had already reconned the area, found a new US Army base, and attacked it with weapons and explosives. Spin Ghul heard about this battle and was ready to join the fight.

CHAPTER FIVE

RAMSES

Agrigento, Italy

The prosecutors, Bitkower and Shreve, took it all in. As soon as Spin Ghul mentioned al Farouq, they wondered which witnesses currently cooperating with the US could corroborate his story about his time in that training camp, or at the very least verify the details as accurate. To Bitkower, that was like the first cylinder opening a prosecutorial lock—they could already imagine the trial witness list taking shape.

On its face, Spin Ghul's story sounded credible. It was one they had heard time and again from al Qaeda recruits. Starting off radicalized at home and school, finding a jihadi connection, figuring out how to get to Afghanistan with almost no idea of what they would find when they got there. Bitkower and Shreve had talked to and read interviews with so many others who made the same basic journey—from Queens, New York City, or Minneapolis, Minnesota, or Denver, Colorado.

They also made note of one particular name Spin Ghul mentioned during his extended monologue: Abdul Hadi al-Iraqi. When Bitkower and Shreve had first worked together in 2009 on President Obama's

Gitmo task force, one of their main assignments was to figure out how to prosecute Abdul Hadi al-Iraqi in a US court. They knew everything there was to know about "Hadi," as they referred to him, and his role in the post-9/11 al Qaeda hierarchy. He was the commander in charge of al Qaeda's frontline operations, leading the battles, as well as the key conduit between al Qaeda and their allies in the region—the Taliban and other jihadi groups. This was someone high up in the al Qaeda organization but whose name only terrorists and the people who hunted them would know, adding a layer of credibility to Spin Ghul's story.

"When did you first have contact with Amerian forces?" Shreve tried to drill down and get more details about Spin Ghul's assertion that he had killed American troops.

"I'm not sure if it was 2002 or the beginning of 2003," Spin Ghul continued. "Abdul Hadi al-Iraqi returned to Afghanistan."

Shreve asked Spin Ghul to describe a specific battle. Spin Ghul tried to recall a more exact date.

"It was before the visit of Francis the Fifth," the interpreter finally said.

Francis?

Spin mumbled another name. Rams-something.

"Ramses," the interpreter said, unsure of what exactly Spin Ghul was saying. "Ramses the Fifth." The interpreter wondered, "He was an African military leader?"

Bitkower and Shreve looked at each other, crestfallen. Was Spin Ghul insane? Bitkower, the former *Jeopardy!* champion, knew that Ramses the Fifth was an ancient Egyptian pharaoh from more than three thousand years ago. Any competent defense attorney willing to take on the US government and defend this man—and there would be hundreds willing to try—might easily undermine their case by arguing this was someone who wasn't even able to provide reliable information about which century he lived in or whether the pharaohs still ruled.

Spin Ghul had been talking for hours, and while he did, Bitkower,

Shreve, and their team had been gathering information, details that could be verified and proved. But just as they were beginning to draft the indictment in their heads, Spin Ghul's mention of a three-thousand-year-old Egyptian pharaoh had thrown everything into doubt. Even if Spin Ghul had done what he said, the man's insanity might make their task of trying him in US criminal court impossible.

"Who led the attack?" Shreve asked, soldiering on.

"Hamza al-Urduni was our leader," Spin Ghul said. "We walked on, on foot when we got out of Waziristan until we reached Angoor Ada. We weren't the first ones to reach that area. There were other groups who arrived there before we did. There were brothers who got there before us and threw missiles."

A group of Uzbeks had wanted to attack the gates of local Afghan forces who were working alongside the Americans. Captain Hamza ordered the recruits to head toward the vicinity of the American forces so that if the US decided to help the Afghans, Spin Ghul's group of jihadis could ambush them.

Spin Ghul, armed with a Kalashnikov, a video camera, and an antitank mine, went to kill the Americans. They fired four Katyusha rockets at the American base. Spin Ghul and an Australian jihadi worked the controls and calibrations while Hamza al-Urduni held the shoulder mount and commanded the operations. Another group behind them had a Soviet surface-to-air missile called a SAM-7. After launching their attack, they all headed back to Angoor Ada. They learned from locals that of the four rockets, two landed outside the US base, one hit an Army vehicle, and the fourth hit the building where many soldiers had taken cover. An American soldier was killed, they were told.

Spin Ghul described a few skirmishes like this before getting to the main attack.

It was dawn of a Friday morning, still dark out. A Pakistani jihadi, Abu Walid, had joined his group. "I was holding an RPG, but Hamza al-Urduni told me to give him my RPG, and he gave me his Kalashnikov," Spin Ghul recalled. He had, frankly, been struggling to carry the RPG and the rockets on his back over the mountainous landscape with his slender five-foot-six frame.

In addition to his Kalashnikov, Spin Ghul carried eight grenades and a Quran.

"The sun was about to come up," Spin Ghul recalled. "We were south of the base where the Americans were located. We heard helicopters." Spin Ghul decided to bury their weapons, hiding them so that local Afghans wouldn't see the weapons and possibly give him away. The jihadis usually waited until nightfall and the time of Maghrib, the evening prayer, to strike.

Spin Ghul turned on his radio and heard their leader, Hamza al-Urduni, speaking in Pashto. Hamza was trailing far behind them.

"Hurry up," Spin Ghul told him. "Bring us some food."

One of his fellow jihadis got onto the radio and started goofing around, saying, "Explosive! Explosive!" in English.

Spin turned down the volume of his radio, sat down, and began reading his Quran.

His companions complained about being hungry and thirsty. They hadn't brought any water.

He heard helicopters and saw a Chinook followed by an Apache. The Katyusha launcher he would need to take down the helicopters was with Hamza, but Spin Ghul decided to try anyway. "I told the Pakistanis to get their equipment ready, and we took out one missile," he said. They struggled to figure out a way to make it work.

"Be careful!" Abu Walid said. "One of the helicopters is coming straight toward us!"

"Should we get under the bushes?" Spin Ghul asked.

They were about to hide when the Apache buzzed over, but the Americans didn't see them. "The bird wasn't low enough and was traveling at a very high speed," Spin Ghul said. "He just whizzed by us." But then he did a loop and "came around us to the left of us, now he was going slower."

Spin Ghul turned to the Pakistanis. "Which one of you has the bullets that can penetrate metal?"

The second Pakistani raised his hand; "I gave him the magazine that was in the Kalashnikov, and he gave me the one that penetrated metal."

"What do you want to do?" his fellow jihadi asked.

"I'm going to shoot at the Apache," Spin Ghul said.

The group thought he was crazy for trying to shoot at a military helicopter with a Kalashnikov. It wasn't going to make any impact other than expose their position.

But Spin Ghul had remembered an old Iraqi from training who recalled firing a rifle at an Apache, forcing the helicopter to make an emergency landing on a farm.

"Everything comes from God," Spin Ghul said, repeating one of the central tenets of the Quran. "I'm going to fire. You can take cover elsewhere. And if it doesn't work, you can go back to the safe house."

He fired, but the Apache crew didn't seem to notice.

"God said if you're thankful, I will reward you more!" Spin Ghul said.

He heard vehicles and saw two US soldiers coming, searching for them stealthily. "After they had a chance to see our position, they went back to their vehicles." Spin Ghul stood and peeked at the soldiers, spotting one of them with his weapon at the ready.

Spin Ghul hatched a plan to outflank the Americans and surprise them from behind. It was a difficult hike, the terrain rocky, and the threat from the Americans real. Then one of the Americans spotted them and began to fire. They took cover, but Spin Ghul struggled to come up with the words to warn Abu Walid, who spoke only Urdu and not Arabic. Abu Walid was hit on his right hand and his right thigh.

The combatants were face-to-face. "The Americans were directly in front of us and we were . . . under the rocks, at a lower position than them," Spin Ghul said. "I had a direct shot, so I opened my Kalashnikov and started firing at them."

Kalashnikovs, AK-47s, are the most used shoulder weapon in the world. Easy to load, easy to fire, and durable, they're manufactured in many countries and have likely been used to kill more people globally than any other weapon. Spin Ghul fired over and over and over.

"I started shooting at them and yelling, 'Allahu al-Akbar! Allahu al-Akbar!'" he later recalled. The Americans were maybe thirty feet away and ducked for cover as he started throwing grenade after grenade at them. Some American troops remained on the ground; he wasn't sure if they had been killed. "There was a Black individual among them—he was a very large individual. I don't know whether or not he was injured or what, but I heard him yelling out to his friends."

Another American soldier came to help him. Spin Ghul took a grenade and "threw it directly at them, and it blew up in between them." Both must have been wounded. Suddenly two other US soldiers had crawled up to them, and they threw grenades at the jihadis. An American was firing his gun and hit Spin Ghul's arm. Shrapnel embedded itself into his torso and head.

He moved closer to Abu Walid, who he now realized was seriously wounded. "The skin and muscle on his foot had separated from the bone." He noticed he also had a large arm wound. "When I tried to move his body, his leg and foot were moving in opposite directions." Abu Walid was nonresponsive. His pupils had become eerily small. He wasn't breathing.

Spin Ghul left Abu Walid behind and crawled to safety as he watched three Apaches flying overhead.

Prepared to cause as much death as he could even if it cost him his own life, Spin Ghul unpinned a grenade, but no one approached him. Hours passed. The time for evening prayers passed.

He eventually tied up the grenade with a piece of cloth and limped back to Waziristan.

Bitkower, Shreve, and the prosecutors had dinner on the water overlooking the Mediterranean Sea, in a dumpy little seafood restaurant with amazing food. Lunch had been in the Italian prison cafeteria, which featured fresh handmade pasta, and was surprisingly delicious, but this was otherworldly—fresh fish, baby octopus, bottles of Nero d'Avola.

They discussed the case. There was often a fine line between zealotry and insanity, and those who volunteered to conduct suicide attacks in the name of a twisted version of Islam were often quick to speed past that line. Spin Ghul's arrogance, even hubris, were one thing, but his reference to "Ramses the Fifth" was going to send off alarms if they tried to have him extradited to New York City.

Despite these reservations, Bitkower and Shreve couldn't shake the bone-chilling credibility of Spin Ghul's story, which included names and information only a jihadi who had traveled to Afghanistan would know. The intensity of the detail seemed impossible to concoct; to Bitkower, it had the feeling of a day Spin Ghul had relived a thousand times—recalling each detail of the terrain, each weapon fired, each encounter with the Americans. The prosecutors and the FBI would now have to figure out which US base Spin Ghul attacked and which American soldiers he'd killed, then amass actual physical proof against him. It was entirely possible they were on a fool's errand, that Spin Ghul was a fabulist. Still, they had to try to gather the evidence and test to see if any of it was factual. If it was, they would need to build the case on the slim chance that they could lock him up. And they had a small window to conduct this investigation—the Italian charges against Spin Ghul were minor, and it was likely he'd be moved from the magistrate's control in the next few months. Bitkower and Shreve had to find corroboration, and now.

CHAPTER SIX

I WANT TO SEE SOME COUNTRY

Antlers, Oklahoma

In one of the cruel ironies of being a directionless young man in America, Jerod Dennis of Antlers, Oklahoma, was encouraged to join the Army to *save* his life.

Jerod grew up on the Choctaw Nation Reservation, the heritage from his dad's side; Dad and Gramma Inez taught the family about togetherness and community. But the divorce between Jerod's parents, Jane and Jerry, had been ugly and difficult for everyone, including Jerod's little brother Renley and sister Jillian. It hit Jerod perhaps hardest of all. The funny little boy with the thick twang—a finalist in the Pee-Wee Spelling Bee at Brantly Elementary School in Antlers, who loved going to the swimming hole or making the four-mile walk to fish in Boggy Creek—started acting out.

He'd always been the class clown. His half-sister Sheila, fifteen years older, had spent time with him when he was an infant and adored him ever since, and she happened to be training as a teacher when she observed his kindergarten class. He got in trouble all the time, but Sheila knew that he was just trying to be a kid. By tenth grade, his discipline problems grew worse. Drinking, smoking pot, missing curfew, skipping school, crashing cars, and failing a drug test for varsity tennis. The goofy kid who had been so full of promise seemed to be on a short path to nowhere.

Part of Jerod's rebellion was against his mother, who had full custody and was stricter than his father. One day, after months of listening to Jerod's threats to go live with his dad, Jane gave in and decided to let him go. Her decision was a bit of tough love but turned out to be not so tough; Jerry lived with Jerod's grandmother, a quarter of a mile away.

"If you work hard and keep your grades up, we'll have a lot of fun," Jerry told his oldest son. "If not, it won't be so much fun."

It wasn't so much fun.

Jerod's behavior got worse. It drove ninety-year-old Gramma Inez crazy. She was always trying to lay down the law, and he was always skipping over it. She would buy him new clothes to replace his shirts that had cigarette burns and his Wranglers with holes in the crotch, but he continued to wear his old grubby gear anyway. It wasn't that her grandson was mean or cruel—he was lovable and funny—but he seemed completely unserious.

The only glimmer of ambition Jerod showed was during his junior year when he talked to a recruiter about joining the Army. This terrified both his parents. Jerry had served in 1968 with the First Infantry in Vietnam, at the base camp in Lai Khê, about thirty miles north of Saigon. He never talked about the war and worked hard to forget his experiences in combat. Still, his service had made an impression on his oldest son, and it wasn't hard for the recruiter to convince Jerod to come to Oklahoma City to take the Army standardized test—the ASVAB—and get a physical. Seeing few alternatives for his son, Jerry reluctantly signed the form to let the seventeen-year-old make the trip.

"I think I'm going to join," Jerod said, calling from Oklahoma City.

"You got plenty of time," his dad advised. "Why don't you come home first and talk to your mom and then you can make your decision?"

Jerod seemed to agree with his dad, but an hour later he called back and told him he'd done well on the ASVAB and that he'd joined right then and there, which he was allowed to do because his dad had already signed the form.

"I just want to see some country," he told his little brother Renley, meaning that he hoped to see the world.

Jerod was thrilled and spent the rest of junior year talking about boot camp, clowning around with his friends, and getting by. Classmates called him "Funky White Boy" after a memorable dance routine at a party.

Soon after the start of Jerod's senior year, in the fall of 2001, al Qaeda terrorists struck the World Trade Center Twin Towers and the Pentagon. Jerod tried to make a joke out of it—"Wouldn't you just know it? I signed up for the Army, and now they're going to send me to war," he quipped to his English teacher, Martha Smith.

When he got home that day, his father was waiting.

"You're gonna see some country now," he said.

As the year went on, Jerod skipped school for days at a time. Two weeks before graduation, his high school principal came to visit Jane in her classroom at the local elementary school.

"Jerod's not going to graduate," he told her.

Initially Jane hadn't liked the idea of Jerod joining the Army. She worried about her baby boy, but she'd since come around. He needed a wake-up call. He needed the discipline. He needed to get away from all these bad habits and temptations. If he stayed in Antlers, she feared, he would dive deeper into the numbing emptiness of narcotics. Addiction, particularly alcoholism, was not new to her family. Jane had lost loved ones to the bottle and was terrified her son would suffer a similar fate. At this point, the Army seemed his only possible lifeline, and to report to training camp, Jerod would need his diploma.

Jane knew her unfocused, often slothful son wouldn't be willing to repeat twelfth grade. He'd already been voted class clown in the yearbook, and it was highly unlikely he was going to return to Antlers High next year and do it all over again. She immediately began reaching out to her son's teachers. Was there anything he could do to get his grades back up? Any projects he could complete? All he needed was to pass, to graduate. The biggest problem he had was a research paper he owed Ms. Smith for English class. She agreed to give him some extra work, but he had to write the paper he owed her.

Ms. Smith thought the problem was bigger than just another kid who smoked too much pot and skipped class. Jerod, she thought, was *trying* to flunk English. Purposefully failing so the Army wouldn't take him and he wouldn't have to go to war.

As luck would have it, Ms. Smith needed some yardwork done, and when Jerod finished, he started talking about wanting to be an Army Ranger. She saw the hope and fire in his eyes. He'd made an about-face, she assessed. She knew he was asking for help without explicitly asking for it.

"You're my boy," she said. "We'll make sure we get you out of here."

In May 2002, Jerod graduated. Weeks later, he headed to basic training at Fort Benning, in Georgia.

As soon as they got off the bus, after being issued uniforms and filling out paperwork, the new recruits split up into platoons and were taught formation procedures, with extra push-ups and leg lifts inflicted whenever there were misunderstandings, all while sweating under the hot summer Georgia sun. Woken up before sunrise, Jerod trained all day and had little time for food or sleep. It was competitive and intense. It was also one of the most structured environments Jerod had ever experienced in his life.

His training consisted of about four months of instruction in combat skills, weaponry, and marksmanship. The course was designed to break down and destroy the parts of Jerod that led him to sneak out of class through a window or blow off a class project so he could smoke a joint and shoot pool. He was instructed in concepts of selflessness and duty, loyalty, and integrity. His individual self was shaved away like his pre-Army mullet, the notion of team embedded in its stead.

Jerod after boot camp with sister Jillian and brother Renley
COURTESY OF THE DENNIS FAMILY

In October 2002, Jane packed up her white Chevy van and drove with Renley and Jill the 750 miles from Antlers to watch her son graduate from basic training at Fort Benning. Jerry had wanted to make the trip but was in Louisiana working on an oil rig and couldn't get away.

Originally built on the site of a former Columbus plantation near the Alabama border, Fort Benning is now 182,000 acres, has more than sixty buildings, and supports more than thirty thousand soldiers and another thirty thousand family members and civilian staff. Jane arrived at this sprawling base to find thousands of young men in the same clothes with identical haircuts, marching in lines and formations. She didn't even know the barracks her oldest boy had been assigned to, so she drove around aimlessly, ultimately stopping at a random building to call her son. She got out of her car and began walking to a pay phone.

"Hey, Mama!" she heard. "Hey, Mama!"

Jane looked up at the barracks she'd parked in front of. Lo and behold, there was Jerod, tall, muscular, joyous. He used to have some of the worst posture in Oklahoma, but there he stood, ramrod straight like a flagpole.

"Your hair!" she commented on his crew cut.

"The guys called me 'Joe Dirt' when I arrived at Basic," he reported, referring to the 2001 cult classic starring David Spade, "account of my mullet."

They drove to the hotel where his mom and siblings were staying for the weekend. He would almost always beat Renley in wrestling, but before he left for Basic his little brother was getting broader and had been able to pin him down a couple times.

"Wanna wrestle?" he asked Renley in the hotel room.

"Heck yeah I do," said Renley, who quickly realized his mistake.

Jillian, twelve, couldn't believe her big brother's transformation. *He'd put on maybe forty pounds of muscle*, she thought. She also liked the way he talked to their mom now—with love and respect.

Jerod was full of stories about training camp. How he'd built up his newly muscled body, his dedication to the routines of the Army, to being a good soldier. He was proud of himself. His voice sounded deeper, too.

Jerod rode home with his mom and siblings and enjoyed a few weeks back in Antlers. His parents were very proud. When it was time to say goodbye, he hugged his mom, told her he loved her, and promised to call as soon as he could. Jane was devastated to see him go. There were no plans yet for Jerod to be deployed, but it was 2002, the US was at war in

Afghanistan, and there was talk of another war in Iraq, too. She had no idea when she would see him again.

"I love you so much," she told her son. "Please take care of yourself and call as soon as you can. And write me!"

"I will, Mom," he said.

"And you be careful on your trip," she said. Jerod would be driving to Fort Bragg, his next stop, and his family reminded him to keep his tank full, because that child was forever running out of gas.

At Fort Bragg, Jerod immediately won over his team leader, Specialist Jonathan Ray, twenty-two. The nineteen-year-old Oklahoman had been one of Ray's best, if not his best, soldiers, shockingly eager to volunteer for even the most tedious duty, from counting ammo cartridges on the range to running back to get the rest of them hot chow. He was giddy to help out.

Not that his transition from high school waste case to exemplary soldier was entirely seamless. At one point, Jerod approached his team leader sheepishly.

"Specialist Ray, I fucked up," he said.

"What'd you do?"

"I'm gonna piss hot," Jerod said, meaning he would test positive for drugs on his next urinalysis. "Specialist Ray, I'm so sorry." There was a good chance this would mean Jerod would be kicked out of the Army, or at least not permitted to deploy. "I want to stay. I want to help out."

Jerod had quickly earned a place in the hearts of his squad, so Ray went to his squad leader, Staff Sergeant Michael Hodge, and argued that the Army would be better off with Jerod Dennis, despite his fuckup.

"I don't need a man down," Ray added. They were not exactly heading to the action at top preparation; many of these new kids were so green they'd been out to the range for training only a handful of times.

When Jerod's failed urinalysis results came to First Sergeant Brian Severino, he notified Captain Scott Trahan and began the paperwork for a disciplinary procedure. The battalion commander, Lieutenant Colonel Richard Clarke, found Jerod guilty of drug use and asked everyone in the chain of command for a recommendation for punishment. Everyone in the chain recommended maximum punishment, including extra duty and docking his pay. Some wanted him kicked out of the Army altogether.

Severino objected to that.

"PFC Dennis is new to the Army and, more importantly, to my company," he told Clarke. "I don't think you should chapter him out." He thought of new soldiers as a lump of clay for the Army to sculpt. He also believed that no one is more loyal than a soldier who is given a second chance.

"Let me work with him," Severino asked Clarke. "I can make Dennis a good soldier."

Clarke ultimately agreed but made it clear that if Jerod messed up again, it was on Severino.

He'd have to earn their trust back, Ray told Jerod, but the private was already eager to pull the shittiest detail with nary a complaint, so Ray was confident that Jerod would make it through.

Jerod Dennis called his mother.

Not to tell her about how he almost got kicked out of the Army, but to let her know when he found out where they were all headed: Afghanistan.

His mom was relieved. *Thank God it wasn't Iraq. Not much seemed to be going on in Afghanistan*, she thought.

Periodically over the next few months, Jerod would write his mother by hand. It was still a common practice in the military, even in the twenty-first century with the advent of email and satellite phones, given the lack of easy access to high tech in low posts.

Dear Momma,

   Hey what's up? Well I arrived in Kandahar yesterday. There are about 10 trees that I have seen and the rest is sand and mountains. But I am OK and everything is just fine. Something really cool is going on tonight. Take a guess. Oh come on you can guess. Well I will tell you. The Outback Steakhouse is flying into Kandahar to cook steaks for all of the new soldiers getting here. . . . I'm going to take my time and enjoy it because that's it for a while. Well I gotta go to a shooting range for target practice will right more later. . . . We are leaving Tuesday to go FOB Salerno which is where we will be for mostly the remainder of the time. I saw a couple locals yesterday and they look just like you see them on TV. Some of them can speak English really well. It is pretty sad when you see them digging through the trash and seeing them overwhelmed with joy when they find old dirty shoes and anything they can salvage. It will make you realize how lucky you are. . . . Just so you know I am not all that far away from home just like 7,500 miles. Well I guess I am going to go I love you and will write again.

Jerod Dennis

CHAPTER SEVEN

THE SLAYERS

Kandahar Province, Afghanistan

Scarcely three months after graduation, Jerod and the other guys in the group they had dubbed "the Slayers"—3rd Platoon, B Company, 3rd Battalion, 504th Parachute Infantry Regiment, 82nd Airborne—were humping over the precipitous terrain of the Adi Ghar Mountains in eastern Kandahar Province, Afghanistan. They were clearing caves in search of insurgents. Their mission was called "Operation Mongoose."

The Slayers' current deployment was spurred when US Special Forces attempted a raid on a compound near the town of Spin Boldak. After the ensuing firefight, Special Forces captured one of the insurgents, who, when questioned, told them that dozens of his fellow fighters were hiding in mountain caves. Apaches had been called to support the operation. After those birds were shot at, the local brass called in more birds and hundreds of troops as they battled the hidden enemy forces at the end of January 2003.

Most of those troops came from the 82nd Airborne, whose mandate it was to deploy anywhere in the world in eighteen hours or less.

Jerod and the rest of the Slayers arrived in January 2003 and had moved throughout the region to various trouble spots. Now they were charged with hunting for Hizb-e-Islami Gulbuddin fighters hiding in caves and crevasses.

Jerod and the Slayers knew next to nothing about Hizb-e-Islami Gulbuddin. Known by the Army as "HIG," the insurgent group had roots that dated back to a former Afghan prime minister in 1976, before most of the Slayers had been born. HIG was affiliated, however loosely, with al Qaeda, and therefore a threat to the US and the new Afghan government the US was trying to help form.

After the US began its counteroffensive, the Taliban government began crumbling in November 2001, retreating to Kandahar Province in the southeast. Taliban troops in Kandahar were pushed back farther the next month, during the same time that the US pursued Osama bin Laden and al Qaeda in the east into the caves of Tora Bora. Bin Laden escaped, but even without his presence, the insurgency began metastasizing, with Islamist fighters coming from Pakistan, often hiding in the mountains.

The Slayers flew to Kandahar Airfield, then loaded into Chinook helicopters squad by squad. Many were under the impression their mission was supposed to last a day or two, after which they'd be picked up by a Chinook on top of a mountain and shuttled back to Kandahar. For whatever reason—a storm that blew through and damaged helicopter blades or continued fears of insurgents in the area—they never got off those mountains and into the action.

By the time they'd arrived in the Adi Ghar Mountains in Kandahar, the fighting was over, but the backbreaking, tedious work was not. Jerod's team—the 3rd Platoon—scoured the mountains to make sure the caves were empty. They always were.

They'd been dropped into the mountains loaded with every piece of gear they had, making their mission humping the terrain even more miserable. This was 3rd Platoon's first big mission, and each man had been ordered to carry more than one hundred pounds on his back, full MOLLE ruck with assault pack, Skedco rescue gear, AT4 rockets, and OE-254 antennas.

A bunch of the Slayers, including Specialist Dwayne McKnight, twenty, from Orange County, California, couldn't even lift their heads fully upright—their helmets would hit the top of their assault packs, tied to the tack of their rucks. One cave was so tight that McKnight had to take off his body armor and put down his rifle to get inside. As usual, it was empty.

It seemed like a tremendous expenditure of energy and effort for nothing. Beyond their mission, few seemed to have a firm grasp of what the rest of their company was doing, let alone the battalion to which they'd been attached. An operation some assumed would last two days turned to three, then into a week. The Slayers were spent, running out of MREs, short on water. They were authorized twelve bottles per man per day, but given the weight they were carrying and the steepness of the ridges, they needed more than that. First Sergeant Brian Severino requested a daily resupply. Even Captain Scott Trahan had to get on the horn more than once to demand more food, rations, water.

As the Slayers' medic, Private First Class David "Doc" Simmons offered morale boosts and advice. The longer they were stuck clearing caves in the mountains, the more the men of 3rd Platoon would check in with him, not only for the wear and tear on the body, but also on their spirit. For every member of the platoon, Simmons memorized his blood type, allergies, family details, hometown, and the last four digits of his Social Security number so he could easily pull his medical records. For kicks, Lieutenant Drew Nathan would quiz him every now and then, marveling at how well he knew each one of them. Simmons was a devout Christian who had pinned to his medic bag an illustration of a resurrected Jesus tending to one of the Romans who'd helped kill him. It was how Simmons viewed his job as a medic—he was there to administer aid to all God's children. Regardless of their faith or their government, he would be there.

Jerod was one of dozens who took Doc Simmons up on the offer to clean their ears from all the wax, sand, dirt, and silt that had accumulated in a few short weeks. What Doc Simmons removed from his ear looked like a rock of crack, Jerod quipped.

Sometimes the whole mission, Operation Mongoose, seemed like a joke. As if it were an exercise back at Fort Bragg—an endurance test to see how long they could survive a drill of futility and stamina, with the possibility of a lurking enemy to keep them on their toes. Thankfully, they had one another to get through it. They embraced the suck together, each man encouraging the others that they could make it, they would make it, they would achieve their mission together.

To the Slayers' team leader, Specialist Ray, this operation was just another opportunity for Jerod to demonstrate his incredible work ethic. Jerod spotted a small hole on the side of a mountain and volunteered to climb up and clear it.

"I can get up there," he promised.

Specialist Ray and 2nd Squad messaged Trahan, who told them to check it out. Jerod took off his gear and climbed up the mountain, some of his squad mates rolling their eyes. He squirmed into the passage, and inside lay a massive cave complex. He called for others to join him. It was huge. Standard operating procedure was to have a soldier remain at each turn so no one would get lost. The cave path was so long, it took the Slayers two and a half squads—more than twenty soldiers—to find its end. There were a couple of AKs and some ammo in there, too.

Classic Jerod, Specialist Ray thought. He worked so hard. He wasn't one to march or stand in formation. He didn't have the shiniest boots; you might not put him on a recruiting poster. But he was a worker. He wanted to get out into the field and be a soldier.

Not long after their stint in Operation Mongoose, the Slayers were moved up to Firebase Shkin. The distance between the base in Afghanistan and Antlers, Oklahoma, was nearly eight thousand miles, but Jerod's new home might as well have been in a different solar system. Across the border from Angoor Ada, Pakistan, a checkpoint in the Waziristan hills, Firebase Shkin was primitive, and the mission was simple. The thirty or so Slayers were assigned to conduct periodic checks of the porous border, made up of steep and rugged mountains through which hundreds of al Qaeda fighters constantly traveled. On any given day, there were up to a hundred servicemembers there, including special ops and CIA. The base sat high up on a plateau on the edge of a mountain range, with a series of dirt roads the US had named after cars—Route Chevy, Route Corvette, and so on. The closest major US base was FOB Salerno, a forty-five-minute helicopter ride away.

The outpost was small. You could probably throw a football from one end of Firebase Shkin to the other. A near-perfect square with guard towers at the corners, the base was surrounded by triple-strand concertina wire and HESCO walls made of canvas, sand, and rocks. Mud huts, pouring rain, piss tubes, one shitter, and a fifty-five-gallon drum where you had to burn it all later. A well and a pump to ensure water for showers and laundry; the small mess hall with a few tables abutted by more picnic tables outside. Breakfast was powdered, brownish-yellow eggs, lunch was a cold meat-and-cheese sandwich or an MRE, and dinner was often a heat-and-serve MRE. Jerod and the other young grunts were thrown into spartan trappings that reminded them of the Alamo. There were flies all over the food and everywhere else, probably because the shitters was so close.

Sometimes the guys would rather starve. Sometimes they chewed tobacco just to curb the hunger.

(Left to right) Andy Kent, Chad Cropo, Victor Belcastro, Daniel Tatro
PHOTO COURTESY OF DWAYNE MCKNIGHT

When they arrived in Afghanistan, it was winter, below freezing at night and windy. A bitter, brutal cold. By the time they got to Shkin, temperatures were easing, at least during the day—but the altitude made Firebase Shkin another matter. Captain Trahan made sure they all got briefed ahead of time about the conditions on the ground, but life at Firebase Shkin had to be lived to be truly understood. To reach a destination three miles away, soldiers sometimes traversed three thousand vertical feet on mostly unpaved roads.

Of course, there were worse threats than the weather. Before the Slayers arrived, in December 2002, about a dozen 82nd Airborne paratroopers with Task Force Panther had been on a nighttime patrol when a team of insurgents ambushed them. Sergeant Steven Checo, the child of Dominican immigrants born in Queens, New York, was hit by enemy gunfire. He died while being operated on in a field hospital.

The enemy attacks increased at the end of 2002 and Task Force Panther was replaced by the Blue Devils (3rd Battalion, 504th Parachute Infantry Regiment) and, soon enough after that, Task Force Devil, which included the Slayers. Three or four times a week, rockets were fired at Firebase Shkin. Luckily, the enemy's aim and technology were both lacking, but there were plenty of close calls.

A routine developed: Insurgents would fire rockets at Firebase Shkin, and 3rd Platoon would return fire and alert Captain Trahan to call in air strikes. Soon a patrol would head out to find and examine the fallen rockets and determine where they'd been launched from. While the risk that they were walking into an ambush was always real, typically the insurgents had fled back to Pakistan, where the Americans weren't allowed to go.

Soon, a large part of the firebase's mission became self-defense. Their very presence attracted bullets, grenades, rockets, and artillery. They'd run missions into nearby villages such as Gharbi Mangretay to search for the enemy, night and day patrols both mounted and dismounted, reconnaissance operations, and ambush patrols.

To many of the grunts, their presence didn't make much sense. "Jesus Christ, we're just sitting here waiting to get killed," as Specialist Eddie Camacho from the Bronx put it.

Some soldiers became resigned to the constant danger. They tried to adapt to the fear by adopting a mentality of considering themselves already dead so it wasn't a matter of if but of when. Lieutenant Nathan, at least, saw it as a helpful adjustment, a way to eliminate any second guessing or hesitations that could ultimately prove fatal.

When the guys from 3rd Platoon weren't returning fire or going on god-awful weeklong missions to see where in the mountains the fire had been coming from hours before, they would play spades in a mud hut, recite lines from *Goodfellas*, goof on each other, and just shoot the shit—Camacho, Dwayne McKnight, Jerod Dennis, and the rest of the guys.

Everybody longed for home. There was nothing to do. Hours and hours of boredom, interrupted by insurgents trying to kill them. This was the worst fucking place any of them had ever been, and they couldn't wait to leave. They would talk about what they would do when they got back home or anywhere with traffic lights—drink, chase girls, eat a burger, play pool. Jerod Dennis was nineteen now; he said he just wanted to go back to Antlers and hug his mom.

CHAPTER EIGHT

I'M SCARED, TOO

Firebase Shkin

Jerod might have had a new physique and level of discipline, but he was still the class clown. Guard duty could be mind-numbingly boring, but he could always be called on for entertainment. A big favorite was "Roy D. Mercer," a character Jerod borrowed from two Tulsa radio DJs who would pretend to be belligerent rednecks, make prank calls, and challenge folks to fights.

One night Jerod came off guard duty with Sergeant Roger Lonergan, who grew quickly irritated with Jerod's struggles lighting the junky propane heater.

"Give me that before you do something stupid," Lonergan said, pushing Jerod aside and trying to ignite the heater himself, which resulted in a propane-fueled plume of fire igniting.

Thankfully he wasn't seriously hurt, but man, did the other guys have a laugh over that. Jerod pretended to be the sergeant, singing à la Bruce Springsteen's "I'm on Fire":

Me and Sergeant Lonergan pulled guard at Gate 3.
He lit the heater and kicked it at me.
Ooh, ooh, ooh, it was a fire.
Well, I grabbed them rockets and them weapons,
I hope that goofball learned his lesson.
Ooh, ooh, ooh it was a fire.
I stood up and turned around
And watched that bunker burning down.
Ooh, ooh, ooh Gate 3 was on fire.
My name is Jerod
And I will tell you true,
Pull guard with Lonergan
And he will burn you, too.
Ooh, ooh, ooh it was a fire.

They had to laugh. What was the alternative? None of the joes thought they were accomplishing much or even anything. They were just getting shot at. None of the enlisted guys seemed to really understand how protecting a patch of land in the middle of nowhere was keeping the US safe.

First Sergeant Severino was thirty-four and had been in the Army for almost as long as these grunts had been alive. He felt protective of his men, wanted them to be motivated, and would try to convince them that it was better to be fighting the bad guys here than having them attack the US homeland again. But his argument was often met with a shrug.

Jerod was "seeing some country" sure enough, or at least a small corner of the world. One day on the satellite phone with his brother Renley, he marveled at how locals branded their livestock. Not with a searing iron scar, but with some sort of dye. Chickens wandering through the nearby town of Shkin might be tagged with green, yellow, or blue, depending on which clan owned them. Jerod thought that was pretty cool. It may have been his upbringing on the Choctaw Nation Reservation that gave Jerod a real appreciation for and an open-mindedness about the Afghans he saw. Unlike some of his fellow soldiers, he didn't see other societies and cultures as inherently bad. While Westerners typically see, say, snakes as threatening, for the Choctaw Nation, the diamond rattlesnake is sacred—Choctaws put them into their gardens to keep other animals from stealing their produce. He was raised to be accepting, nonjudgmental.

He wrote home again, expressing both his fascination with his surroundings and the latent homesickness of a teenager.

> Dear Momma,
>
> Well it's me again how is it going? Good I hope. . . . I'm kinda tired but that's allright because we only have 5 1/2 months left. . . .
>
> The mail helicopter just flew in a few minutes ago. We went to the Hodgy shop yesterday which is a little Afghanistan flea market that is pretty cool. When it is closer to leaving I am going to buy y'all some stuff. Well it is another day at the fob and we are listening to George Straight and cleaning our weapons. We have guard duty in a few hours so we are just waiting for that. . . .
>
> I haven't had a shower in quite some time now but it doesn't really bother me because there's no one here to impress you know what I mean. Well momma I just want you to know I love you and you can never know how much I appreciate your thorough support and love you have given me. I know there are alot who doesn't have that and for that I know I am lucky. So thank you. I will write again soon.
>
> Love ya
> Jerod

It got warmer. One week, the rain was so heavy it literally melted much of the mud-hut barracks the platoon called home. It was a mess.

On the night of April 8, a nearby Afghan checkpoint came under attack and an American quick reaction force began chasing insurgents toward the Pakistan border, eventually pushing them into the village of Shkin.

Sergeant Konrad Reed, twenty-two, was attached to what's called a "maneuver unit," responsible for directing artillery mortar fire and aviation support onto enemy targets in accordance with the maneuver commander's plans. Reed would, if they came under fire, call in the enemy location for the artillery unit. The University of San Diego dropout had joined the Army in November 1999 and was at the base of a rappel tower at Pope Army Airfield in North Carolina when the first plane hit the World Trade Center. And here he was in Afghanistan, just over a year later, preparing for battle.

Firebase Shkin

The quick reaction force chasing the insurgents was also being supported by a joint terminal attack controller or JTAC team, which helped direct air attacks and make sure the right targets were hit and the soldiers out on patrol were spared. As Reed and his team listened to the radio traffic, gunfire echoed in the distance. Then several of the insurgents ran into a compound in the village. The troops wanted to engage, but their presence in the village posed obvious risks.

There were a couple of Harrier jump jets in the area, US Marine Corps planes that allowed short takeoffs and vertical landings. Once the Harriers were told there were US troops in contact in the town of Shkin, they zoomed over.

The soldiers on the ground had no way of talking directly to the Harrier pilots on their bombing run but were able to speak to the JTAC team, who then relayed the information to the pilots. The military restricted direct communication with the Harrier pilots on a bombing run, so the process of helping them locate their targets was convoluted, inefficient, and potentially confusing.

The JTAC team led the Harriers on a strafing run toward where a forward observer thought the enemy was. The Harrier machine guns fired at the target as helicopter gunships also engaged in the fight. Insurgents inside the enemy compound continued to return fire. Nothing the Americans did seemed to have much impact. One of the officers in charge grew frustrated. He wanted the Harriers to drop a thousand-pound bomb and take out the entire building. Using infrared laser pointers, the forward observers tried to direct the Harriers to the target. The planes flew over the target once but couldn't find the red dot. They tried again. Again, no dot.

At Firebase Shkin, Reed started expressing concern. He felt they were rushing it.

The officer got onto the radio and told them to just drop the damn bomb already.

Reed expressed his doubts again.

The JTAC team gave the clearance.

Reed was kicked out of the tower.

They all watched; it took only a couple of seconds for the bomb to hit.

But it hit the wrong spot. It hit a building maybe four hundred meters away from the target.

Reed tried to understand what he had just witnessed—maybe the pilot was frustrated; certainly the officer and the JTAC team seemed so. Dropping bombs from twelve thousand feet in the air at night in a war zone could lend itself to mistakes. *But holy shit*, Reed thought. *This could be bad.* Everyone braced themselves for what they might have done.

The US soldiers waited until daylight, then rolled over to the village to survey the damage. It was likely going to be so ugly, officers decided to make it a leaders' recon, meaning the team leaders and squad leaders went to the village before the rest of the enlisted men.

The Harriers had hit the wrong house, killing eleven innocent civilians. Afghan families were weeping, pulling civilian bodies out of the rubble. Captain Trahan was later told the building served as a sort of hostel for families and individuals traveling between Pakistan and Afghanistan.

All the Americans could do was stand there watching, helpless. They were told not to go near the bodies. It was a horror. Specialist Victor Belcastro spied an Afghan man lifting up a blanket under which lay what appeared to be the body of a child. The locals glared at Belcastro with a hate he'd never seen. The troops were told not to approach the house.

Second Squad—Hodge, Ray, Jerod, and the rest of the team— guarded the perimeter around the block where the tragedy took place, just to control a crowd in case one formed. No one talked. It was all too awful.

Eventually, the guys from civil affairs came by the village with suitcases full of money. It didn't do much to salve the grief or anger.

The rest of April brought less rain but more chaos. The insurgent traffic ticked up, as did the attacks. Sergeant Reed acted as a forward observer for the Slayers, which meant he was the guy who would go where a rocket had landed and try to figure out where it had been fired from.

Reed worked to coordinate artillery with the men on the ground. If troops needed artillery from the air, they had to rely on the two Air Force guys to communicate with the planes. Tech Sergeant Lee Marvin Blackwell and his wingman, Airman First Class Ray Losano, were there to do a job. Since they were Air Force, not Army, they tended to dress more casually. Blackwell would bop into the TOC, the tactical operation center, with his beard and orange Texas Longhorns baseball cap, gold Oakleys, badass Sportiva shoes, no name tag, no branch of service on his uni. Captain Trahan would roll his eyes and shake his head.

"Fucking Air Force," he'd mutter under his breath.

Blackwell and Ray Losano were inseparable, rooming in the same grim hooch decorated with art by Laura Losano, age two. Sarah Losano was pregnant with their second, so her husband took every chance he could get to grab the sat phone to ring her up. He felt guilty being away. He'd joined the Air Force to make ends meet after quitting his job at the front desk at the Studio 6 Hotel in Tucson, the salary not really cutting it.

Ray Losano wasn't just Blackwell's sidekick, he was also his wingman on the ground at the firebase as they worked side by side. Blackwell's call sign was Hardrock 1-1; Losano's was Hardrock 1-1-Bravo.

Blackwell would assess the terrain, and Losano would call it in back to "Tombstone," the air support operations center, where the birds were kept, at Bagram Air Base. Before missions, Blackwell and Losano would huddle with artillery, operations, and intelligence to get all the data they needed, and Losano would call in what was referred to as a "1972": the target of the mission, the target type, where it was on the grid, its elevation, how it was dispersed—Was it a column? A tank formation? A couple of troops in the open? They'd paint the picture so Tombstone would be prepared.

On April 20, as much of the world celebrated Easter, Ray Losano turned twenty-four, and Firebase Shkin came under the most serious rocket attack they'd ever experienced.

The first blast sounded like two large trains crashing together, and the force of the impact knocked everyone back. Glass windows shattered.

Losano and Blackwell ran to the closest tower, Blackwell assessing the situation while Losano—Hardrock 1-1-Bravo—radioed to Tombstone. The rockets were being fired from across the border, in Pakistan, so their responses were limited as US retaliation against targets in Pakistan was strictly prohibited. It was infuriating, frankly—whether they were Taliban or HIG or al Qaeda, teams of insurgents were right across the border in Waziristan, firing rockets at the Americans, or sometimes sneaking in, taking potshots, and sneaking back. Once they were on the other side of the line (a 1,640-mile border concocted by British diplomat Sir Mortimer Durand in 1893), there was nothing the American troops could do.

Still, Blackwell thought close air support might at least stop them, so Losano called in the details, the 1972. Losano was at the far end of the tower, exposed, while Blackwell was safer behind the sandbags. Blackwell grabbed Losano and pulled him behind the sandbags.

"Sergeant Blackwell, I'm scared," he said.

"I'm scared too," Blackwell admitted, "but you need to send that CAS request in."

And he did. Two A-10 Warthogs showed up, and Losano called in the nine lines—giving the pilots very specific information about the terrain.

The Warthogs couldn't fire into Pakistan, where the mortars were coming from, but their presence stopped the incoming.

Blackwell looked at Losano. He was proud of him. He'd worked through his fear. They both had.

After the attack stopped, Reed and his team went to analyze the craters and easily determined they were 107-millimeter rockets, known as Katyushas. Measuring the trajectory and reverse engineering the distance, he figured they were fired from this one spot the local insurgents seemed to like a whole lot, up in the mountains maybe four miles away.

As night descended, Ray Losano called his wife and parents to hear them say happy birthday and Happy Easter. He revealed nothing that he had gone through that afternoon.

Jerod called his dad around that time as well. He didn't say a word about the attack from earlier that day.

"I'm so bored," he told his father. "We're just lying around in camp not doing anything. I want some action."

"Naw, you don't," Jerry told his son.

CHAPTER NINE

284 OUT OF 285

Washington, DC

The detainee center at Guantánamo Bay was so removed from US and international law that one former State Department lawyer called it "the legal equivalent of outer space." The courthouse that held Spin Ghul in Agrigento, Sicily, was quite the opposite. Though the courthouse-glued-to-a-prison construct appeared menacing, it was defendant-friendly in comparison to what suspected terrorists like Spin Ghul typically faced in detainment after 9/11. Sicilian courts had a wide array of rules and procedures to protect defendants, with defense counsel provided and a high bar for any extradition requests. Spin Ghul was savvy enough to understand this, vaguely aware that he had rights and protections. He asked the judge under what Italian law he was being held and requested to speak with an official from the government of Niger. Generally, he seemed unbothered throughout the proceedings.

The contrast with how Spin Ghul would have been handled at Gitmo was chasmic and more than symbolic given the task Bitkower and Shreve were facing. Unlike the many terrorists captured and imprisoned without trial over the past decade, the two young attorneys would have to build a criminal case in order to prevent Spin Ghul from killing again. They would have to meet a series of requirements usually reserved for US citizens, or people who commit crimes on US soil, who are on trial—admissibility of statements, sufficient corroboration, proof beyond reasonable doubt. And because Spin Ghul was a foreign combatant, they had the additional challenge of being asked to play the role of both prosecutors and police detectives—there was no local law enforcement precinct they could call in the Wild West of that part of Waziristan, Pakistan, to see what kind of record this guy had. Spin Ghul's testimony was only beginning to scratch the surface of what they would need. Without question this was going to be the most difficult case of their careers, with life-and-death consequences.

The reason that Spin Ghul was credibly able to ask about his rights in Italian court rather than receiving a one-way ticket to Gitmo, was rooted in policy changes President Obama had ushered in. It was also the reason Bitkower and Shreve had to worry about the mental state of the defendant who seemed to be ranting about Egyptian pharaohs—the insanity defense yet another privilege that terrorists hadn't previously been afforded.

To Obama, and to many Europeans, the US after 9/11 had become completely untethered from international law. Before that fateful day in 2001, Americans were committed to upholding the minimal standard treatment of prisoners of war established by the Third Geneva Convention in 1949. Those who violated the laws of war were tried in military courts accordingly—including even the most heinous war criminals tried after World War II in the Tokyo and Nuremberg Tribunals. Meanwhile, terrorists both foreign and domestic historically had been arrested and tried under US criminal law. Whether the far-left Marxist terrorists of the Weather Underground in the 1970s or the far-right Oklahoma City bombers in the 1990s, it was the police, the FBI, and the US Justice Department who pursued them, caught them, and put them away.

But with the size and scale of the 9/11 attacks, the distinction between terrorism and warfare—and between criminal justice and the laws of war—was blurred. In the wake of new foreign threats on US soil, President George W. Bush and his legal team decided that current laws, both international and domestic, were insufficient. So, using the argument that they were building on precedents from past conflicts, they created and ushered in an almost entirely new legal framework and language to coincide with the wars in Iraq and Afghanistan.

"Enemy combatants"—including American citizens so designated—were treated differently under this new framework. Once detained, some of these prisoners were turned over to allied governments, who then tortured them. Others were tortured by their American captors using "enhanced interrogation techniques" at CIA black sites, where the American legal system had no jurisdiction. Then, in 2002, the detainee center was set up at the Guantánamo Bay Naval Base on Cuba, where terrorist suspects could be interrogated using various methods of torture and detained indefinitely without trial.[1]

"Extraordinary rendition," which the CIA began during the Clinton administration as a way of pursuing al Qaeda, was expanded significantly during the Bush years. The Italian courts had just weighed in on what they thought of the practice by convicting those twenty-two suspected or known CIA agents of kidnapping the Egyptian imam Abu Omar. To many in Italy, including prosecutors, Abu Omar—who was snatched off the streets of Milan and flown to Egypt, where he was imprisoned for fourteen months—became a symbol of the extralegal excesses of the Bush administration.

---
[1] This book will use the word "torture" colloquially and in accordance with international standards with the understanding that the Bush administration had a highly-parsed definition that differed.

Running for president just a few years later, Senator Barack Obama, Democrat of Illinois, pledged to dispose of the Bush administration's new legal dictionary. But this shift in policy was anything but smooth.

During the Bush years, dealing with Spin Ghul would likely have been a snatch-and-grab with a connecting flight to Gitmo. No risk to innocents, no expensive process to try to prove the homicidal crimes and conspiracies to which he was confessing.

To Obama, the American judicial system was a cornerstone of democracy and not an obstacle to be avoided during tough times. He ordered the end of "enhanced interrogation techniques." And one of his very first official acts as president, surrounded by flag officers, was to order the Gitmo detainee center shuttered. On January 22, 2009, Obama introduced a process under which he optimistically declared that "Guantánamo will be closed no later than one year from now."

As Bitkower and Shreve would witness firsthand, Obama's pledge to shut Gitmo down came into direct conflict with his simultaneous instruction to close the base "consistent with the national security . . . interests of the United States." In addition to making sure the US lived up to its ideals, the president is primarily tasked with protecting the American people. Those two imperatives were not always easy to square. Some of the detainees were considered so dangerous that the US could not release them, nor would they be able to transfer them to other countries. Trying most of the prisoners in court would be impossible because either they had been tortured or the evidence obtained against them was otherwise sullied.

Obama's plan was to stand up a task force that would provide him with recommendations on how to deal with those problem cases.

"The American people," Obama said, "understand that we are not, as I said in the Inauguration, going to continue with a false choice between our safety and our ideals. We think that it is precisely our ideals that give us the strength and the moral high ground to be able to effectively deal with the unthinking violence that you see emanating from terrorist organizations around the world."

Surrounded by senior military officers, many of whom were skeptical that their new commander in chief would be able to achieve what he was promising, the president concluded by saying, "We intend to win this fight. We're going to win it on our terms."

But could they?

Throughout 2009, Bitkower and Shreve served on the Guantánamo Review Task Force, which recommended that 126 of 240 detainees be transferred or released to other countries—either their home country or somewhere else. They referred forty-four cases to the Justice Department for potential prosecution either in US criminal federal court or in military commissions. The glaring issue was the final forty-eight, whom the task force recommended be held indefinitely under the "laws of war."

These were forty-eight tremendously dangerous men, the task force concluded. Forty-eight individuals who were dedicated to the slaughter of Americans and had the intelligence and means to carry out attacks.

In their work on the task force, Bitkower and Shreve also made recommendations about who could potentially be prosecuted. Two of the Gitmo detainees whose cases they explored were Abdul Hadi al-Iraqi, or "Hadi," and Abu Faraj al-Libi, or "Faraj." The Obama administration decided to keep both Hadi and Faraj at Gitmo and not send them to the US for trial.

The task force's report had been completed by January 2010 when the nation was in something of a panic. Days before, on Christmas 2009, on a Northwest Airlines flight from Amsterdam to Detroit, a Nigerian affiliated with al Qaeda named Umar Farouk Abdulmutallab tried to ignite chemical explosives sewn into his underwear. His plot failed, and he was arrested. Ultimately, he ended up being convicted in federal court, but the administration handled the near miss clumsily.

The secretary of the Department of Homeland Security claimed "the system worked" when it hadn't. The political climate was not ripe for a rational discussion of the need to transfer accused terrorists to prisons on American soil, much less for their release, the Obama White House decided, so they kicked the announcement to June 2010.

Later that same year, the Obama administration got mugged by reality again.

With much fanfare, Obama had ordered the transfer from Gitmo to New York City of a man named Ahmed Khalfan Ghailani, a Tanzanian who'd played a key role in the bombings of the US embassies in his home country and Kenya. Ghailani—captured in Pakistan in 2004, detained abroad by the CIA or US military until 2006—would be tried in the Southern District of New York.

Ghailani would be the first Gitmo detainee tried in a civilian court. The Obama administration had high hopes that his easy conviction would lead the public and elected officials to have more confidence that other detainees, including 9/11 coconspirators such as Khalid Sheik Mohammed, a.k.a. "KSM," could be flown north, tried, convicted, and locked up forever at a Supermax.

"Preventing this detainee from coming to our shores would prevent his trial and conviction," Obama said in May 2009, standing in front of the US Constitution at the National Archives. "And after over a decade, it is time to finally see that justice is served, and that is what we intend to do." He insisted that "in the long run we cannot also keep this country safe unless we enlist the power of our most fundamental values."

Less than two miles away, a different view was being presented that same day. Standing at the American Enterprise Institute, former vice president Dick Cheney lambasted Obama's moves. "In the fight against terrorism, there is no middle ground, and half measures keep you half exposed," Cheney said, predicting that "the president will find, upon reflection, that to bring the worst of the worst terrorists inside the United States would be cause for great danger and regret in the years to come."

The US attorney for the Southern District of New York was Preet Bharara, and his prosecutors were confident. They had a key witness against Ghailani, a man named Hussein Abebe, who sold Ghailani the TNT that blew up the US embassy in Dar es Salaam. But in October 2010, US District Judge Lewis A. Kaplan ruled that the prosecution would not be allowed to introduce Abebe's testimony. Ghailani had divulged his name while being interrogated in a CIA black site during a period when Ghailani said he had been subjected to enhanced interrogation techniques. This made calling Abebe as a witness in US criminal court impossible, one of the difficulties the task force had foreseen.

Abebe's testimony was too directly linked to Ghailani's statements while in CIA custody, the judge said. "The court has not reached this conclusion lightly.... But the Constitution is the rock upon which our nation rests. We must follow it not only when it is convenient, but when fear and danger beckon in a different direction. To do less would diminish us and undermine the foundation upon which we stand."

Deprived of its star witness, the prosecution over the four weeks of the trial introduced a largely circumstantial case. One of the prosecutors told the court that without being able to include the testimony from Abebe describing selling the TNT to Mr. Ghailani, "the government has no way of putting such evidence in front of the jury at all."

On November 17, 2010, the jury of six men and six women came into the courtroom to render their verdict on each of the 285 charges. The jurors avoided eye contact with anyone but the judge.

Count one: conspiracy to kill US nationals.

"Not guilty."

Count two: conspiracy to murder, kidnap, and maim at places outside the US.

"Not guilty."

Count three: conspiracy to murder.

"Not guilty."

Count four: conspiracy to use weapons of mass destruction against US nationals.

"Not guilty."

The jurors shocked the world. Counts 11 through 223 were for the mass murders in Kenya. Not guilty.

Counts 224–234, for the murders in Tanzania. Not guilty.

And on and on.

In all, they found Ghailani guilty of only one of the 285 counts: for conspiracy to damage or destroy US property. This charge had a possible sentence of twenty years to life. Ultimately, Ghailani would be sentenced to life in prison, but it was tough to sell to the public that the glass was 1/285th full. The prevalent take was that Obama's Justice Department had made a gamble the American people almost lost.

"The Obama Administration recklessly insisted on a civilian trial for Ahmed Ghailani, and rolled the dice in a time of war," said the leaders of a group called Keep America Safe, which included Debra Burlingame, sister of the pilot of the hijacked plane that crashed into the Pentagon on 9/11, and Liz Cheney, a former State Department official and daughter of the former vice president. "This result isn't just embarrassing. It's dangerous. It signals weakness in a time of war."

Even before the verdict, Obama's principles of a new protocol for prosecuting terrorists faced headwinds—and fear. The mayor of New York City, Michael Bloomberg, ran like a purse snatcher in Times Square from the plans of Attorney General Eric Holder to try 9/11 detainees in Manhattan. The NYPD cost estimate for the trial suddenly skyrocketed to a billion dollars, with Police Commissioner Ray Kelly presenting a proposal for a two-tiered security perimeter in lower Manhattan that guaranteed gridlock to the point of paralysis. New York Democratic senator Chuck Schumer, he of the 2009 local TV headline "Schumer Not Afraid of Gitmo Goons," flipped even before the Ghailani verdict, and by January 2010 he declared it "obvious" the trial shouldn't be in Manhattan. A few weeks later he opposed the trial being held anywhere in the Empire State.

Some Democratic allies of the president would come to see this, in retrospect, as a colossal political error by Team Obama. While Obama's supporters would rightly argue that Republicans were almost always in lockstep opposition to Obama's efforts to close Gitmo and shift to civilian courts, Democratic fingerprints were all over the knife as well. It's a lot easier for a politician to criticize the existence of an American extrajudicial prison somewhere in the Caribbean than to agree to ship its terrifying prisoners to the courthouse down the street. Observers would later suggest that Obama's presidential transition team should never have let him make the pledge he did on day one of his presidency, with great fanfare, without ensuring that there was sufficient congressional backing for details of the plan in full. President Obama, however, was always assured of the correctness of his views and the power of his persuasive abilities.

After Ghailani's trial, the Obama administration went into crisis mode. Congress was telling them that the only way to deal with captured terrorists was by shipping detainees to Gitmo and trying them in military commissions. The Senate Armed Services Committee was chaired by an ally, Senator Carl Levin, Democrat of Michigan, but the politics of this issue were tough, with the arguments of GOP senators Lindsey Graham of South Carolina and Kelly Ayotte of New Hampshire winning the day. Assistant Attorney General Lisa Monaco saw the arguments that US courts couldn't handle terrorist trials as cynical and playing on the public's fears, painting the FBI and seasoned prosecutors as soft and the American justice system as weak for allowing terrorists basic rights.

John Brennan, a grizzled CIA veteran who served as President Obama's counterterrorism adviser, went to the US Senate on October 18, 2011, with two other top national security advisers, Denis McDonough and Avril Haines, to try to explain their point of view. Sitting in Senator Graham's waiting room, C-SPAN 2 on the TV, they watched the South Carolina Republican on the floor of the Senate attacking the Obama administration for pushing back on the changes the Senate Armed Services Committee was making to the defense bill. Graham accused the Obama White House of having "an irrational view of what we need to be doing with detainees."

"They've lost the argument," Graham said, noting that he had tried to work with the White House on closing Guantánamo Bay. "It's not going to close. We're not going to move those prisoners inside the United States. The Congress has said no. The American people have said no." He noted the plan to try Khalid Sheikh Mohammed in New York City "blew up in their face."

"The reason Mr. Brennan objects," Graham said, is that the Senate's actions would "create a presumption for military custody, and the reason we're doing that is because the Obama administration has been hellbent on criminalizing this war," he said. Graham noted that the legislation had a waiver to allow the exemption. "What I don't want to do is start reading rights to everybody we capture in the United States as part of a terrorist organization's plot."

Upon Graham's return to his office, Brennan told the senator they'd seen his floor statement.

Years later, Brennan would claim that Graham chuckled and said,

"Oh, don't pay any attention to what I say on the Senate floor. It doesn't mean anything. It's just politics." Graham told me he never said that. Either way, Obama administration officials would ultimately come to see many of the criticisms as unfair and not grounded in fact.

"We don't want to tell a terrorist you have the right to remain silent," said Ayotte, the former New Hampshire attorney general and the wife of a reservist fighter pilot who flew missions in Iraq, during Senate debate in November 2011.

Monaco went to Capitol Hill one day to brief Levin on how the system actually worked. Ayotte's concern was unfounded, she explained to Levin. A 1984 US Supreme Court ruling—*New York v. Quarles*—provided that a law enforcement official's reasonable concern for public safety can justify an exception to the requirement to give Miranda warnings. In that case, a woman who had been raped told police in Queens that Benjamin Quarles, the man she identified as having committed the crime, had a gun and had entered a supermarket. After finding Quarles, police asked him where the gun was before arresting him and reading him his rights. As a result, the trial court judge wouldn't allow the gun or Quarles's confession to be introduced into evidence. But that decision was overturned; public safety could take precedence over Miranda warnings, a 5–4 majority ruled. It's not true that a terrorist immediately gets to lawyer up, Monaco explained to Levin. Law enforcement tools actually can be used effectively to generate more intelligence. The FBI and prosecutors had demonstrated time and again an ability to secure cooperation from suspects to learn more to protect the public.

But it was a tough sell.

A straight line could be drawn from the failure to convict Ghailani on all but one charge on November 17, 2010, to Congress's decision a few weeks later to pass a defense bill banning the use of federal funds to transfer detainees from Gitmo to the US. Indeed, the events were building to a crescendo—bipartisan outrage and alarm following the November 2009 Justice Department announcement that 9/11 defendants would come to Manhattan to be tried; the December 2009 failed Christmas Day bombing; Ghailani being convicted of just one charge in November 2010.

By March 2011, Obama had lifted his ban on new military charges against Gitmo detainees. In April, Attorney General Holder announced he'd told military prosecutors to file war crimes charges against the 9/11 terrorists in custody. At the end of 2011, President Obama signed into law—reluctantly, he said—a defense bill that included a provision allowing the indefinite detention of terrorist suspects.

None of this was encouraging news for Bitkower and Shreve, who now not only had a difficult case to put together but also hundreds of officials in Washington, DC, primed to be skeptical that they could succeed, significantly increasing the likelihood that they wouldn't be permitted to prosecute Spin Ghul—thus all but ensuring he'd end up a free man in Europe, determined to kill as many Americans as possible.

CHAPTER TEN

WHAT ONE RADICALIZED MAN COULD DO

Agrigento, Italy

Five months later, sitting in that Sicilian courtroom, Bitkower and Shreve were well aware of the Ghailani debacle. On top of that, both men were fairly certain that no one had ever been tried in a US criminal court for killing American servicemembers on a foreign battlefield. To amass enough evidence to convince Attorney General Holder—and Congress—that they should fly Spin Ghul from Sicily to Brooklyn seemed not just practically, but politically impossible.

They were relatively young—Bitkower had just turned thirty-six, Shreve thirty-five—on the middle rungs of a career in the Justice Department. If one were to create a sort of scale for prosecutorial counterterrorism views, Bitkower and Shreve were by 2011 closer to Obama than Bush, but decidedly in between the two. They understood why Gitmo had been created, even if by now they agreed that it had become too much of a liability in the larger war, a terrorist recruiting tool to underline American hypocrisy. They viewed the nomenclature of "enhanced interrogation techniques" as absurd and torture as obviously illegal. But as the ones who actually put together the cases to prosecute terrorists, they knew criminal law was not always adequate to wage the war on terror. They knew there were prisoners at Gitmo who could not be tried in criminal court because there was no usable evidence, but also that there was enough reliable intelligence that these men were too dangerous to be released. Retroactively attempting to fix every one of the sins of the past in the purest way wasn't feasible, nor would it be safe, so they understood the rationale behind using the law of war detention in such cases.

They also knew that their personal opinions didn't matter. The rules were what they were, set by the current administration, and their job wasn't to change them but to work within them. Bitkower and Shreve were determined to try those who could be tried, and they were confident their boss, US attorney Loretta Lynch of the Eastern District of New York, had their back. They were less sure about the pressure politicians in Washington, DC, might bring to bear on the US Justice Department. Of course, they also worried about pushback from the White House as President Obama geared up to run for reelection. They worried their job would be for naught if Obama didn't have the willpower to carry through with the domestic prosecutions as public backlash to bringing terrorists onto US soil swirled. Bitkower admired Obama's ideals but worried that the president was politically naïve, both too enamored of his ability to reason with anyone and too fearful of GOP attacks on him.

Would President Obama and Attorney General Holder back them if they built a case? Was it worth their time, or were they putting their careers in jeopardy? The potential consequences went beyond professional risks. Both men had new wives at home and were starting families. Bitkower had a one-year-old boy. The two prosecutors weren't the only ones who might face the consequences of taking on such a high-profile and politically charged case.

And yet what choice did they have? The victims, whoever they were, deserved justice. And homicidal terrorists could not just be allowed to stroll into another bar, another train station, another airport, to blow it up.

Hearing Spin Ghul invoke the 1998 embassy bombings as some sort of career goal was resonant on a deeply personal level for Bitkower, who, during law school, had worked on the International Criminal Tribunal for Rwanda, based in Arusha, Tanzania. While there, in July 2000, he visited the memorial for victims of the US embassy bombing. He walked in the garden of the new embassy, saw the photographs of the carnage, the slabs of concrete, the flag-draped coffins, the bloodied survivors. It was a sad, solemn place commemorating unspeakable cruelty. He was deeply moved and well aware that many of those responsible for the bloodshed remained on the loose. Men like Ahmed Khalfan Ghailani.

Meanwhile, Bitkower's partner remembered a different case from Africa. Shreve had worked to prosecute the men behind the gruesome attacks from just a year before, suicide bombings coordinated by al Qaeda–affiliated al-Shabaab targeting crowds in Uganda who had gathered to watch the FIFA World Cup at a rugby club as well as a restaurant popular with foreigners. The attacks slaughtered seventy-six people and wounded nearly one hundred, including several Americans.

Even if Spin Ghul wasn't able to connect to the al Qaeda network—and surely he would if released back into Europe—one radicalized man could do a ton of harm, as Shreve and Bitkower knew all too well. Just a month after Spin Ghul asked Officer Morgese for water on the deck of *The Excelsior*, a thirty-two-year-old white supremacist named Anders Breivik detonated a bomb in a van next to a government building complex in Oslo, Norway, killing eight people and wounding more than two hundred. And that was nothing compared to what he did next, taking a Glock 34 pistol, a Ruger Mini-14 rifle, and more than one thousand cartridges on a ferry to an island housing a youth summer camp. There, with ammo partly bought from the US, Breivik mowed down sixty-seven people, many of them teenagers.

Most members of the team investigating Spin Ghul had come face-to-face with the horrors that he sought to inflict. Many were haunted by them. For instance, a week before FBI agent Greg Paciorek first got the call from Ari Mahairas to visit Italy in September 2011, he was in Lagos, Nigeria, to make sure US personnel in the area had sufficient safety policies, procedures, and equipment. Days after Paciorek arrived, on August 26, 2011, a suicide bomber with the terrorist group Boko Haram rammed a Honda Accord packed with explosives through gates and into the United Nations compound in Abuja, damaging at least three floors of a seven-story building, killing twenty-three people and wounding more than eighty others. Paciorek was sent to the scene of the crime to lead the post-blast investigation, digging through the rubble, seeing the horrifying, bloody remains of the innocent UN workers targeted by this rising extremist group.

As shocking as the images from the attacks were to the public, what the general populace sees on TV or in newspapers is always a sanitized version of the horrors. Few have seen the worst photographs and videos of the people who jumped from the World Trade Center towers, the pulpified remains of their bodies on the ground, the carrion mixed in with the debris, the green meadow on which lay the corpses of teenagers. In their line of work, Bitkower, Shreve, and their colleagues were always exposed to images of blood and lost souls with law enforcement failures hovering over their heads.

This case was different. It wasn't a post-crime mystery where the murderers had to be located and the conspiracy deduced. Here they had a dangerous person in custody, and they feared the Italians were going to—ultimately, essentially—let him go. And when they did, there was no question that Spin Ghul would do everything he could to kill as many innocent people and as many innocent Americans as possible. Here they had a chance to prevent the next tragedy, not sort through the wreckage of its aftermath.

So they had to do it.

But what exactly did they have? As of then, just a confession from a possible madman. They had a few credible details to be sure, names and locations, but they would need more. Witnesses. Physical evidence. Evidence from a battlefield thousands of miles away from events that took place more than a decade ago. The fog of war was complicated enough, but add in time and post-traumatic stress, and it was tough to imagine any of the surviving servicemembers being able to pick Spin Ghul out of a lineup. If anyone in the Obama administration expected detainee information to resemble a police file, they would have been disappointed—military and intelligence operators who made the captures were not trained or directed to create files. And why would they be? A soldier or operative can hardly be expected to bag evidence and establish a chain of custody while they are getting shot at, particularly when the established policy had been to avoid federal court prosecutions. And good luck trying to pry out of the black box that is the CIA any information they might have on individual cases.

Maybe all these reasons were why no one had ever prosecuted an enemy fighter for killing a US servicemember on a battlefield.

But that was all yet to come. They still didn't have any idea which battle Spin Ghul was referring to. More than 1,600 Americans had been killed in Afghanistan by September 2011; for all they knew right then, it could have been any one of dozens of potential firefights that matched Spin Ghul's description.

And they didn't know exactly when the battle had taken place.

Above all, they still didn't even know if Spin Ghul's "Ramses the Fifth" comment would lead to ruin before they even established the most basic fact of their case.

With the pressure of past and future terrorist attacks, the burden of proof of a criminal trial, and the political weight all bearing down on him, Shreve sucked in a breath and questioned Spin Ghul again.

"Could you just clarify the date when this took place?" Shreve asked. "Do you remember when it was in context with, like, Ramadan?"

Spin Ghul said, "I don't use European months, January, February. That's why the history is a little foggy."

Shreve pushed.

"It was a Friday," Spin Ghul said, remembering prayers during that special day of the week for Muslims, *Yawm al-Jum'ah* in Arabic, the Day of Assembly. But he didn't know the month. He didn't know the year. He thought about it, though.

"I'm not sure," Spin Ghul said, "but at that point, Ramses the Fifth was intent on visiting the American forces, but he decided not to come."

There it was again. Ramses the Fifth.

"Do you know what season it was?" Shreve asked.

"I'm not sure," Spin Ghul said, "but I know that was his first attempted visit."

"And again, who is Ramses the Fifth?" Shreve asked. He couldn't ignore this bizarreness any further. Ramses the Fifth?

The interpreter pressed Spin Ghul on the name of this would-be visitor to US forces in Afghanistan.

And then the interpreter had a revelation: Spin Ghul wasn't saying Ramses—he was saying "Ramsfeh," which the interpreter now realized was "Rumsfeld."

And the five fingers Spin Ghul kept holding up, that wasn't to convey "the Fifth"—those digits represented the five sides of the Pentagon.

"Oh, Rums—Donald, he said Don, Donald Rumsfeld," the interpreter explained.

Bitkower and Shreve breathed a sigh of relief. This was an issue of translation, not sanity. And now they could better identify which battle this was—it was around the time of a visit to the region by Secretary of Defense Donald Rumsfeld.

That would be easy enough to google. Sometime early in the war, Rumsfeld visiting US forces.

Shreve was puzzled as to how Spin Ghul knew this: he'd been hunkered down in a safe house in an obscure town in a remote part of the developing world. It wasn't as if he were getting CNN news alerts on his phone.

"How did you know that Rumsfeld was planning on coming to Afghanistan at that time?" he asked.

"Our commander Abdul Hadi al-Iraqi speaks English, and he listens to stations," Spin Ghul said.

Hadi, of course, was one of the two detainees Bitkower and Shreve had studied on the Gitmo task force. Spin Ghul was describing real terrorists serving roles and in places that matched biographies that weren't anything close to common knowledge. Spin Ghul also mentioned Faraj—and a bombmaker who schooled him on how to use poisons such as ricin for mass murder. The expertise that Spin Ghul might possess sent a shiver down Shreve's spine.

For the rest of that day and the next, Spin Ghul detailed his terrorist exploits after the battle: After tying up the grenade, he had limped back to the terrorist safe house. While the coast cleared, he began having visions of greater terrorist feats than taking potshots at American soldiers. He soon left Afghanistan and embarked on an international adventure to replicate the 1998 US embassy bombings in a new country.

After Shreve carefully went over with him the name of every fellow jihadi Spin Ghul had encountered in his travels, adding to the ever-growing list of potential sources, the Americans drove back to their hotel, exhausted. But neither man took the opportunity to rest. Shreve went for a run. Bitkower began research to figure out in which battle Spin Ghul had participated. Without this first and crucial step of the investigation, knowing where and when the battle took place, there was nothing they could do with their mountain of leads.

Their biggest clue happened to be the miscommunication that made Bitkower and Shreve fear the case would be thrown out. "Ramses the Fifth" was actually a reference to Rumsfeld's trip to the region. After his run, Shreve found an *Irish Times* story online from AFP detailing the defense secretary's flight to the Gulf and ultimately Afghanistan being delayed in Shannon, Ireland, for technical reasons. Spin Ghul had said something about Rumsfeld's attempted visit. Bingo. They were looking for a battle around April 27, 2003.

As he sifted through Spin Ghul's testimony, details emerged that narrowed it down considerably: an ambush, near a ridgeline, walking distance from Angoor Ada in Waziristan.

And there had been American casualties. Shreve made a list of any American casualties from around that time: In December 2002, Sergeant Steven Checo was killed during a patrol at Firebase Shkin. An ambush in Helmand Province, March 29, 2003, two men killed.

But only one battle took place around the time of Rumsfeld's trip: an ambush outside Firebase Shkin on April 25, 2003. A Combat Studies Institute interview with a Major Gregory "Scott" Trahan that Bitkower found online provided details. An attack on his patrol on "hilly terrain." US helicopters present. Two men killed, several wounded, including Trahan. Most of the insurgents got away.

Right near the Afghanistan border. Firebase Shkin. April 25,

2003. This had to be the setting of the horrific attacks that Spin Ghul described. But any thrill that Shreve might have felt of discovering this crucial fact would have been short-lived. It wasn't just a question of if or where Spin Ghul's atrocities happened anymore. It was a question of whether Shreve and Bitkower could prove it.

CHAPTER ELEVEN

GOATS OR WHATEVER

Firebase Shkin, Afghanistan

The man who went only by "John" came into the tactical operations center, or TOC, and told the Slayers that there were insurgents in the area. John was a "contractor" who lived at Firebase Shkin, and the Slayers all took that to mean he worked for the CIA. True to stereotype, John was hard looking, former Special Forces. People took him seriously. He had access to information they didn't.

Immediately one of the officers went and found Captain Trahan in his room, reading a book about a team of British Special Forces hunting for SCUD missiles during the Gulf War. Insurgents had been spotted, he was told, although in Captain Trahan's experience, reports like this often turned out to be complete bullshit. The Americans worked with Afghan militia in the area who were ethnic Tajiks, and, to Captain Trahan, they usually seemed a tad too eager to share any bad news about the local Pashtuns, something of a rival ethnic group. Time and again the US special ops working with the militia would share reports of unusual behavior, Trahan would send a patrol to check it out, and they would find nothing.

Trahan went to the TOC and learned this report was quite different. John's intel came from a CIA predator drone.

"Ten to twelve guys, dressed in black. Crossing the border."

The assumption was they were hostile forces. John pointed to a spot on the map where the insurgents were seen. It was the same spot where soldiers at Firebase Shkin had found caches of rockets, from a location where they'd been fired upon many times before, just off Route Chevy.

Trahan suspected they were the same insurgents who'd launched rockets at Firebase Shkin a few days before. No one had been hurt, but the attack was intense. The blasts had shattered windows.

John wanted to investigate. After talking to Trahan, they decided to conduct a patrol to see what they could find. The patrol would be made up of a portion of 3rd Platoon, the military policemen (MPs) in Humvees, and a section of soldiers from D Company already on patrol near the border crossing.

Trahan also requested that fifty Afghan soldiers accompany them as 3rd Platoon rolled out.

Word rapidly spread throughout Firebase Shkin. Airman First Class Ray Losano came into the hut where Specialist Eddie Camacho and other Slayers were relaxing. He told them that drone sensors had picked up more than a dozen objects seemingly on their way to the camp from the mountains.

"They don't know if it's goats or whatever," Losano said. "But it's a lot, so we need to check it out."

Losano jumped into the Special Forces Humvee, with Camacho driving, newly-promoted Sergeant Jonathan Ray in the front passenger seat, Private First Class Matthew Emry in the back, and Jerod Dennis on the .50-cal.

"What the fuck you doing in my truck?!" Camacho asked the airman.

"C'mon, man," Losano said. "Don't be a dick."

"I don't care," Camacho said. "Get out."

Losano hopped out and found another Humvee.

A convoy of Humvees rolled out of Firebase Shkin, heading north, taking a right onto Route Corvette to a border checkpoint manned by Afghan militia members, then headed south down Route Chevy. Trahan was in the lead with his fire support officer Lieutenant Mike Dolan and a couple of others.

Trahan was radioed by Battalion Executive Officer Major John Hanson. Helicopters were coming to Firebase Shkin with mail and food. Two Apaches were providing escort, on standby if Trahan wanted to call them in for the search. Then Trahan asked Dolan to tell the Apaches to circle the area where they thought the insurgents might be, to see if they could find them. While he and his team waited for word from the birds, they drove to the homes of some locals.

Trahan had concluded that the Afghans near them were ambivalent about their presence. They were a destitute people, obliging but aloof when approached. Whenever possible, he would try to take the sting out of their searches by bringing a doctor or offering humanitarian aid. He knew the ugly fact of armed American soldiers going to a village and demanding that everyone gather, separating the men from the women and children, searching their homes, was bound to piss people off. Ambivalence was the best they could hope for.

They drove on Route Chevy, stopping to ask locals if they knew anything about insurgents who had crossed the border. No one knew anything. The Slayers covered several more miles of terrain but found nothing. The Apache pilots soon called back: they didn't see anything, either.

The birds circled and moved on—helicopters are big targets on the landing zone and would drop and go as fast as they could. Trahan was ready to pack it in. As long as they were out there, though, he thought it would be smart to check out the spot where the rockets had been coming from, up the hill.

Camacho drove up to the ledge where the drone had picked up the goats or whatever. They were at the top of a steep hill, the expanse of the Pakistan mountains clearly visible in the distance. It was a gorgeous day. Sun shining, not too hot yet. Jerod started talking about his mom, as he often did. How much he missed her, what a waste of time this all was.

The others arrived at the top of the hill, which was narrow and bumpy. Only a couple of Humvees could fit on the path. Large mounds of dirt, rock, and scrub brush sat atop the hill, obstructions so big a soldier might not be able to see the person thirty feet in front of him. The road was so steep a soldier couldn't see over the crest or anything directly on the other side of the hill unless he walked around to the other side.

Doc Simmons was driving the Humvee behind Trahan's, inside of which were Belcastro, Sergeant First Class John Setzer, Private Andy Kent, and Private Second Class James Elphick. Their vehicle broke down about one hundred meters from where they were headed.

Trahan's Humvee came to a stop, and they all exited the vehicle, splitting up to cover as much territory as they could, as did the US and Afghan teams behind them.

One of the MPs' Humvees pulled up and out popped Staff Sergeant Michiru Brown, a giant of a man, built like a middle linebacker, to help assess the situation.

Trahan walked to where they'd found caches of weapons before and there were the remnants of an insurgent camp—scattered canteens, burlap sacks for either camouflage or sleeping, three rockets already set up to be fired on Firebase Shkin with another cache of maybe ten with firing points set up.

Trahan turned to signal for Mike Dolan to come check it out, double time.

"I'm so sick of this shit," Jerod Dennis said.

At that moment, Sergeant Jonathan Ray felt a bullet snap by his ear, the opposite ridgeline exploded in gunfire and chaos, and the ground beneath them all erupted with gunfire.

To Trahan, it was like being in a sudden downpour, but those weren't raindrops jumping from the dirt, they were bullets from AKs and RPK machine guns. He hunched down and ran back toward the three Humvees, where he saw that a bullet had taken down the hulking Staff Sergeant Michiru Brown.

Sergeant Konrad Reed was just a few feet away when Brown went down, and in that split second he saw an insurgent, maybe ten to fifteen feet away, wearing military-style clothing and carrying a magazine holder across his chest.

And it was the damnedest thing; Reed was used to seeing Afghans, Pakistanis, even folks who looked like they came from the Middle East in the local insurgency. But the guy standing in front of him with the gun was Black. Not just Black—the blackest person he'd ever seen.

Reed hit the ground, and so did the insurgent. Then Reed started yelling for help for Brown.

"MEDIC! MEDIC!"

The hillside began lighting up with gunfire.

Blackwell and Losano had hopped out of their Humvee and had been walking toward Trahan when the ambush started. They hit the ground immediately. Bullets, grenades, explosions—they heard American soldiers crying out, cursing, screaming.

"Get Tombstone on the radio!" Blackwell yelled at Losano. "Tell 'em troops in contact 1972 when able!" They needed close air support as soon as humanly possible; it was vital that Losano alert the airbase at Bagram that they were in a TIC—troops in contact—and to give them the 1972—the full details of where to strike.

Losano began setting up his radio to call Tombstone at Bagram while Blackwell tried figuring out where the insurgents were and looking for cover. He would need to be able to give whatever air support showed up a clear picture of the ambush—where all the friendlies were, as well as the insurgents. There wasn't much on the road that they could hide behind. Bullets snapped and whizzed by them, kicking up plumes of dirt. An insurgent stepped out from behind a large rock, aimed his RPG launcher at them, and squeezed off the rocket. Thankfully it sailed past both men, but it was clear they couldn't stay in the road.

The 82nd's military police had driven two up-armored Humvees there, and Blackwell realized one of them was close enough to run to, maybe seventy yards away.

"Grab your ruck!" Blackwell yelled at his friend. They began sprinting to the MPs' Humvee. Enemy gunfire continued to target them. As they ran, their destination felt impossibly far, as if they were running in mud. Finally, they arrived at the Humvee, which was facing east, toward Pakistan, and ran to the back of the vehicle. Blackwell patted down Losano to make sure he hadn't been hit; Losano did the same to Blackwell. They both then crawled up the passenger side of the Humvee, with Blackwell beside the front tire and Losano just to his right. Losano resumed radioing Tombstone.

Suddenly cognizant that they were huddling near the front tire of a giant Humvee that might back up at any moment, Blackwell flashed back to a horrible moment in the early 1990s during a Joint Readiness Training Center Army exercise back at Fort Polk, Louisiana. One night, a young soldier drove through their camp without waking up his buddy to put on night-vision goggles and help guide him through the area. He drove over two soldiers in their sleeping bags. Their screams still haunted Blackwell.

Blackwell backed up to the rear passenger door to yell at the driver, Specialist Matthew Meyers.

"We're laying on the ground near the front tires!" he yelled at Meyers. "Lay on the horn if you need to leave, and we'll jump in with you!" Above Meyers, Private First Class James Torbet manned the Humvee's .50-cal turret gun.

Tombstone radioed back to Ray Losano. Aircraft were being directed to them, F-16s, each carrying two GBU-12s, five-hundred-pound laser-guided bombs, and equipped with the M61A1 twenty-millimeter six-barreled Gatling gun.

"Blues 03 ETA five minutes!" Losano shouted to Blackwell.

Through the driver's side backseat window, Blackwell saw US soldiers moving forward to return fire. He looked toward the insurgents. He needed to determine the best way to guide the F-16s to take out the enemy. They were looking east toward Pakistan. The best way to attack was north to south, he figured. But given the proximity of the enemy—maybe fifty yards or even closer than that—Blackwell knew he and his fellow servicemembers were well within "Danger Close," making it extremely risky to call for any bombs to be dropped. Their best bet was to have the F-16s buzz as low and fast as possible—a show of force—to chase the enemy away and then bomb them once the minimum safe distance could be established for a Danger Close engagement.

"Stay behind your ruck, you'll be fine!" he yelled at Losano, when suddenly Private Torbet, still standing above them in the .50-cal turret, got shot in the head.

CHAPTER TWELVE

THE GOLDEN HOUR

Paktika Province, Afghanistan

Blackwell hopped into the Humvee to check on Torbet, who was wobbling. Expecting Torbet's head to be split open, Blackwell rolled the young man over and was surprised to see him looking back with wide-open eyes. The round had hit his helmet's rim, and the force of it had knocked him back, but the bullet hadn't penetrated the helmet.

"You're good, brother!" Blackwell said happily, patting Torbet. "You just got knocked out."

"I'm good!" Torbet said. They both laughed.

"Get on the fifty!" Meyers yelled. Someone needed to return fire.

"I have CAS coming, *you* get on the fifty!" Blackwell shouted.

Doc Simmons and the guys in his Humvee—Belcastro, Setzer, Kent, and Elphick—had run up from their broken-down truck as soon as they heard gunfire. Simmons heard Reed yelling for a medic and ran to

Sergeant David Cyr Jr. behind a tree. Who needed help? Who was yelling "medic"? Cyr directed Simmons to Staff Sergeant Michiru Brown, and Simmons instinctively ran toward the sound of the cries for help, almost forgetting that they were under fire. Brown was bleeding heavily from his left leg, just above the knee.

Simmons knew the leading cause of death for soldiers in battle was uncontrolled blood loss, so he immediately tried to stop the bleeding with direct pressure and field dressings. That didn't work, so he fashioned a tourniquet out of a cravat and a whittled stick he had, just to do what he could and get Michiru Brown the hell out of there.

In Jerod Dennis's Humvee, everyone had gotten out to patrol except for him and Eddie Camacho. Jerod was standing in the turret, manning the .50-cal. When they first heard the machine-gun fire, Camacho thought it was an accidental discharge by the US.

Ooh, someone's going to get in trouble, Camacho thought, having learned that occasionally the safeties of exhausted soldiers can get snagged on branches, accidentally popping off a round.

But then Camacho spotted holes in the hood of his truck and realized they were under fire. Rifle fire was soon enough replaced by machine-gun fire. Camacho expected Jerod to return fire, but nothing happened.

"Dennis, you gotta shoot!" Camacho yelled.

"I can't get it to fire!" Jerod yelled back.

An insurgent down the embankment on the left began throwing grenades up the hill.

Camacho looked out the window and saw Ray Losano right at the moment a bullet hit him.

Blackwell was taking cover, leaning inside Meyers's Humvee as the door behind him slammed against him. Then it began slamming into him again. And again. He didn't know what the hell was going on.

He stepped out of the back of the Humvee and saw it was Ray Losano kicking at the door. He was holding his face with his hands as blood sprayed from his mouth and poured out of him.

Losano was gravely wounded. A bullet had hit the top of the radio, deflected through several fingers on his left hand, then hit him in the left side of his face, taking off his lower jaw. His eyes revealed desperate panic and terror.

Blackwell ran to Losano and grabbed him by the top of his kit, dragging him behind the Humvee. He kept falling down. Losano was heavy and the earth beneath his feet rocky and uneven. Blackwell was racked with guilt. Why hadn't he made his friend sit in the Humvee?

"MEDIC!" he yelled. "MEDIC!"

He knew Doc Simmons was busy. So many guys had been shot up. But Blackwell kept yelling and yelling because if he stopped, he knew no one would ever come help Ray Losano.

"MEDIC!"

Amid the chaos of the battle and the bullets and the grenades, Simmons didn't hear him. He was focused on Brown right then, and doing quite a bit of yelling himself.

Camacho had heard someone tell him Brown needed to be picked up, rescued from the line of fire, given medical care. Foot on the gas, Camacho went to them immediately.

Emry, too, responded to Simmons's shouts for help. Soon the three of them were carrying Brown to the Humvee—Camacho carrying his arms, Emry trying to hold his bad leg up, Simmons with the good leg.

Bullets hit the Humvee, and Simmons snapped back into the moment, realizing the degree to which they were under heavy enemy fire. He remembered from training to create a casualty collection point away from danger. Emry got behind the wheel, and they tore down the road.

"The truck's shaking so much I can't put in the IV!" Simmons shouted.

Camacho had been manning the .240 on the front-right passenger side, so he jumped into the back to help.

But then smoke started pluming out of the hood; they'd been hit. The Humvee came to a stop down the road, thankfully out of the line of enemy fire. But they were stuck.

"I'm going to bleed out!" yelled Brown, still very conscious.

"Go find help," Camacho commanded Jerod, who hopped out and ran down the hill.

Blackwell was screaming for the medic, holding his friend in his arms. Ray Losano was dying. He was pulling at Lee Marvin Blackwell, clawing at him. Staring at him. Begging him wordlessly to save him.

"I love you, Ray," Blackwell said. "I'm proud of you."

Losano was losing so much blood. The life was leaving him.

"Your family loves you, Ray," Blackwell said. "Hang in there, Ray. Calm down." He began holding him tighter.

"MEDIC! MEDIC!"

Shrapnel from a grenade had peppered Reed's left foot early in the ambush, but he kept going, returning fire and trying to stay alive. Now he was scrambling back to Trahan's Humvee to call for artillery fire against the insurgents.

As he arrived, Trahan was telling Dolan to report back to the base that they were in contact with enemy fire, which was intensifying, not just rifles but also machine guns—the rounds more rapid, higher velocity.

This was significant. Trahan had worried this was a friendly-fire event, having suspected the Afghan militia of firing at them accidentally.

But when the attack kicked up again, Trahan knew these were not the lower-caliber rifles of the militias but the heavy machine guns of insurgents. This was an ambush.

"Prepare an indirect fire mission," Trahan told Dolan, meaning a request for the artillery unit to fire rounds nearby so the Slayers could escape while the insurgents took cover. They had two M119 howitzers back at the base, "lightweight" 105 mm howitzers, meaning they weighed only two tons.

Before Konrad Reed left the firebase that morning, he'd given potential target information to the artillery unit at the firebase. He didn't have his radio any longer, so Dolan grabbed his own radio out of the Humvee and handed it to Reed. The target they'd originally planned for was too far from them and the insurgents.

"I'm going to get a better look where the enemy's at," Trahan said. He stood and began walking to the crest of the hill.

A bullet immediately grazed his arm, and then two insurgents popped up roughly 150 feet away, one firing his AK-47, the other throwing hand grenades.

Reed saw a spray of red mist burst from Trahan's leg as he went down.

The captain was hit in his legs once, twice, three times. A fourth bullet hit his helmet, grazing his head.

"Grenade!" yelled Dolan.

Reed looked around to see where the incoming might be coming from, but before he could spot anything a grenade exploded a few yards away, throwing him fifteen feet, knocking him unconscious, and spraying his body with dozens of pieces of shrapnel.

Meyers and the driver of the second MP Humvee, Private Stephanie Pavliska, low-crawled to Blackwell and Losano.

Pavliska plugged one of Losano's wounds with her fingers while simultaneously plugging an IV into his arm.

Hovering over Losano, Blackwell looked around and motioned to Belcastro, who was lying prone thirty feet away. Signaling with his hands—pointing at the Humvee, then Ray Losano—Blackwell told Belcastro to get Losano out of there. Belcastro, Kent, and Elphick then high-crawled to Losano and picked him up.

Ray Losano was a big guy. It was tough. They dropped him a bunch of times on their way but finally got him loaded up, after which they ran back to their squad, which was backed against a steep ravine.

The Humvees began rolling down the hill to the casualty collection point.

A Humvee pulled up to Camacho, Simmons, Emry, and Brown.

SFC Setzer poked his head out from the passenger side. Doc Simmons could see from the damage on his vest that rounds had hit him there. On his face he had what appeared to be burn marks, likely from the same rounds, burning his face but not puncturing his skin, what passes for luck in battle.

"What's going on?" Setzer said.

"We got a guy shot bleeding out," Camacho said. He didn't know Brown, since the guys at the firebase pretty much kept to their small teams. "And we're stuck, so we sent Dennis to get help. We sent him to get you guys."

"We didn't see him," Setzer said.

Setzer hopped out, and Brown was carried to the Humvee, tended to by Doc Simmons. They turned around and zoomed down the hill.

But within a few seconds, a Hilux pickup driven by an Afghan soldier pulled up, containing Jerod Dennis.

"Shit yes, Dennis," Camacho said.

"You need to help me pick who comes with us," Setzer said to Camacho.

"What do you mean?" he asked.

"We're going back up the hill and flank these motherfuckers," Setzer said.

Camacho wondered how they were going to accomplish that with only three soldiers, but he told Setzer to bring Jerod Dennis, who had an M249 light machine gun.

Back in the tactical operations center at Firebase Shkin, it was chaos and confusion. Lieutenant Nathan was desperately trying to understand the situation on the battlefield, miles away. He and his team were trying to chart all the activity on a map, dashing off the ten-digit coordinates to pinpoint each engagement. For Nathan, the feeling of helplessness was overwhelming.

First Sergeant Severino led a handful of Humvees packed with extra Class 1 (MREs and water) and Class 5 (ammunition) to a small farm with a structure that had walls that would give some protection. It was in his mind a position that was somewhat defensible, if need be, not far from the ambush site but far enough. He'd brought with him a physician assistant and a senior medic. The surgeon stayed back at Firebase Shkin, prepping for whatever might come his way.

They waited for the wounded.

In medicine, particularly combat medicine, there is an intense focus on the "Golden Hour," those pivotal minutes after any traumatic injury where prompt medical and surgical treatment can prevent death.

Severino was acutely aware of the Golden Hour and the ugly fact that Firebase Shkin was remote. Once loaded on a chopper from Firebase Shkin, a wounded soldier would have a forty-five-minute flight to Forward Operating Base Salerno, the trip a Golden Hour unto itself.

Every minute, every second, could mean life or death.

Fueled by adrenaline and the simple desire to survive, Trahan managed to pick himself up and run hunched over to his Humvee, where Dolan was waiting.

Knowing Doc Simmons was long gone, Cyr ran to Trahan to help him out and got to work bandaging up Trahan's legs.

Reed woke up, his ears ringing, in intense pain, his arms and legs covered in blood. He had no idea what kind of shape he was in, but he did know if they didn't get some type of artillery fire or some additional support in the next few minutes, the enemy would advance, more Americans would be shot, and they might be completely overrun.

He grabbed the military FM radio again to call the artillery unit back at the base, grabbing his GPS. But his device had been blown up by the grenade—the screen was cracked, the rubber holder burned and twisted. The screen had frozen at the moment of contact, so Reed was able to read some coordinates, presumably in the neighborhood of accurate, developing a target location to feed back to the base.

The artillery guys back at Firebase Shkin fired two artillery rounds at the coordinates for the enemy, but they were way off, about two football fields away, so Dolan and Reed told the firebase to bring them about three hundred feet closer. Those next shots seemed to do the trick, with the enemy scurrying down the hill into an area where the US couldn't get them.

Suddenly the Americans were being fired upon by a heavy machine gun from across the border, by Pakistani forces. Trahan assumed the Pakistani border guards mistakenly thought the Americans were trying to shoot them, rather than the insurgents, and were returning fire. Either way, with Losano and Reed wounded, not to mention himself, Trahan figured it was high time to get the hell out of there.

Setzer was sitting shotgun—which in the Hilux truck was the left front seat—as the Afghan soldier veered their vehicle off the path to the ambush.

"Whoa!" Camacho yelled from the back seat. "Whoa!"

"I told him to do that," Setzer said. "To flank. We gotta save our brothers."

"Get down!" Jerod Dennis yelled from the back of the pickup as he started firing his gun and a rocket headed toward the Hilux.

Camacho looked toward the front of the truck and saw a rocket headed right for them, almost as if in slow motion. It missed the Hilux at the last minute, with Jerod continuing to spray fire with his machine gun, but insurgents unleashed a punishing spray of bullets and rockets and RPGs. The Hilux crashed into a tree. Men in the truck got hit, but it wasn't clear who and how bad.

Jerod continued to provide cover fire. Camacho got out of the truck. He saw the Afghan driver and Setzer sprinting down the hill. He saw Jerod get down from the truck bed.

"I'm shot," Jerod said.

Camacho saw that Jerod's pant leg was soaking wet with blood, a dark red, almost a brown.

"Fuck," Camacho said. "Go run to where Setzer ran while I hold 'em off."

"I'm not leaving you," Jerod said.

"Go!" commanded Camacho, running behind the truck and firing as much as possible at the enemy.

Jerod Dennis began hopping down the hill as best he could, as fast as he could, shot in his leg, bleeding severely.

CHAPTER THIRTEEN

THE ROMAN

Firebase Shkin, Afghanistan

At the casualty collection point, Doc Simmons was monitoring Brown's leg wound, adjusting the tourniquet a bit at a time, trying to keep some circulation in his leg.

"Fuck!" Brown yelled, in intense pain.

Simmons filled a hypodermic needle with a sizable dose of morphine and jabbed Brown's butt.

That was when the Humvee containing Ray Losano arrived.

Simmons removed his tracheotomy kit from his bag and began checking Losano's vital signs—breathing, airway, and circulation.

He immediately realized Losano wasn't breathing at all. He had no pulse.

Panicking, Simmons pulled out a chest tube to insert into Losano's chest to drain the blood from his lungs. But he heard a gurgling sound from his neck: blood was bubbling. He then realized it wouldn't do any good. Losano wasn't moving. He wasn't breathing. Simmons wanted to perform CPR and attempt to breathe for him, so he tried to lift his chin to open his airway but his lower jaw was so damaged, he couldn't. There was no way to carry out any serious first-responder action without being in an OR.

"If you can hear me, God loves you, I'm here for you," Simmons said. "Everything's going to be okay. Put your trust in Jesus, and everything's going to be all right."

As a last resort, Simmons grabbed a pocket mask from his kit. He tried to push air into Losano's lungs, but it didn't work. There was no rise and fall in his chest.

There was nothing he could do.

Simmons tried to hide the fact from everyone else that Losano was dead, especially from Brown, who needed to stay as calm as possible if he was going to survive.

Soon enough, the incoming from the enemy was so overwhelming, Camacho couldn't even return fire. He sprinted down the hill.

He came to the Afghan driver, lying on his stomach on the ground, Emry putting pressure on his ass, soaked in blood. Before he could get to them, Setzer approached him, speed-walking. He was holding his face. It looked as though half his jaw had been blown off; when Setzer tried to talk, Camacho could see his tongue.

"Where's Dennis?" Camacho asked.

"He's dead," Setzer said, thinking Jerod was still back in the truck up the hill. "He's dead."

"No, he's not," Camacho said. "He followed behind you."

Camacho tried to patch Setzer up with gauze. Humvees started rushing up and down the road.

"Dennis is still out there," Camacho said to anyone who would listen. "He ran, but we can't find him."

When Severino heard Jerod was missing, he decided to immediately send a mounted element to a spot up the road where Afghan coal burners served as a landmark, and another dismounted element over rougher terrain. The goal was to approach Jerod's last known position from two different directions, hoping to find him on the way. Severino approached one of the MPs, Staff Sergeant Keith Graf, to helm the mounted element.

"We got a Humvee broke down by the coal burner," he said.

He told Graf to take his MP squad to tow the Humvee, maybe a kilometer away from the point of the ambush. By now the better-targeted artillery as well as an influx of A-10 Warthog attack planes and helicopters had chased the enemy off.

Graf grabbed his gunner, Specialist Nathan Petty, and the rest of his squad, and they drove up the hill in two Humvees. Petty knew Jerod Dennis a bit, thought he was a sweet kid, thought of him as very young, green, and super country. They quickly ran into Camacho, Setzer, and the Afghan driver. Setzer tried to talk to Graf, but his jaw injury was so severe, Graf couldn't understand a word he was saying. Graf and the other MPs began loading Setzer and the Afghan into their truck, when Camacho approached him.

"Dennis is still out there," Camacho said.

"Are you fucking kidding me?" Graf asked.

"He ran down the hill," Camacho said.

Graf had the other Humvee rush Setzer and the Afghan back to the casualty collection point. He radioed for another truck to tow the broken vehicle, and while he waited, he and Petty yelled for Jerod Dennis.

"Dennis!" they screamed. "Dennis!"

They separated and yelled for Jerod Dennis for maybe five minutes. Graf wanted to hear Jerod's voice so badly, he could feel it in the pit of his heart. At one point he thought he heard an answer, from up the hill to the left, maybe eleven o'clock. Was his mind playing tricks on him?

He didn't feel comfortable heading farther up the hill until more of his MPs joined him; he thought about doing "reconnaissance by fire," firing rounds in the direction of where they'd seen plumes of dust from before, hoping to get the enemy to reveal their location. But it wasn't worth risking hitting Jerod Dennis, so he thought better of it. Jerod could be hurt, he could be bleeding out.

"Sit tight," said a call from Firebase Shkin. "Infantry joining on foot."

Graf knew what that meant: don't go looking for Jerod Dennis.

But Petty thought he'd heard something, too.

"You're coming in broken and unreadable," Graf said, "I'm going to go ahead and go."

Petty, Graf, and some of the other MPs drove up the hill, stopping when they arrived at the demolished Hilux, and got out of their trucks. The dirt was littered with AK brass, the casings from enemy bullets, hundreds and hundreds. An M4 carbine sat on the roof.

Graf walked down the hill, looking for Jerod Dennis.

As soon as he got out of eyesight of the others, Graf thought to himself, *Son of a bitch, this is not the smartest thing I've ever done.*

He'd walked maybe three hundred yards down the hill when he spotted what looked like a pair of red pants jutting out from behind a tree. He figured it was an Afghan; they sometimes wore colorful sweatpants. He scanned the area, looking for insurgents, remaining as quiet as a church mouse. As he got closer to the red pants, he saw they weren't sweatpants—they were US Army issued, soaked red with blood.

Then he saw the standard-issue desert boots. Then a brown T-shirt.

Then Jerod Dennis came into full view.

His chest was moving.

He was breathing.

He was alive.

Graf bent down and rolled Jerod toward him, pulling him out from under the tree. Jerod was lethargic, moving slowly but on his own. He gave him a once-over, quickly coming to the conclusion that Jerod had lost so much blood, there wasn't much he could do for him there. They needed to evacuate him at once.

"Buddy, we found you," Graf said. "We're going to get you out of here."

Graf called out to the rest of his squad at the top of the hill.

Petty came down. He'd never seen so much blood before in his life.

"Hey, man, it's Petty," he said.

"Hey, man, nice to meet you, I'm suckin'," Jerod Dennis said, always the class clown.

They carried him up to the Humvee and put him into the back, on the gunner's platform. Petty had to sit on top of the Humvee, since there wasn't any room inside. He kept talking to Jerod, trying to keep him awake, trying to keep him alive.

"Hold on!" Petty said. "We're almost there!"

Jerod seemed in and out of consciousness, squirming on the gunner's platform.

"Dennis!" Petty shouted. "Hold on! Hold on!"

"I am! I am!" Jerod said.

Back at the casualty collection point, after Jerod Dennis was given blood and stabilized, he was ground evac'd back to Firebase Shkin. The medevac helicopters were on their way, but there was time to have the surgeon look at him before the choppers arrived.

As the medic bandaged his leg, Severino talked to Jerod.

"Hey, man, you're going up to Bagram," he told him. "You're young, you're strong, you're going to be sleeping in a nice warm bed with actual sheets, not these nasty cots."

Severino could see Jerod was scared. Some of it was shock, but he also knew getting shot had to be terrifying; his eyes were wider than he'd ever seen them. Still hopeful, the first sergeant kept talking up the young private.

"You're going to be eating good food at Bagram, having ice cream," Severino told him. "You'll be all healed up and you'll join the team again. We'll see you in about a week."

Soon enough, Jerod, John Setzer, and Konrad Reed were loaded up and medevac'd from the base in a Black Hawk helicopter to FOB Salerno. Reed was crouching in a corner of the Black Hawk, Setzer sitting in another, a bandage holding his jaw in place, a sad, shitty look on his face. In front of them the medics hovered over Jerod Dennis, trying to keep him breathing, filling his body with fluids and blood.

Staff Sergeant Michiru Brown and Captain Scott Trahan were driven from the casualty collection point to the firebase. They needed surgery but were stable enough to be flown all the way to Bagram.

Setzer and Jerod were in such bad shape, they would have to stay on longer at FOB Salerno, which had a level-two medical facility where surgery would be necessary.

When they landed at Salerno, they were taken to three separate tents. John Setzer's rough wound but stable condition meant he was then also whisked to Bagram, where they could better repair the damage. Konrad Reed's arms, legs, and torso were spotted with shrapnel. Some big chunks, loose in his skin, were removed, but most of the dozens of pieces of metal were too tiny to remove at FOB Salerno. His condition was stable but he, too, would have to head to Bagram. Reed's wounds were bandaged; he was given painkillers and told he would need to wait for Jerod Dennis.

The medical unit was a series of tents with their sides rolled up. Reed headed to a picnic table area where soldiers took smoke breaks and attempted to clear their heads. Reed sat there with some soldiers he happened to know and was able to look into Jerod Dennis's tent, where doctors focused on giving him oxygen and blood and stopping the bleeding.

From what Reed could ascertain, Jerod Dennis had been hit twice in his femoral artery, in his groin area, causing massive blood loss. For hours Reed watched doctors and surgical teams rotating in and out of Jerod's tent trying different things to stop the bleeding. To him it appeared the teams would work for an hour or two, find some success in stanching the bleeding. Then thirty or so minutes later, Jerod would reenter dangerous territory, and the medical teams would go at it again.

It took them all day before they thought Jerod was safe for transport. They'd arrived in the morning, but Reed and Jerod Dennis didn't load up into a Black Hawk to head to Bagram until night. It was a specially rigged helicopter for medical transport, with two bunks on top of each other where stretchers could be fastened. In intense pain, Reed was on the top bunk. He could move a little, but his arms, legs, and chest were throbbing. Jerod Dennis was on the lower bunk, consuming most of the attention of the nurse who accompanied them on the agonizing thirty-minute flight.

The bird finally landed. The surgical hospital at Bagram, too, was a series of tents. Konrad Reed watched Jerod Dennis be whisked away to the right, straight to surgery, while he was taken to triage on the left. Reed was terrified for his friend. Having witnessed everything Jerod had to go through that day, he didn't think it possible he would survive.

The next few hours were a blur. After being examined, Reed was given some medication. Someone from division headquarters for the 82nd Airborne stopped by to see how he was doing. Two guys who seemed to be with intelligence, maybe CIA, also came by to debrief him on the attack.

Around midnight, a doctor came in to check on him. The next day, he said, they'd get some X-rays of Reed to see how bad his wounds were.

Only then could they determine whether they should send him to Landstuhl Regional Medical Center, a US Army post in Landstuhl, Germany, near Ramstein Air Base.

"Hey," Reed said, "the other guy I came in with—how's he doing?"

There was a grim expression on the doctor's face as he shared the news. "We weren't able to stop the bleeding," he said. "He didn't survive the operation."

Konrad Reed broke down in tears. The doctor kept talking, but Reed didn't hear a word he said.

Doc Simmons had returned to the hill with some other soldiers, looking for bodies or anything left behind from the battle, taking photographs of any evidence of the firefight. Called a TSE, or "tactical site exploitation," it's the military version of what law enforcement does at a crime scene.

Just hours before they'd all been ambushed, but now all Doc Simmons could hear was wind.

He couldn't stop thinking about the impossibility of saving Ray Losano, the horrific things bullets did to him, and Jerod Dennis, and John Setzer. Michiru Brown and Konrad Reed would likely survive, but their bodies would never be the same.

None of them, really, would ever be the same.

On the far side of the hill, Doc Simmons saw the dead body of an enemy fighter. The bottom half of one of his legs was blown off, and jutted out at a right angle from his body. He had a bizarre, evil grin on his face. Simmons looked in his pockets, finding a toothbrush and about a dozen grenade pins. Grenades that had been used with the express purpose of killing Americans. His fellow soldiers. His friends.

Doc Simmons looked down at his aid bag, with the four-by-six-inch image of Jesus embracing the Roman soldier ensconced in plastic and neatly framed by white medical tape. He thought about why he'd fastened it to his bag, about his belief that he was there to tend to every one of God's children, even those who sought his destruction, as with the Romans and Jesus.

But the battle had changed his heart. He ripped that picture off his bag, folded it up, and put it away forever.

CHAPTER FOURTEEN

THE LOST ARK

New York, New York

The pressure from the Italians was polite but relentless. They would reach out to Bill Nardini—the US Justice Department's presence in Rome—on a regular basis and check on how the case was proceeding. The subtext—and sometimes the text—was clear: they'd been holding Spin Ghul since June and did not want to hold him much longer. Legally there were also questions as to how much longer they could do so.

Italy was going through its own turmoil and rash of homegrown terrorism. Uncertainty about spending cuts pushed by Prime Minister Silvio Berlusconi caused markets to roil. By November 2011, Italy's borrowing costs were reaching dangerous levels. The European Union was demanding reforms, and Italian labor minister Maurizio Sacconi was warning it all "could lead to a new wave of attacks" from leftist terrorist groups.

Sacconi's alarm was merited. Less than two months later, letters containing bullets were sent to the mayor of Rome and the justice minister. A package bomb was mailed from Italy to the Greek embassy in Paris. Mail bombs were sent to the director of the state tax collection agency, seriously wounding him, and to a Deutsche Bank chief executive. The Italians had a terrorism problem, but it wasn't related to Spin Ghul, and its government wasn't exactly flush with cash to indefinitely hold on to prisoners whom America had interest in.

The political realities and limitations on Italy's desire to hold Spin Ghul created constant pressure for Bitkower and Shreve, a ticking time bomb with the release of an al Qaeda terrorist at stake. Every day of their investigation that didn't get them any closer to an indictment was a failure, one that could ultimately result in Spin Ghul getting out and committing a horrific act of violence. Thankfully, it wasn't just the two of them doing the detective work.

When FBI special agent Raushaunah Muhammad was fourteen months old, her father died under suspicious circumstances.

The details of his death in Okinawa, Japan, were obscured by the time they hit the pages of his hometown newspaper, the *Baltimore Sun*, in 1980. His obituary noted that the twenty-two-year-old communications technician served with the National Security Agency at Fort Meade and had turned down an athletic scholarship to join the Army in 1974. His death was attributed to a "short illness." Lots of uncomfortable facts came to light after her father's death. But for whatever reason—Raushaunah Muhammad would attribute it to happenstance—this child born amid secrets would end up dedicating her career to uncovering them—and preventing murders.

Generations of her family had set an example by serving their country. Her granddaddy served in the Korean War, her great uncle had been a POW, and her mother worked for the US Air Force. Raushaunah had always been on the path to public service. Recruited by the FBI at a college job fair, the Morgan State ROTC student had thought the Bureau would assign her to the cybercrimes squad given her degree in engineering. But perhaps because her maternal grandparents had converted to Islam during the 1970s, the powers that be sent her to counterterrorism instead. She wasn't a particularly religious Muslim, but she was happy to work wherever she was needed, in this case on the New York Field Office "Rest of Africa" (ROA) squad, West Africa team at the FBI's Joint Terrorism Task Force site in Manhattan, where she and her fellow agents teamed up with Bitkower and Shreve.[1]

In May 2011, Raushaunah had had surgery for thyroid cancer. Scar on her neck notwithstanding, she was back at her desk weeks later—just in time for the squad's IA—intelligence analyst—to inform them at the morning briefing that Spin Ghul had been picked up by the Italians.

Raushaunah was a case agent, building folders on criminal activities from scratch, interviewing witnesses, gathering evidence, building out files on suspected bad guys, and bringing the materials when ready to the relevant US attorney. She and her team kept tabs on anything criminal going on in the vast majority of the African continent that might hurt the US or its allies. If something terrorist-related happened in Africa, there was a better than 50 percent chance that she had worked on it—kidnappings, hostage takings, murders, bombings, piracy, narco-terrorism, and attacks on embassies. She'd deployed to Kampala for the 2010 bombing, worked on the Benghazi investigation, briefly assisted with the case against the Somalis who on April 8, 2009, hijacked the *Maersk Alabama* container ship in the Indian Ocean and took Captain Richard Phillips as a hostage, until a team of Navy SEALs had stepped in.

Spin Ghul was exactly the kind of individual the West Africa team would be tracking. He was from Niger and flew to Nigeria after his time in Waziristan. There he met with like-minded Islamist terrorists,

---

[1] At the time of the Spin Ghul case, the ROA squad covered all countries outside of the Horn of Africa (Djibouti, Eritrea, Ethiopia, and Somalia). The West Africa team was part of the ROA. Later on, the continent would be split up into further teams. For simplicity, this book will refer to the West Africa team.

such as the "Nigerian Taliban," which would soon become Boko Haram, and the "Salafist Group for Prayer and Combat," which had its origins in Algeria and would within a few years become al Qaeda in the Islamic Maghreb, or AQIM. He was very much on the FBI's radar before he'd vanished. In the summer of 2011, Raushaunah was extremely interested to learn Spin Ghul had been picked up.

Later that day, walking in the hall, she ran into the brand-new guy on the team, Bert LaCroix. Trinidadian by birth, American by choice, LaCroix had served in both the US Army in Iraq and the NYPD. Now he was a counterintelligence special agent with the US Army, a civilian job, assigned by the Department of Defense to the JTTF.

The forty-five-year-old was carrying his boxes to his desk. It was his first day.

"Hey," she said, "you're DOD, right?"

"Yeah," said LaCroix.

"Come with me," she told him.

Agent Raushaunah Muhammad had a new case for them to work on. One that would end up consuming their lives. And just like that, LaCroix's next seven years of work at the DoD were set in motion before he could even unpack his stapler.

Jim Hodgson's grandparents were quick to notice that he had a special kind of brain, one extraordinarily wired for detail. As a kid in rural Indiana, that meant being able to recite all sorts of baseball statistics, such as the fact that Pittsburgh Pirate Roberto Clemente had only 240 home runs among his 3,000 career hits, before his tragic plane crash at age thirty-eight while delivering aid to survivors of the 1972 earthquake in Nicaragua.

As an adult, it meant a similarly encyclopedic knowledge of known terrorists.

Bitkower and Shreve met Hodgson when they served on President Obama's Gitmo task force to shut down Guantánamo Bay. They found the soft-spoken, bespectacled redhead unusual for a US Army Criminal Investigative Division expert—a kind of military detective who tended to fit the type A machismo mold.

In this case, Bitkower and Shreve found that Hodgson, peculiarities and all, was utterly indispensable. The files on the detained terrorists in Gitmo were thin and wanting. The CIA contractors and Navy SEALs who had caught suspected terrorists had not been trained to, nor were they required to, build legal cases. So that job fell on Bitkower, Shreve, and others on the task force, who needed to ascertain what actual evidence existed.

And for that they had Hodgson. For hours, the three men would sit with a translator in dusty rooms packed with overflowing file cabinets looking for documents, and Hodgson would call out, with incredible accuracy, ones that might contain a fingerprint, a signature, or a contemporaneous account.

Hodgson's path to the team investigating Spin Ghul began when the criminal justice major joined the Army, ending up within a few years at the Criminal Investigative Division. He soon acquired a reputation for excellence and was tapped for high-level assignments.

In April 2003, after the start of Operation Iraqi Freedom to remove Saddam Hussein's regime from power, Hodgson was flown from Pope Air Force Base in North Carolina to Camp Arifjan, Kuwait. In September, he flew to Baghdad. Lodged in an old police barracks near the Baghdad International Airport, he worked at the Al-Faw Palace complex, the grounds of which included a lake fully stocked with what were referred to as "Saddam's bass." But Hodgson wasn't there to fish. He was assigned to the Army CID's War Crimes Investigation Team. The man who was once obsessed with every stat on his Topps baseball cards was now focused on the deck of cards the Defense Intelligence Agency produced of the "Most Wanted Iraqis" for US soldiers so they would be able to recognize key figures in Saddam Hussein's network.

Hodgson's mien was mild and deferential. When he would interrogate prisoners at Camp Cropper, he would put his hand over his heart when he said *Salaam aleikum*. He greeted these wanted men by shaking with two hands. He picked their brains, asked them about their opinions on various subjects. He found this approach effective. His rapport with detainees elicited testimony about Saddam, other senior leaders, and their decisions to commit horrific atrocities—including the mass slaughter and torture of citizens of the Shiite town of al-Dujail in 1982. Hodgson was integral to the US's Coalition Provisional Authority's ability to build the case against Saddam, one utilized by the Iraqi High Tribunal after Saddam was captured in December 2003. Two of Hodgson's reports were used in the trial. Saddam Hussein was convicted of crimes against humanity and hanged in December 2006.

His work was just as vital on Obama's Gitmo commission. Hodgson would mumble something like "This batch of documents might be interesting; it was found in a particular safe house known to be associated with" a specific terrorist—and the documents not only would be where he recalled they were, as he described, but also would often include a key piece of evidence.

Before they even flew to Italy in September 2011, Bitkower and Shreve invited Hodgson to New York City to prepare. They needed to assess what they already knew about Spin Ghul. The information at the time was deeply classified, but Spin Ghul had been mentioned by name by other al Qaeda operatives captured in previous years.

A member of al Qaeda mentioned in the 9/11 report, a Pakistani from the Waziristan region named Mustafa Hajji Muhammad Khan, or Hassan Ghul, was captured in January 2004 and handed over to the CIA. Khan knew quite a bit about al Qaeda facilities and procedures in the border area of Pakistan, and—under CIA duress—shared enough information to fill at least twenty-one different intelligence reports. These included many details about the al Qaeda operatives who lived in or traveled through the Shakai Valley near Angoor Ada, a town in Pakistan along the Afghan border near Firebase Shkin, a specific fact that was included in at least sixteen of the intel reports. Khan also described in detail the career ambitions and workplace tensions of Spin Ghul's boss in Angoor Ada, Abdul Hadi al-Iraqi, or "Hadi."

Hadi—the same man Bitkower and Shreve had discussed in detail on Obama's Gitmo commission. The man from whom Spin Ghul allegedly took orders and sought guidance during his days in the Angoor Ada al Qaeda safe house.

And Hadi himself also talked about Spin Ghul.

Long after Spin Ghul left the Afghan battlefield hoping to fulfill his wish of carrying out a more serious bombing attack, Osama bin Laden ordered Hadi to travel to Iraq to help the local al Qaeda affiliate there. Hadi's journey required a flight through Turkey, where he was detained in late October 2006 before being handed over to the US.

Hadi was held in a CIA black site for 170 days, then transferred to Gitmo in April 2007. His 2007 charging document asserted that Hadi, "during 2002-04, was in charge of cross-border attacks in Afghanistan against Coalition forces." He had a lot to share. Especially after the CIA had at him.

Hodgson knew all these obscure details almost by heart and had given a nonclassified briefing to Bitkower, Shreve, and others from the Justice Department and FBI before they flew to Rome. The way Bitkower and Shreve pictured Hodgson hunting down the potential evidence was almost like the last scene of *Raiders of the Lost Ark*—Hodgson facing down an impossibly immense warehouse full of everything the US government had ever collected, boxes and crates as far as the eye could see. Keys to the universe stacked away and ignored forever. Hodgson was their guide to that warehouse.

For Hodgson it was more zeros and ones—the database he could access either with his computer or his brain.

The one in his brain was a marvel.

The one he could access from his desk was called DOMEX.

DOMEX means "Document and media exploitation," and it was an ever-expanding part of intelligence work in the information age.

The summer before, in an issue of the *Military Intelligence Professional Bulletin*, one colonel had argued that the US needed to recognize that the documents they could capture, translate, scan, and make digitally accessible were worth infinitely more than what they were gleaning from interrogations, which were regularly marked by "deception, exaggeration, and misdirection."

The point, the colonel argued, was that these documents were unfailingly true—"terrorists, criminals, and other adversaries never expected their material to be captured."

American fighting men had learned this as far back as the Civil War, though it wasn't until World War II that it became truly appreciated and prioritized; documents recovered from a Japanese plane shot down during the 1941 attack on Pearl Harbor ultimately helped cryptographers break the Imperial Navy operational codes. One officer noted of the Japanese in 1944—the same year that the US Department of War directed the publication of *The Exploitation of Japanese Documents*—that "Fortunately, the enemy as a nation is addicted to keeping diaries and converting everything into writing."

They would find them in the pockets of dead or captured Japanese soldiers, on abandoned bases, on sunken boats. In March 1944, for example, US soldiers found on the dead body of a Japanese battalion officer a field order he'd issued for an attack on American forces for later that afternoon, one that the US was thus able to beat back.

The US tried to replicate this success a generation later in Vietnam, with less effectiveness. In 1966, to provide a home for the documents seized from the North Vietnamese and Vietcong enemies, the US Army established the Combined Document Exploitation Center near Saigon. More than three hundred Vietnamese and Americans were trusted with analyzing, translating, and logging photographs, documents, letters, and diaries.

But nothing could match the explosion of access to information that occurred with the advent of the internet, coinciding with the US "Global War on Terror." Or the need for it, given the shadowy, underground nature of the terrorist threat. Hodgson first became acquainted with the DOMEX system when it was set up in Iraq for the tribunal that had been working to build the case against Saddam.

Then the DOMEX database expanded.

Servicemembers were trained in collecting CED (captured enemy documents) and instructed to bag and tag any piece of recorded information. That meant everything from books, newspapers, pamphlets, to operation orders, identity cards, passports, driver's licenses, letters, diaries, notes, computer files, tape recordings, video, voice recordings, and on and on. The location, the date, the relevant details about the battle or the materials would all be part of the filing before the intel was analyzed and, if need be, translated.

The goal was such that if a grunt found a library card in an obscure nook of Afghanistan, any intel officer with the appropriate clearance could at some point have access to it thousands of miles away.

That goal, of course, was far from the reality.

It took months to find the information, even with the detailed logs. This was the US government, and there were millions upon millions of files to sift through.

Hodgson had been on the case since August 2011, when he received a copy of the original testimony Spin Ghul had given the Italians. Based on the rough timeline and geography, he'd taken a cursory look and determined it was possible Spin Ghul had been involved in various attacks near the Pakistan border. There was Sergeant Steven Checo, killed in an ambush outside Firebase Shkin in December 2002. In September 2003, Private First Class Evan O'Neill had been killed on patrol in an ambush outside Firebase Shkin. The very next month, two CIA contractors—William "Chief" Carlson and Christopher Mueller—former special ops guys on the hunt for al Qaeda, were killed. Abdul Hadi al-Iraqi and his al Qaeda cell likely had been involved in those attacks.

Having sat through Spin Ghul's testimony in Italy, Bert LaCroix, now four months on the job, called Hodgson at Fort Belvoir, in Fairfax County, Virginia, and told him to focus on the April 25, 2003, attack that had resulted in the deaths of Jerod Dennis and Ray Losano. The team currently in Italy was pretty sure that was the right battle.

Hodgson got to work. He ordered some records from the Pentagon and saw others had been wounded in the 2003 attack, some grievously. Setzer was shot in the face. Brown and Trahan and Reed had been seriously injured in action as well. Maybe Spin Ghul's claim that he'd killed four or five Americans was based on those seriously wounded, who in a previous era would likely have died of their injuries. Maybe he thought he'd killed some guys who had ultimately survived.

At Hodgson's request, the Medicolegal Investigator Office sent over autopsy reports, photos, and death certificates related to Jerod and Losano. Hodgson studied them, but it didn't take long to figure out that grenades had been involved in the battle.

Spin Ghul had mentioned throwing hand grenades.

Yeah, this was it, Hodgson thought. This was the attack. It was the only one that made sense for that time period, for that geography, for that method of killing.

At his desk in Fort Belvoir, Virginia, Hodgson plugged "25 April 2003" into the DOMEX database to see what evidence might exist.

"We think we found the battle," Bitkower told his boss, US attorney Loretta Lynch. He told her about the ambush outside Firebase Shkin on April 25, 2003, the deaths of Jerod Dennis and Ray Losano.

Lynch was herself a member of a military family. Born in 1959, one of her earliest memories was of a military funeral for an uncle who had served in World War II. She also recalled a prayer service at her home that her minister father hosted before her cousins and an uncle shipped off to Vietnam. Her older brother Lorenzo Lynch Jr., who had just passed away in 2009, had been a Navy SEAL for more than a decade, leading an underwater demolitions unit and traveling the world.

The Lynch family had been relatively lucky—all the servicemembers in their family returned home, even if their service had exacted physical and psychological tolls. But it made Lynch acutely aware of the human costs of decisions to send men and women to war. It made her see the Spin Ghul case as a way to bring closure of some small sort to the families of Jerod Dennis and Ray Losano. Losing someone on the battlefield was often experienced as an opaque matter, with few details ever shared. Rarely do Gold Star families get a chance to find out the specific person who killed their loved one.

This case could offer a different sense of justice. Lynch knew of no other case where a combatant had been prosecuted for killing American servicemembers on a battlefield. That made this job potentially more difficult, but no less sacred. She also knew that both KIA servicemembers had been young, with their parents still living. Ray Losano had a wife and two young girls. So often in her work as US attorney, she would encounter crime victims who'd become convinced that their government had no interest in what had happened to them, and she was determined that the Dennis and Losano families would never feel this way.

CHAPTER FIFTEEN

PINK CHICKENS

Washington, DC

For the rest of 2011, the FBI—Raushaunah Muhammad, Bert LaCroix, and others on the FBI's West Africa Team, which had already been working on the Spin Ghul case—seamlessly melded into Bitkower and Shreve's team with the US attorney's office.

From her desk, Raushaunah worked to confirm every detail Spin Ghul gave them, adhering to the strictest of FBI standards. This meant, for instance, that when Spin Ghul testified that he left Waziristan and arrived in Lahore, Pakistan, on Independence Day in 2003, Raushaunah would assign a possible date to that—August 14 or 15. When Spin Ghul detailed the battle, she would find every ambush that could fit that description—including his claim that a large Black American soldier had been shot. Every assertion needed to have a corresponding fact based in her research. After looking into several battles that nearly fit Spin Ghul's description, she too had separately concluded that only the April 25, 2003, battle matched. It had occurred on a Friday, and there had been indirect fire beforehand followed by a direct insurgent attack, with one insurgent killed and a handful of US servicemembers killed and/or wounded including a large Black male, near that specific border crossing, during the time frame of Donald Rumsfeld's Afghanistan visit and before Pakistani Independence Day.

With the battle now confirmed with a high degree of certainty, LaCroix made a list of soldiers who could provide details about that horrible day, what they called "victim witnesses." But as LaCroix quickly discovered, the victim witnesses were not eager to talk about the worst day of their lives.

Since being shot up on April 25, 2003, Scott Trahan had gone through multiple surgeries: at FOB Salerno that day and then later at Bagram, then on to Landstuhl Regional Medical Center in Germany for a week and a half. He arrived at Walter Reed National Military Medical Center in Maryland on May 1.

On May 17, 2003, Trahan was one of a handful of wounded servicemembers bused from Walter Reed to the White House at the invitation of President George W. Bush. They were in the Oval Office as the president recorded his weekly radio address honoring Armed Forces Day.

Captain Scott Trahan (fourth from left)
visiting the White House with George W. Bush
GEORGE W. BUSH WHITE HOUSE ARCHIVES

"Here in the Oval Office, I'm joined by some distinguished Americans, eight members of the military who fought bravely during the battle of Iraq," President Bush said, even though Trahan had been wounded in Afghanistan. "All of them were wounded in battle and are recovering from their injuries. All of them have earned the respect and the gratitude of our nation."

Trahan found the experience surreal and embarrassing. He felt responsible for having caused the death of two of his servicemembers and the serious wounding of several others, irrevocably impacting countless lives. And despite that, the president—and others who visited him at Walter Reed—thought he was a hero. It was quite possibly the lowest point of his life. The guilt was almost equal to if not greater than the physical pain and recovery.

He did physical therapy for several months and underwent seven surgeries at Walter Reed. One day, his battalion commander called to relieve him of command—the company needed to appoint a new commander. In August, Trahan was healthy enough to return to active duty, and upon his arrival at Fort Bragg, he was offered an opening with Headquarters and Headquarters Company (HHC), 82nd Airborne Division. In September, they went to Al Anbar Province in Iraq. Just five months after being shot, Trahan was back on a battlefield.

He tried to avoid thinking about the battle, but April 25, 2003, was not done with him.

In February 2007, he spoke with the Combat Studies Institute of Fort Leavenworth, Kansas, and the interviewer wanted to know more about the ambush.

Then in November 2011, prosecutors and the FBI reached out to him. A guy named Dave Bitkower held a video conference with him from the FBI's New York City office. Bitkower seemed really interested in all the details from the battle, about the guy who crouched down from over the ridge, grenades being thrown, and a big Black American soldier getting hit early. Trahan hated talking about this, but he tried to help, which seemed to please the prosecutor.

"Who else are you in touch with?" Bitkower asked.

As guilt-ridden and traumatized as Trahan was, Specialist Eddie Camacho was in a far worse place.

After his deployment in Afghanistan ended, the specialist was sent to Iraq. He left the Army after that deployment and became a police officer in Raleigh, North Carolina, but was called back from the inactive Ready Reserve.

"I'm scared shitless," he told friends. "I don't want to do this again."

He was depressed and experiencing post-traumatic stress. But he wasn't seeking any help, nor did he think the Army was eager to help or even acknowledge what he was going through.

Then he received an email from the FBI. A special agent named Raushaunah Muhammad said she needed to speak with him. Her email didn't go into detail about what she wanted to know.

Holy shit, Camacho thought. *Am I in trouble? Is one of my battle buddies in a jam?*

He called his buddy Dwayne McKnight in California.

"What is this?" he asked.

"Bro, I don't know," McKnight said. "They want to meet with me, too."

"I'm not going to meet with them, are you crazy?" Camacho said. "Do we need an attorney?"

Camacho asked Raushaunah what this was about, but she was cagey. She would tell him when they spoke, she said. They would be coming to North Carolina. Could they meet?

Eddie Camacho refused to set up a time.

Bert LaCroix phoned him.

"I don't know what the problem is here," LaCroix said. "We need to talk to you."

"Buddy, it don't work like that," Camacho told him. "You don't call me and scare the shit out of me and expect me to cooperate. You won't even tell me what this is about."

Raushaunah was on the call, too. "Listen," she told him. "We caught a guy who we think was in the firefight from April 2003. They want to bring him to trial. We need to debrief you guys. You're victim witnesses. We need your testimony to put this guy away."

But at that point Camacho was already on edge.

"No no no no no no," he said. "I'm good."

She pushed.

"I don't want to meet," he told her. "I don't want to talk about this."

After their conversation, Camacho butt-dialed Raushaunah. She couldn't make out everything he was saying, but it was clear he was stressed and not interested at all in talking to them.

In October 2011, Raushaunah and LaCroix began a road trip. Calling ahead of time, they spoke with soldiers and veterans around Fort Jackson in South Carolina, Fort Bragg in North Carolina, and Fort Gordon in Georgia. Shreve joined them on video conference or in person whenever possible.

At Fort Benning in Georgia, they showed a photograph to now–Command Sergeant Major Brian Severino and asked him if he knew anything about it. He studied the image; it was a cropped and close-up picture of a small brown book.

Does this look familiar? he was asked.

Severino requested more details about the picture, but they wouldn't give him any, which annoyed him. Obviously, this was important—the FBI wouldn't fly to Georgia for nothing—but they wouldn't tell him why. He didn't know what the image was. He told them that. They left their business cards and told him to call them if anything rang a bell.

The image of the book nagged at him. What was it? There was something familiar about it, but he couldn't figure out what.

Later that night, after dinner, Severino grabbed his laptop and perused the photos from his deployment. Scrolling through the hundreds of images, he came across the very same image. It was the Quran found after the ambush of April 25, 2003. The other FBI officials had cropped the other objects out.

Memories started to flow back into his mind.

The sounds, the smells, the images of that day came back to him.

The next morning, Severino called LaCroix. He remembered the photo—it was a Quran belonging to one of the guys who ambushed them.

Yes, he said, he remembered the photograph. He had taken it.

Raushaunah and LaCroix also spoke with Dwayne McKnight via teleconference; he was in California. He called Camacho to tell him why the FBI had been trying to reach him.

"It's about the firefight," McKnight told Camacho.

Raushaunah and LaCroix told Camacho they were willing to meet him in Raleigh during their Fort Bragg leg of the trip. He continued to be reluctant, but they insisted. They agreed to meet at a Starbucks. Raushaunah and LaCroix got there first and grabbed seats where they could get a good look at Camacho as he came in, with their backs against the wall. They didn't know where his mind was at.

The first thing Raushaunah did was show Camacho a photograph she'd found of him in his Raleigh PD uniform, from a police department newsletter she'd found during her internet sleuthing. She was trying to establish that they were all law enforcement, all on the same team. That's not how he took it.

"How'd you get this?"

"We're the FBI," she said. She hated it when people didn't treat others with the basic respect they deserved.

"You trying to scare me to cooperate?"

Raushaunah was surprised at his reaction.

"Not at all," she said.

"Listen, you don't know what I've been through, you don't know who I lost," Camacho said. "I don't want to talk about this."

"Look, Eddie, you just need to relax and help us out," LaCroix said. "We just need your help. We're on the same side here. We're all in law enforcement."

But Camacho would not budge. He had nothing for them. He didn't want to share anything. He was hostile, and Raushaunah and LaCroix left the Starbucks frustrated and a bit pissed off.

The interviews were difficult for Raushaunah, and not just because of the reaction of Eddie Camacho. The testimony from these men who had served weighed on her. These were tough guys who had been through hell. They would choke up, they would weep, they would say that because of her, their nightmares were coming back. She felt like she was reinflicting old pains on them.

But talking with the soldiers also reminded her that the work had a purpose. The soldiers and veterans were able to fill in blanks and provide contemporaneous details that corroborated Spin Ghul's account of the battle, from the other side of the ambush. These were glimpses of the evil that had been done and the men they were seeking justice for.

One of the soldiers told her all about Jerod Dennis and gave her a photograph of one of the Afghan hens, dyed to distinguish which farmers they belonged to.

"Look, Sergeant, they dye their chickens pink," Jerod Dennis had told him, he recalled sadly.

She kept the photograph of the chicken on her desk for the rest of the case, a reminder of the sweet soul Spin Ghul and his fellow terrorists took from this earth.

Bitkower and Shreve had returned from Italy and continued to work the case from their Brooklyn offices with the US attorney EDNY, the FBI team at the Joint Terrorism Task Force in Manhattan, and at the Justice Department in DC as needed.

One gray afternoon, on December 7, 2012, at his top-secret government facility in Northern Virginia—one of many nondescript gray buildings in the cookie-cutter office parks throughout the suburbs—Hodgson presented what he'd found to Bitkower and Shreve.

He had many documents to show them. Whether any of them would be enough to secure an indictment, let alone a conviction, was another matter. DOMEX document number one was based on Spin Ghul's description of his plan to go to Nigeria to blow up the US embassy. DOMEX had retrieved a journal recovered by US forces in Kandahar, Afghanistan, which detailed plans to go to Lagos, Nigeria, to kill Israeli officials. But this wasn't tied to Spin Ghul and seemed to be a completely different mission. Bitkower and Shreve shrugged it off. What else did he have?

He had Jerod Dennis's and Ray Losano's autopsy information. He had details about the Malik terrorist training camp in Afghanistan.

What else?

From DOMEX he had the class roster from the al Farouq training camp, 2001. But Spin Ghul was not on it.

The DOMEX system included VHS videos showing reconnaissance and surveillance of the countryside near Firebase Shkin. Spin Ghul was not in it.

Hodgson also had something he knew they would love.

DOMEX listed what was commonly referred to as "pocket litter"—items found on or near fighters, alive or dead.

In this case dead.

An insurgent killed near Firebase Shkin in April 2003 had in his pocket a recruitment pamphlet with an image of Osama bin Laden on a phone talking to a small boy. There were many different groups of insurgents shooting Americans in Afghanistan. The Taliban, HIG, the Haqqani network. This flier essentially identified the dead man as a member of al Qaeda.

That same insurgent had a journal. A yellow logo on a black cover depicted a rocket-like minaret, the letters *MCH*, and the word *NOTES*.

Inside were thirty-five pages of details. An FBI agent had translated its contents from Urdu.

The KIA al Qaeda fighter's name, or kunya, had been Abu Walid. The son of Walid.

The same name of the Pakistani jihadi Spin Ghul had fought with, the one killed in battle, who Spin Ghul had said he left behind.

The journal documented a militant's travel from Shakai to Angoor Ada and listed other fighters present at the safe houses he visited along the Afghanistan–Pakistan border. It described missions conducted under the cover of night, firing rockets. It also mentioned names: Noor Muhammad, Haji Farooq Abu Hamza Shafiq, Abu Al Hassan, Abdul Rehman Hussain Salman, Khalid Waleed Hamza al-Australi, Abu Tamim . . .

Abu Tamim.

The alias—the kunya—of Spin Ghul.

In Italy, on September 16, Spin Ghul had told the court, "My friends call me Abu Tamim."

Hodgson looked over at Bitkower. He had never seen a bigger smile on his face.

He wasn't sure he had ever seen him smile before, for that matter.

Bitkower and Shreve couldn't believe it. The journal must have belonged to the Pakistani jihadi Spin Ghul had fought alongside, the one killed in battle who had been left behind. The man Spin Ghul had referred to as Abu Walid.

They now had physical evidence that seemed to show Spin Ghul was at the battle he had claimed to have fought in. The evidence in Abu Walid's journal matched many of the details in Spin Ghul's story, from the jihadis he met, to the safe house where they stayed, to the earlier missile strikes before the battle. And then of course there was the fact that Abu Walid had stopped writing anything on April 22, 2003—three days before the attack.

It showed his path from Lahore to Waziristan to south of Firebase Shkin. It showed that he was with al Qaeda. It showed clear intent to kill Americans.

This was no longer just a case based on a confession. This was a case based on physical evidence.

Would this be enough for an indictment? That was their entire focus right now. It was a circumstantial case—not a weak one, necessarily, but circumstantial nonetheless. A skilled defense attorney might be able to have a jury doubt Spin Ghul's sanity and thus his confession.

They considered the "victim witness" testimonies they had received from Raushaunah and LaCroix. Their interviews confirmed the details that Spin Ghul had been involved in the ambush that had killed Jerod and Losano. But there wasn't much more there than that. No one so far had recognized Spin Ghul. The Abu Walid journal Hodgson had found was a breakthrough. A rare find. But was it enough?

They had the political capital to take this to the Justice Department and the Obama White House, but there was a risk. If they moved too early with too little evidence, Spin Ghul would go free. If they waited, the Italians might let Spin Ghul go before they even got off the starting block.

Bitkower and Shreve had to make the biggest call of their professional lives. They decided to gamble.

CHAPTER SIXTEEN

KOBIE WILLIAMS

Houston, Texas

As Bitkower and Shreve prepared to take a risk, the winds from Capitol Hill continued to blow against indicting and extraditing Spin Ghul. In December 2011, the US Senate, controlled by Democrats, passed a defense bill that sought to require that any suspected terrorists be automatically turned over to the military for detention, as opposed to law enforcement. President Obama had threatened to veto the $662 billion spending package, the White House trotting out statements of opposition to the "political micromanagement" from the secretary of defense, director of national intelligence, FBI director, and Attorney General Eric Holder, but the Senate didn't care.

Obama's record as the commander in chief who ordered the deaths of Osama bin Laden and Anwar al-Awlaki didn't seem to matter. The Senate bill passed 86–13. The White House tried to save face before final passage by securing a provision that would allow the president to transfer a suspect to law enforcement if he submitted to Congress a waiver declaring the move to be in the national security interests of the United States.

From Italy, Nardini would constantly remind Lynch, Bitkower, Shreve, and anyone who would listen that the Italians still very much wanted Spin Ghul out of their prison—and that a US military facility, and presumably a tribunal of sorts, was not an option for them. The Italian government saw military detention as part and parcel of what many perceived as the lawless Bush legacy: a package of torture, indefinite detention at Gitmo, and extraordinary rendition. It didn't matter that President Obama was trying to infuse the process with new credibility, appointing a man with a reputation for reform—Brigadier General Mark Martins—to the position of chief prosecutor of military commissions in September 2011, to deal as best he could with the more than 170 detainees still in custody. The Italians simply didn't trust the Americans, and they weren't going to send Spin Ghul to the US for anything other than a civilian trial. And the death penalty—long abolished within the European Union—had to be off the table, too. There was nothing anyone could say to convince them otherwise.

The man who would help Bitkower and Shreve convince the Obama administration to seek an indictment of Spin Ghul would just a few years before have looked askance at these same prosecutors.

As a civil rights activist, Alamdar S. Hamdani had begun by defending cases against the US government.

Born in England to Indian Muslim parents, Hamdani came to North Texas with his parents at the age of eleven, his mother and cabdriver father raising him and his little sister in a modest two-bedroom apartment. In no small way, Al Hamdani was the embodiment of the American dream. After he graduated from the University of Texas–Austin, then the University of Houston Law School, Hamdani sought to make as much money as possible at a big firm. He did and was well on his way to climbing the economic ladder just one generation later.

Then came 9/11.

For Al Hamdani, it seemed like the entire Muslim community in the US was suddenly unfairly under suspicion for the actions of a handful of al Qaeda extremists. He knew firsthand how unjust this was—he was himself, after all, a brown-skinned Muslim who loved the US, but in airports he was often met with suspicion.

He started to do civil rights work on the side, representing Muslims accused of various crimes, becoming the first Muslim member of the board of directors of the ACLU of Texas. The group protested when US attorney general John Ashcroft sought to interview five thousand young men who had entered the US from countries where al Qaeda was active, based on their nationality alone—which the ACLU called racial profiling and against Texas law.

Watching the FBI ask his clients what he deemed "inappropriate questions" was transformative. One of his clients was visited and questioned by the FBI just for videotaping a sunrise while his hijab-clad wife watched. After two Muslim Americans complained about the sales staff to an apartment manager, the FBI got involved—asking the two about their mosque, their politics, how often they prayed, whether they were Sunni or Shiite. Hamdani understood it was a fraught time, and that common citizens might not be able to discern the differences in culture or religion between American Muslims and 9/11 terrorists just by appearance. But it was quite another matter for the FBI or National Security Agency to treat every Muslim American as a potential suspect in the midst of plotting acts of terrorism.

He was passionate about pushing back against the Bush administration and what he saw as unconstitutional abuses that amounted to legal bigotry. Most of his practice was commercial litigation, where he lived and died by the billable hour. But the civil rights and civil liberties cases allowed him to feel like he was actually pursuing justice. It was important, impactful. The billable hours filled his belly, but this work fed his soul.

And then he agreed to defend Kobie Diallo Williams, and everything changed.

Kobie Williams was thirty-two, a bearded, bespectacled, Black US citizen and student at the University of Houston–Downtown. Al Hamdani represented Williams when the FBI interviewed him to talk about his travels. Hamdani was convinced that, as with many of his pro bono clients, the FBI was unfairly targeting Williams for his religious views.

In 2006, Hamdani became better informed about the investigation conducted by the US attorney's office in Houston against Williams. The FBI began presenting its evidence.

Recorded conversations. Financial records.

According to that evidence, in May 2005, Williams went camping outside Houston, firing guns with three other young men, including a Pakistani student who wasn't allowed to be in possession of a firearm. According to the FBI's evidence, Williams hadn't just been camping and firing guns for recreation—he was in training, learning how to shoot and conduct reconnaissance for a trip to Afghanistan. Kobie Williams, a.k.a. Abdul Kabir, saw US servicemembers in Iraq and Afghanistan as "invaders" and wanted to kill them in the name of Islam. He wanted to join the Taliban.

The details of the case against Williams flipped a switch in Hamdani's heart and head.

The case shattered Hamdani's assumptions that the government's motivations behind the interrogation of Muslims, South Asians, and Arabs in the wake of 9/11 were all baseless. He began to believe that their targeting might be far from arbitrary.

His case defending Williams represented the beginning of the end of his pro bono work, and the beginning of his path to the US Justice Department.

He decided that he wanted to be on the other side, the government, the prosecution. He wanted to use his skills to protect the US and those who fought for her.

The calling was so strong that he left his corporate job behind for a different kind of American dream, applying to be an assistant US attorney in Houston. But he didn't get a second interview. Hamdani was undeterred and called Amul Thapar, a Bush appointee who was the US attorney in the Eastern District of Kentucky. Hamdani knew Thapar through the South Asian Bar Association of North America. Thapar invited him to Kentucky for an interview and, soon enough, for a job.

Hamdani's wife understood this was a new dream of her husband's and sacrificed selflessly. She begrudgingly came to love Kentucky and gave birth to their second child there. When a position opened up a few years later at the counterterrorism section of the National Security Division of the US Justice Department, he interviewed for that, too, and was hired.

The Hamdanis moved to the DC area on Christmas Day, 2009, the same day Umar Farouk Abdulmutallab boarded Northwest Airlines Flight 253 from Amsterdam to Detroit and tried to detonate explosives hidden in his underwear, an attempt that would have taken the lives of all 290 people on board if he had been successful. He had been trained by al Qaeda in the Arabian Peninsula, a fact that underlined to Al Hamdani how important his new charge was.

For Bitkower and Shreve, it didn't matter how Al Hamdani came to be on their side, it was just their goddamn good luck that he was.

Immediately after Spin Ghul was picked up on the cruise ship, Hamdani's boss at "Main Justice"—the hallowed halls of the US Justice Department building in Washington, DC—a guy named Joe Kaster, told Hamdani about the case.

"This is out of New York, reach out to them," Kaster told him.

Kaster knew Shreve and Bitkower and the work they'd done. Bitkower had been at the Counterterrorism Section of Main Justice from 2008 to 2009 and was part of the team that helped put together a major case out of Minneapolis. A case that started with an American who joined al-Shabaab and became a suicide bomber in Somalia and ended with more than two dozen indictments of Somali Americans who were part of a group that would recruit, train, and fight for al-Shabaab. Bitkower had also later joined the team investigating the would-be New York City subway bombers, Najibullah Zazi and two others.

Shreve's biggest terrorist case at that point had been two Brooklynites, sons of immigrants from the former Yugoslavia, radicalized online and determined to take up arms against the US abroad. Aggressive investigations and one flipped witness stopped them before anyone got hurt.

Hamdani had called Shreve and then traveled to Manhattan to meet with Raushaunah, LaCroix, and the team. He went to Sicily to meet with Italian authorities and emailed updates to his bosses back at Main Justice—Kaster, deputy assistant attorney general in the National Security Division George Toscas, and counterterrorism chief Mike Mullaney—about Spin Ghul's claims as he made them.

The two assistant US attorneys from EDNY were known by Main Justice to be very aggressive. That wasn't necessarily a bad thing with respect to Spin Ghul—it meant that if there was a criminal case to be made, the EDNY team would run through walls to make it. But this bullishness also put the EDNY at odds, as it often did, with the more cautious attorneys on Pennsylvania Avenue in Washington, DC. The closer to the White House attorneys got, the higher the political stakes climbed and the less they could afford to make mistakes when bringing cases to Attorney General Eric Holder and beyond. So they applied a healthy skepticism whenever the Brooklyn attorneys promised they could get enough evidence to charge a case.

Hamdani was the middleman helping Bitkower and Shreve negotiate these differences, conveying and anticipating any Main Justice concerns about the weakness of their case and advocating for their case to his superiors.

Hamdani had learned how to navigate these choppy administrative waters from a previous case involving a Somali terrorist named Ahmed Abdulkadir Warsame. Warsame had been picked up on April 19, 2011, by Navy SEALs in the Gulf of Aden as he made his way back from meeting with the terrorists of AQAP in Yemen. He was taken on board the USS *Boxer*, a US Navy amphibious assault ship, where he was interrogated for two months. Worried about the near miss in the Ghailani trial, the chief prosecutor of the Guantánamo military commissions, Judge Advocate General John Murphy, had ordered Warsame to Gitmo. President Obama overruled him and in December 2011, Warsame pleaded guilty in U.S. criminal court to nine counts of providing material support to al-Shabaab and AQAP, conspiring to teach bombmaking, and more.

The process was instructive—Hamdani learned how to get a sign-off from the assistant attorney general, who would then need to get a sign-off from the attorney general, and how the necessary approvals didn't end there. Hamdani also recognized that to bring an alleged al Qaeda operative into the US for prosecution, a case like Spin Ghul's would also need blessings from the Deputies' Committee (a group of the deputy directors of all national security–related agencies), then the Cabinet-level Principals' Committee (the same, but all the directors), and finally the blessing of the president of the US himself.

Hamdani knew it was theoretically possible to get a terrorist overseas charged and brought to a federal court. The most perilous trap, in his experience, came from the intelligence community, which feared that any such prosecution might expose the fabled and ever-guarded "sources and methods." Hamdani was prepared to provide a road map for Main Justice prosecutors to protect said sources and/or methods knowing that was exactly the first thing they'd pick over.

Bitkower and Shreve also sought guidance from their direct boss at the US attorney's office EDNY, Marshall Miller, the deputy head of the criminal division in Brooklyn. Long focused on terrorist cases, Miller had fought the same battles, pushing aggressive prosecutions through skeptical chambers of folks with political careers of their own—and their bosses—to worry about. Bitkower and Shreve knew that they would get one shot at this; it needed to be perfect. For now, the indictment would serve as a general outline in which they would encircle all the various countries, terrorist organizations, and plots that Spin Ghul had traversed to enact his terrible mission. And they knew they needed to do much more work to find evidence regarding Spin Ghul's failed plan to bomb the US embassy in Nigeria. In testimony he had shared details of this failure, dropping dozens of clues that Bitkower and Shreve would have to follow up on and fill in before they presented the indictment in court.

After all, not only had Spin Ghul killed two Americans on the battlefield, he had also intended to commit mass murder.

CHAPTER SEVENTEEN

DIPLOMATIC DRIVE

Lagos, Nigeria

After returning from the ambush of April 25, 2003, securely ensconced in the safe house in Angoor Ada, Pakistan, Spin Ghul heard war stories from a Saudi terrorist who had claimed to have destroyed a military installation where fifty soldiers were killed.

Fifty was a lot more than the four or five Spin had attacked on the battlefield. It was much more in the style of the 1998 truck bomb attacks on the US embassies in Nairobi, Kenya, and Dar es Salaam, Tanzania, where more than 4,500 were wounded and 224 killed. And all the jihadis had required was a few trucks, TNT, and the motivation.

One thing was for certain: Spin Ghul thought he was a bigger deal than a common foot soldier. He was meant to be a global operator. He told Hadi, who ran the safe house, that he wanted to meet with Osama bin Laden. If not bin Laden, then perhaps with the mufti of al Qaeda, Abu Hafs al-Mauritani. Spin Ghul wanted to appeal to them, to have them send him to the al Qaeda cells working around the world.

He told this to Abu Faraj al-Libi at his next stop, at a different safe house in a different part of Waziristan.

"I want to attack any American installation anywhere around the world," Spin Ghul told him.

So Faraj connected Spin Ghul with a higher-ranking al Qaeda operative called Hamza Rabia, the head of external operations for the terrorist group; he worked near Wana, in Waziristan, southwest of Islamabad near the border with Afghanistan. Hamza Rabia invited him to join him there and trained him.

In August 2003, Hamza Rabia organized a trip to Lahore, a city then in the throes of Pakistani Independence Day celebrations. Hamza Rabia and Spin Ghul plotted ways he could best fulfill his jihadi fantasies. Hamza Rabia shared some books with Spin Ghul, books written by those who had fought the Soviets. The books were referred to as *Mossouat al Jihad*—the "Encyclopedias of Jihad." He trained him on what to do if he was being tailed by law enforcement. Earlier that year, al Qaeda released an audiotape believed to have been recorded by bin Laden, in hiding, giving an update on their struggle against the West. Bin Laden quoted the Quran and urged "true Muslims" to act to "break free from the slavery of these tyrannic and apostate regimes." He cited six countries where Muslims should rise up: Jordan, Morocco, Nigeria, Saudi Arabia, Yemen, and Pakistan.

Spin Ghul's family was originally from Niger, which borders Nigeria—Africa's most populous country, where many locals also spoke Hausa. Of those options laid out by bin Laden, Nigeria made the most sense as a place where Spin Ghul could operate. Spin Ghul and Hamza Rabia hatched a plan where they would fly to Lagos, Nigeria, rendezvous with local jihadis, obtain explosives, and target the US embassy there. They devised a code so they could communicate on the phone or by email without detection from prying authorities, if anyone was listening in to their phone calls or reading the drafts folders in the email accounts they shared on Yahoo!

In the summer of 2003, Spin Ghul got onto an Asia Airlines flight from Islamabad to Dubai. There he hopped onto a Kenya Airways flight to Nairobi, and then a connecting flight to Lagos, on the coast in Southern Nigeria, and finally to Kano, near the border of Niger, to begin carrying out this plot.

Through Hamza Rabia's connections, Spin Ghul met a man named Mohammed Ashafa Suleiman who ran a local safe house and was affiliated with the Nigerian Taliban—years later Boko Haram. They were all staying in a safe house for like-minded jihadis, one that had other members of the Nigerian Taliban. He also met members of the "Salafist Group for Prayer and Combat," soon renamed al Qaeda in the Islamic Maghreb, or AQIM. The Salafist Group for Prayer and Combat ran a terrorist training camp in Niger, and Ashafa helped recruit and sponsor members of the Nigerian Taliban to travel there. Mohammed Ashafa was a useful man for Spin Ghul to know. He asked Ashafa to travel with him the three hundred miles to Abuja, the capital, to scout out the US embassy. But that proved more complicated than it sounded. Spin Ghul and Mohammed Ashafa crisscrossed Abuja, a city of more than one million people, and saw the embassies of other Western nations on Diplomatic Drive and in the surrounding area, but they could not find their target. There were no signs or markers alerting any members of the public where the US embassy was located. It was as if the US embassy did not exist.

They returned to the safe house. Spin Ghul would need to figure out what to do next. Perhaps he would need to seek guidance from Hamza Rabia. In the meantime, he would begin the search for explosives.

Using his connections, he met a contractor who dug toilet wells for local homes, a man named Maradone, who seemed to have an in, low-level enough to be of use, high-level enough to have some knowledge.

Maradone told him of a local quarry that used explosives to extract rocks from the ground for construction. Spin Ghul went there, but an employee at the company told him that he wasn't allowed to sell explosives to just anyone. Spin Ghul would need to get permission from either local police or the construction company headquarters in the Hausawa neighborhood between a roundabout and "the only tall building in Kano." Spin Ghul sent Maradone to the company to see what he could get. He returned empty-handed but noted that given Nigeria's reputation for corruption, it was possible that a payoff would work. The only problem was that Spin Ghul had no money with which to bribe anyone.

These were complicated issues, and Spin Ghul would need more direction than he could get in a phone call or email, especially when any communication might be monitored. He decided to send Mohammed Ashafa, as a messenger, back to Lahore to get guidance. Members of the Salafist Group for Prayer and Combat also took advantage of Ashafa's trip to have him deliver a message to be passed on to bin Laden, as well as Mullah Omar, head of the Afghan Taliban, and Abu al-Walid al Ghamdi, the new emir of the Arab mujahideen fighting the Russians.

Ashafa's trip was successful, and al Qaeda members in Pakistan gave him $1,500 to help with Spin Ghul's plans. The Pakistani cell also gave him messages to pass back to other Islamist groups in West Africa.

But on his way back to Nigeria, Ashafa was arrested by Pakistani intelligence, deported, and handed over to Nigerian authorities. As soon as he heard the news, Hamza Rabia phoned Spin Ghul and told him to get out of Nigeria immediately, suggesting that he try to get to Algeria if he could. He gave Spin Ghul a number to reach them on their satellite phone, which Spin recorded in one of the two travel notebooks he carried with him. One included the phone number for his parents' place in Saudi Arabia.

Contemplating his future, Spin Ghul decided that Europe might be a better place for him to set up shop. He considered a man named Zayn al-Abidin Muhammad Husayna a role model. A Saudi-born Palestinian better known as "Abu Zubaydah," he'd risen from the low ranks to emerge as a major player in the world of jihadists flocking to the Afghanistan-Pakistan region for training until the FBI and Pakistanis captured him in 2002 in Faisalabad. Spin Ghul figured he would get to somewhere in Europe, maybe Italy, familiarize himself with the area, make friends, and then get back in touch with Hamza Rabia to formulate a new plan.

When he made it to Libya, on his way to Europe, Spin Ghul emailed Hamza Rabia and told him that he was in the land of Abu Laith—a fellow jihadi in Afghanistan but originally from Libya. He didn't have enough money to make the next leg of his journey, so he took a job unloading bags of beans at the dock. There he met a man named Basim Sha'ban, in whom he confided about his plans for jihad in Europe.

"I'll help you," Sha'ban told him. "But do you have enough training?"

Ghul described his training in the rocky terrain of Pakistan, but Sha'ban said he'd need to learn how to operate in urban terrain. Terrorism in a city is different from terrorism in a mountainous place like Afghanistan or Pakistan. Sha'ban told him he'd help make up the difference.

Sha'ban was generous, buying Spin Ghul a DVD player, TV set, and jihad DVDs to study. He also came up with simulated missions for him to perform in Tripoli. He would give Spin Ghul a target to fictionally "strike" and challenge him to figure out the exits and entrances. They would conduct these exercises around the city—on Omar Mukhtar Street, near the presidential palace, and elsewhere. None of this was for an actual attack; it was just a way for Spin Ghul to advance his studies. After all, European capitals have much tighter security than a firebase in Afghanistan.

On one such training exercise, Muammar Gaddafi's intelligence services took notice of this strange man sniffing around town. Concerned by what was in his notebook—he appeared to be planning an attack on the Libyan government or Libyan forces—they grabbed him off the streets. That was Spin Ghul's last day as a free man until that June day in 2011, when Libyan forces grabbed him from prison, brought him to the docks, and put him on a refugee boat that ended up at Lampedusa Island.

CHAPTER EIGHTEEN

THE RWANDAN PRECEDENT

Brooklyn, New York

Spin Ghul's yarn about his efforts to blow up the US embassy in Nigeria was a compelling tale, but not one part of it was verified. Bitkower and Shreve, Raushaunah and LaCroix would need to pursue leads in Africa, but that took time they didn't have. The Italians had made it clear that there was not much left.

From the beginning, Bitkower and Shreve knew the indictment would need to be vague and broad—what's called a "nonspeaking indictment." They wrote of Spin Ghul's participation in the battlefield attacks and his ultimately fruitless trip to Nigeria to attack Americans. They laid out the bare bones of Spin Ghul's offenses. More details would be provided at trial—if they found the evidence they were looking for. In gambling terms, they had to make significant wagers without looking at their cards.

"This is enough to get it done, right?" Bitkower asked his boss, Marshall Miller, while he worked on the indictment with Shreve.

"Yes," Miller said. "Do it!"

Bitkower and Shreve then got the sign-off from Miller's boss, Rich Donoghue, then his boss, US attorney Loretta Lynch. Then they sent it to Al Hamdani, who shepherded the document through Main Justice: from his boss, Joe Kaster, to his boss, George Toscas, to his boss, assistant attorney general in the National Security Division Lisa Monaco, to her boss, Attorney General Eric Holder, to, ultimately, President Obama.

None of these folks were easy sells, but for Hamdani the toughest obstacle would be Toscas, a legendarily hard-boiled prosecutor always pushing for every argument to be as tight and stress-tested as possible. A faction of Congress remained angry that Gitmo was no longer an option, while others wanted military commissions to be the only prosecutorial avenue for terrorists. If they were going to bring Spin Ghul to the federal courthouse in Brooklyn, they had better be near 100 percent sure they were going to get a conviction.

Toscas knew the indictment wasn't the strongest in the world, but he was also aware that the patience of the Italians was not infinite. There was a serious risk that if Spin Ghul was released in Italy, an act of mass murder would follow in his wake. Now that there was a paper trail that the Americans had been given a chance to try him, the consequences of setting him free could be laid at their feet. There were political dangers either way.

Toscas's boss, Lisa Monaco, would be on the hook and have to explain the case to President Obama if he grilled them for the details. This was by no means a weak case—they had Spin Ghul's confession and some contemporaneous evidence that he was telling the truth—but it was an incomplete one. Were they ready to take the risk? Under the brand-new defense bill, the president would have to formally declare a waiver to bring this terrorist from overseas to Brooklyn. Were they ready to face off against the Pentagon, which was still pushing military commissions as the safest way to proceed?

Luckily, that issue was cautiously and quietly addressed.

When they served on Obama's Gitmo commission, Bitkower and Shreve met Mikael Clayton, who worked for the chief prosecutor in the Office of Military Commissions. While they were evaluating the cases of Hadi and Faraj for potential prosecution in courts, Clayton had been preparing to try them both in the military commissions. Instead of leaning into the natural competitive tensions that might exist among prosecutors, the three men agreed to work the cases side by side and support one another whatever the decision on Spin Ghul's case was from up above. After all, one of the key recommendations of the 9/11 Commission was for everyone in the intelligence and national security infrastructure to improve information sharing, and that needed to be a principle and an attitude, not just a box to check by rote.

Shreve spoke regularly with Clayton, who continued to work on the prosecutions of Hadi and Faraj. Spin Ghul was from the same world as Hadi and Faraj, so the prosecutors often troubleshooted with each other about potential internal roadblocks. They even speculated on how the prosecution of Spin Ghul might help Clayton with his prosecutions of Hadi and Faraj, whose evidence had been tainted by information garnered through coercive techniques.

In these conversations, Shreve—a natural charmer—explained the reality of the Spin Ghul case. It was going to be a heavy lift internally. The Italians had made it clear that an extradition to a military commission trial was a nonstarter. To them, it had the stink of torture. The Obama administration needed to take the risk of a court trial. And perhaps Spin Ghul would become a cooperating witness and help the commission with the Hadi and Faraj cases. Either way, his testimony could only help.

Clayton explained these views on the matter to General Martins, who had met US attorney Lynch, Bitkower, and Shreve after he was assigned the job and visited the Brooklyn offices at EDNY.

It was a touchy situation, the general knew. The near miss in the Ghailani trial had everyone on edge, but with Clayton and the military courts supporting Bitkower and Shreve, their appeal to higher-ups was stronger. Martins and Clayton worked on an official letter and sent it to Lisa Monaco, the assistant attorney general in charge of the National Security Division. The general forcefully made the argument that he, the chief prosecutor for the US military commissions, fully supported the indictment, extradition, and trial of Spin Ghul in a civilian federal court. He also hoped Spin Ghul's testimony could buttress the cases against Hadi and Faraj. Either way, the trial would be in the service of counterterrorism.

Whatever decision Main Justice would make, it would now be with the blessings of the Pentagon.

The deliberations in Main Justice were made initially with Toscas, Hamdani, counsel to the National Security Division David Newman, and others. They'd heard from the US ambassador to Italy, a businessman named David Hoadley Thorne, who confirmed for the Italian government that this would not be a military commission but a criminal trial in New York.

They discussed matters related to Spin Ghul's potential defense. There was no question that his defense attorneys would suggest that his confession was a result of his treatment and likely torture in Libyan custody. Though the Americans certainly couldn't be blamed for that, a good defense lawyer in front of the right judge could argue that the confession was tainted anyway. Military commissions had yet to show themselves able to resolve such complex issues, whereas there was substantial US case law on the issue in American criminal courts.

The precedents had been set almost seven months to the day before 9/11, when US District Court Judge Leonard Sand of the Southern

District of New York, for whom Bitkower had clerked, had ruled that foreign terrorists captured abroad who were to be tried in the US had the Miranda rights bestowed on any defendant. The cases this ruling was based on dealt with four suspects in the 1998 US embassy bombings.

Judge Sand threw out as inadmissible five different FBI interviews of one of the defendants, Mohamed Rashed Daoud Al-'Owhali, "deeming the 'advice of rights'" the agents offered as too weak. Essentially, the judge found that basic Miranda rights should apply anywhere, to anyone who might be tried in the US. Subsequent interviews, in which an assistant US attorney made a better effort at informing the suspect of his rights, were permitted.

It was quite possible that a future judge might look at how Spin Ghul was treated by the Libyans and find relevance in how Al-'Owhali was detained by Kenyan officials. Al-'Owhali's lawyers said the conditions had been far too harsh, since he'd been kept from communication for two weeks, first in a ten-by-eleven-foot cell and then in a smaller, eight-by-eight-foot cell, both of which imposed "terrible psychological and coercive pressures" on him. The district court found his conditions "non-ideal" but far from oppressive. It should be considered "only one data point—albeit a significant one—in our totality-of-the-circumstances analysis," Judge Sand ruled.

How a court might find the conditions of Spin Ghul's Libyan detention prior to his capture by the Italians was anyone's guess. There was some precedent for admissibility but also for inadmissibility.

George Toscas wondered about Spin Ghul's confession, given the treatment of inmates in the Libyan prison, where torture and other horrific abuses were common. In 2006, Toscas had watched helplessly as three murderers he was prosecuting were freed because of confessions deemed fruit of a poisonous tree. The case had begun in March 1999, when Hutu rebels attacked a campground at a national park in Uganda, seizing and ultimately killing hostages, including Intel executives Robert

Haubner and his wife, Susan Miller. Three Hutu men, captured by the Rwandan government in a later, separate attack, confessed after being interrogated by Rwandan officials from the rival Tutsi clan. But in 2006, US District Court Judge Ellen Judith Huvelle ruled that "the conditions under which defendants were held . . . and the abuse and mistreatment they endured while being interrogated shock the conscience and therefore render the statements involuntary and inadmissible." The defendants were ultimately sent to Australia, free men.

The Rwandan precedent weighed heavily on George Toscas. He was resolved that such a case would not happen on his watch again.

In the end, it would not be left up to Bitkower and Shreve, or even US attorney Loretta Lynch, to decide whether to try to extradite Spin Ghul and prosecute him in a criminal court. It would be up to the Commander-in-chief. President Obama would be blamed if the trial went south. So it was Obama who would need to pull the trigger.

At the time, Obama's homeland security and counterterrorism adviser, John Brennan, was preparing for a big promotion: CIA director. He would be replaced in his White House role by Assistant Attorney General Lisa Monaco. The two were already in close communications, but especially so as 2011 came to a close.

Brennan and President Obama were of one mind on the need to try terrorists in US criminal courts. Brennan, a twenty-five-year veteran of the CIA, had come to share the view that Bush-era policies had made the US less safe. Having joined the Agency out of college, Brennan had worked his way through the ranks—two tours in Saudi Arabia, a presidential daily briefer for President Clinton, executive assistant and then chief of staff to CIA director George Tenet. But he had been shocked to his core when he read the horrific techniques CIA operatives had used on terror suspect Abu Zubaydah—who had been waterboarded and locked inside a small box until his body was disfigured—finding the practices "brutal and inhuman" and "morally repugnant." To his eternal regret, he had pulled his punches when discussing those interrogations with his boss Tenet, never saying what he really thought: that the coercive techniques were unethical, wrong, and un-American. CIA torture, calling the extremists "jihadists"—all this played into the enemy's hands by sullying American ideals and bestowing religious legitimacy on their enemies.

Which was not to say Brennan didn't push aggressive counterterrorism measures. President Obama ordered many drone strikes, innocent civilian casualties notwithstanding, proving that he took the threat seriously, and Brennan backed the president on this as well.

Monaco and Brennan had numerous conversations about Spin Ghul and the case—pros, cons, potential pitfalls. They agreed that the criminal court was the place to try him, to signal that President Obama was committed to taking terrorists off the battlefield—and not just with lethal strikes. It was the best option: the Italians could bring only a low-level case against Spin Ghul, so the US needed to prevent Spin Ghul from going into the Italian justice system, where he would be guaranteed just a slap on the wrist.

A criminal court trial was the only option. With all the appeals and challenges, the process was certain to be long and drawn out. Monaco was already pushing her team to come up with plans, procedures, and protocols for this route. The new defense bill would require that President Obama issue a waiver to bring him to the US from Italy, but that was just a formality.

If they did this, Monaco and Brennan agreed, the Obama administration needed to be prepared. Any indictment would initially be sealed, but soon enough the public would find out about it. None of this was without risk—judges and juries were fallible and capricious, the justice system unpredictable, the politics risky.

But what other option did they have? Spin Ghul was a dangerous man. This was truly the only way to lock him up and prevent him from killing again, President Obama agreed.

Monaco met with the Deputies' Committee one last time to make sure everyone was on board and every procedure was in place. Then she told Hamdani to give their friends at EDNY a call.

In February 2012, Hamdani called Bitkower and Shreve to tell them they were good to go.

They in turn told Lynch they were going to a grand jury to seek an indictment and ultimately extradition of Spin Ghul.

"Go get 'em," she said.

Twenty-three random US citizens sit on a grand jury. Only twelve of them are needed to indict. And they often don't know why they are there until the very last minute. Usually, the cases in Brooklyn are what you might expect for a jurisdiction of eight million people—weapons, assault, drugs. Prosecutors in the Eastern District of New York know that when they bring a terrorism case in front of the grand jurors, their eyes will likely light up and they will look up from their smartphones and pay attention.

In February 2012, Bitkower and LaCroix helped prepare Special Agent Raushaunah Muhammad to be a witness before the grand jury. Shreve explained to her that this would be the first time since the defense bill passed that President Obama had sought a waiver from the ban on bringing terrorists into the US for a trial in a civilian court.

Despite Raushaunah's nervousness, Bitkower didn't think the actual proceeding would be all that big a deal. The cliché is that prosecutors can get a grand jury to indict a ham sandwich. As far as Bitkower and Shreve saw it, the burden had been the okay they'd already received from President Obama and Attorney General Holder to seek the indictment. The grand jury indictment would be more of a formality.

On February 21, the grand jury in Brooklyn did indeed hand down an indictment against Spin Ghul, with six distinct charges: (1) conspiracy to murder Americans (American servicemembers in Afghanistan); (2) conspiracy to bomb a US government facility (in Nigeria); (3) conspiracy to provide material support to al Qaeda (all his activities since leaving Saudi Arabia); (4) providing material support to al Qaeda; (5) using firearms in furtherance of crimes of violence; and (6) using explosives in furtherance of one or more felonies (his attempts to purchase explosives in Nigeria).

The indictment was sealed. For security reasons, the American people would not be informed about the indictment until March 2013, more than a year away. Bitkower and Shreve commenced the extradition process, and Raushaunah and LaCroix prepared to fly to Italy to formally arrest Spin Ghul and take him to a Brooklyn prison.

The indictment was written a mile wide and an inch deep, with—theoretically—very few details confirmed and verified beyond a reasonable doubt. The entire team was aware that a conviction was far from guaranteed. Bitkower and Shreve would not be able to add charges to the case once Spin Ghul had been indicted and extradited, so they hoped they'd have enough to try and convict him. There was no time to celebrate the indictment. They now had to present it before a judge and jury, with Spin Ghul likely afforded fierce defense attorneys. Their journey to prove it all, to form an airtight case, was only just beginning.

CHAPTER NINETEEN

THE ARREST

Naples, Italy

Okay, so this is how I'm going to die, Special Agent Raushaunah Muhammad thought as she sat on a private jet chartered by the FBI. Bouncing through a torrential storm, her body was tossed up and down, and she avoided a concussion only by the grace of her seat belt. Raushaunah was on her way to Italy to escort Spin Ghul back to the US.

A few months earlier, she had held what's called an ROC, or "rehearsal of concept," drill to go over every detail of the transfer. In a surreal moment for Raushaunah, a Black, thirty-two-year-old Muslim woman, she'd stood at a long table of senior leaders of the FBI and other agencies, most of them middle-aged white men.

I'm the one running this, she thought.

Well, shit.

After several delays, the day finally came on Tuesday, October 2, 2012. Agent Raushaunah Muhammad and Bert LaCroix reported to a small tarmac in Northern Virginia in the early hours of the morning.

The downpour was so heavy that they could barely see in front of them, and Raushaunah was unsettled as their small US government aircraft took off. That day would end up seeing record-setting rainfall with fog so thick that Vice President Biden's Air Force Two 757 would be diverted to Dulles from Joint Base Andrews in Maryland.

Rocking and rolling in the plane, they were headed overseas to formally arrest Spin Ghul and take him back to Brooklyn to stand trial. In addition to the flight crew, she and LaCroix were also joined by Carlos Fernandez, the assistant special agent from the FBI's Joint Terrorism Task Force (JTTF), multiple members of the FBI's hostage rescue team, a member of the FBI's fly team, and their translator Mo. Under normal circumstances, there was no way Raushaunah would have voluntarily gotten onto this plane. But today she was thrilled.

When they landed in Italy, jet-lagged and still a bit motion sick, they were driven to a local hotel. Raushaunah was just conscious enough to notice the Mediterranean style of the tall ceilings before passing out.

The next day, they met with officials both American and Italian, making sure all terms of the MLAT were being honored and upheld. Once everything was settled, they set their work aside and strolled down a cobblestone street for a nice authentic Italian dinner. That would be their only opportunity for sightseeing, as Spin Ghul would be transferred to their custody the following day. That next morning, Raushaunah awoke excited. She'd been working on the case for more than a year, had known about Spin Ghul for longer than that, and was thrilled to be placing him under arrest.

She'd played out the scene in her mind dozens of times: *My name is Raushaunah Muhammad, I am a special agent with the Federal Bureau of Investigation. You have been indicted by a Brooklyn grand jury for the murders of Private Jerod Dennis and Airman Ray Losano, on April 25,*

2003, in Afghanistan, and for plotting to blow up the US embassy in Lagos, Nigeria. I hereby place you under arrest.

Raushaunah had a sense that she was part of something historic—it would be the first time in the US Global War on Terror that the US military was deferring to the FBI, an action so controversial that Attorney General Holder had to sign a waiver under the new defense bill to allow them to bring Spin Ghul into the US. Arresting Spin Ghul could end up being the crowning moment in Raushaunah's FBI career.

Raushaunah and LaCroix had dressed up for the occasion. Raushaunah was in her FBI "uniform" of a black pants suit and white button-down shirt, though this time she was also wearing high heels instead of her boots. LaCroix, who was more likely to wear khakis and a plaid shirt, donned a suit and tie. They stood outside the transfer building, watching the van belonging to the carabinieri—the national gendarmerie of Italy—as it crossed the tarmac to them.

Raushaunah was ready to enact the scene she'd spent days fantasizing about, preparing to make the positive identification of the prisoner and arrest him. She was intensely focused on making sure she did everything correctly and by the book.

The carabinieri removed Spin Ghul from the van. *That's him*, she thought to herself, catching her breath.

She was about to step forward to arrest him, but before she could one of the guys from the HRT, the hostage rescue team, stepped toward Spin Ghul, handcuffed him, and placed him into custody. The HRT took him inside to use the restroom.

Well, ain't that a bitch, she thought.

Raushaunah was dismayed but determined. She had been flown all the way from Northern Virginia in a Tilt-A-Whirl to arrest an al Qaeda terrorist, and she would do just that. She had been working this case for a long time. She wasn't going to miss her chance.

So as soon as Spin Ghul was escorted out of the bathroom and back to the waiting area on the tarmac, Raushaunah held up her FBI billfold—gold badge on the outside, FBI photo ID on the inside—and approached him.

"I am Special Agent Raushaunah Muhammad," she said, "and I hereby place you under arrest."

Mo translated her remarks seamlessly into Hausa, as well as what she told him next, the advice of rights per the FBI form FD-395, the same ones Americans know by heart from TV police procedurals, the right to remain silent and on and on. Did he understand his rights?

He did.

He was then taken back inside, where the hostage rescue team medic gave him an examination to assess his health and physical condition. Raushaunah went to make copies of the advice of rights she had read to Spin Ghul, the Italian transfer of custody paperwork, and the arrest warrant to give to her Italian counterparts.

While she was gone, Spin Ghul was turned over to LaCroix, the terrorist's face betraying a flash of recognition. A year before, at the September 2011 hearing in Italy, Spin Ghul at one point was close enough to ask LaCroix, in broken English, whether he was going to go home with him. Not then.

But this time you are, LaCroix thought with satisfaction as they all boarded the plane.

After dealing with the paperwork, Raushaunah was the last to get onto the plane. Spin Ghul was given a change of clothes so he could get out of his prison scrubs. Raushaunah and LaCroix offered him earmuffs for the noise and chill of the flight. They also gave him a new Quran.

"We have halal foods for you to eat," Raushaunah told him.

"Coming to America was part of my fate," he told her.

More than ten hours later, the jet landed at John F. Kennedy International Airport in Queens. After Raushaunah handed the proper paperwork to immigration officials, Spin Ghul was taken into the custody of an FBI SWAT team, and a caravan of law enforcement vehicles headed to the New York FBI field office downtown, in the Jacob K. Javits Federal Office Building at 26 Federal Plaza, a.k.a. "26 Fed." Raushaunah had to walk down some long halls at this stop and, still in her high heels, her feet were killing her.

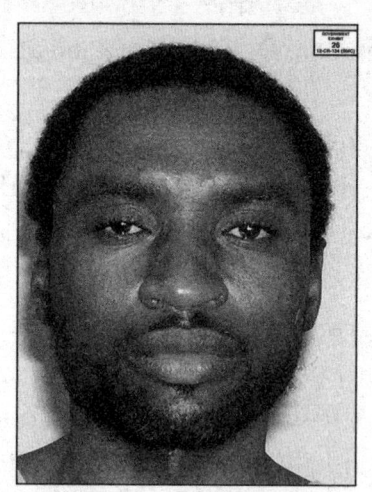

Ibrahim Suleiman Adnan Adam Harun, aka "Spin Ghul"
U.S. ATTORNEY'S OFFICE FOR THE
EASTERN DISTRICT OF NEW YORK

After Spin Ghul was fingerprinted and processed at 26 Fed, the caravan drove him to the Metropolitan Correctional Center in Manhattan, where the Bureau of Prisons processed him and put him in a section for the highest-security prisoners—in the past, 1993 World Trade Center bomber Ramzi Yousef, in the future, the drug lord El Chapo.

Spin Ghul was finally behind bars in New York City. And now the terrorist detectives and their team had to make sure they could keep him locked up forever.

CHAPTER TWENTY

WE NEED THAT

Grand Forks, North Dakota

"Man, you're the hardest person to get ahold of," said Bert LaCroix.

LaCroix, with his golden retriever nature—cheery, ebullient, but relentless—was finally on the phone with Major Drew Nathan, who'd served at Firebase Shkin as a lieutenant nine years before. It was October 2012, and Nathan was at his government job in Grand Forks, North Dakota, helping fellow veterans seeking employment. He and his wife and young son lived about forty minutes away in Hillsboro, population just over 1,600, tucked on the far east side of the state, near the Minnesota border.

For months, LaCroix had been trying to track down the soldiers involved in the battle near Firebase Shkin with varying success, but he never let the lack of leads deter him. One of the lessons he'd picked up as a soldier in Iraq was to remain cool under fire. Since then, he'd realized that very little was worth panicking about. He simply wouldn't stop until he achieved his mission. The call with Nathan was quick, a surface-level explanation of the basics of the case. Spin Ghul was in custody, and

LaCroix and others with the Joint Terrorism Task Force were hoping for Nathan's insights about the April 2003 battle. Did he have any photographs from his time at Firebase Shkin? Did he take any souvenirs home? Could they meet if he came to North Dakota? Nathan said yes, so LaCroix made immediate plans to head to Grand Forks.

LaCroix understood war souvenirs. Back when he'd been in Iraq, out on patrol, out of the corner of his eye he noticed a Montblanc pen that had been partially crushed by a truck. He grabbed it, put it into his pocket, and repaired it with Krazy Glue. He used it all the time and made sure to bring it back with him to the war zone both times he returned as a civilian employee. There was something about using the once-smashed detritus that connected him to his deployment and brought him a joy that he couldn't quite explain.

In North Dakota, LaCroix met Nathan at his office, sat down with him in a conference room, and went over all the photographs Nathan had from his time in eastern Afghanistan. Nathan had also brought his "war box," where he kept artifacts from that time. In the aftermath of the battle, Nathan had collected from the enemy camp a canteen, binoculars, and a scarf.

As long as men have been fighting in wars, they've been grabbing souvenirs from the battlefield as keepsakes, with reasons as disparate as the soldiers themselves. Some see such items as a final "screw you" to the enemy, while others see the objects as sacred talismans. There are those for whom an item from battle is proof that their memories, which evaporate like smoke, are real.

As the Slayers departed Firebase Shkin in August 2003, there was a free-for-all as troops grabbed battlefield souvenirs that had already been inventoried. The only rule was against bringing back firearms. LaCroix copied and downloaded Nathan's photographs of souvenirs and other images onto a thumb drive and photocopied some of the paper items—maps and such.

Then they drove separately to Bonzer's Sandwich Pub for lunch, where Nathan and LaCroix continued their conversation and Nathan shared the names of other soldiers who might have information as well. One of those names was Dwayne McKnight, an NCO with whom Nathan would trust his life.

"Is this Dwayne McKnight?" LaCroix asked.

"Yeah," said McKnight. On that awful day in 2003, then-Specialist McKnight had speeded to the casualty collection point with First Sergeant Severino and tried to find Jerod Dennis after he disappeared. Since then, he'd done two tours in Iraq, returned to California in 2007, and was trying to put the war behind him. That proved impossible. The war was always on his mind. The pain was always present. When LaCroix called him, McKnight was sitting in his home in Victorville, California, about ninety miles northeast of Los Angeles, where he lived with his wife and young son. They'd moved from Orange County so he could take a job as a correctional officer with the federal penitentiary there, a high-security facility that housed almost a thousand convicts.

"Were you in the 82nd Airborne?" LaCroix continued. "B Company, 3rd Battalion, 504th Parachute Infantry Regiment?"

"Yes," McKnight said, sounding uneasy.

"And were you in Afghanistan, in battle on April 25, 2003?" LaCroix continued.

"Yes," McKnight said. "What's this about?"

LaCroix introduced himself, told him that he got McKnight's phone number from his old lieutenant, Drew Nathan. He explained they were building a case to prosecute Spin Ghul for killing Jerod Dennis and Ray Losano. McKnight's apprehension gave way, and he shared his story of the battle. The ambush. Trying to defend himself and his unit. Helping clean up once it was all over.

"Did you bring anything home with you from Firebase Shkin?" LaCroix followed up.

In the aftermath of the battle, several soldiers had walked up the hill to the scene of the ambush and picked up stray items they found at the makeshift al Qaeda camp. AK-47s, flashlights, knives. A journal, a Quran, miscellaneous items. The weapons and military objects were inventoried by Severino and sent to Bagram. The other stuff ended up packed away in the supply closet.

For Dwayne McKnight, these objects had intense meaning as a way to remember his time in war. Having possessions formerly belonging to al Qaeda fighters also brought him some personal satisfaction—*this was yours, and now it's mine.*

In August 2003, when the 82nd Airborne was being relieved by the 10th Mountain Division, Severino announced that if anyone wanted anything from the storage room, the time to grab it was now. Otherwise, it would become property of the 10th Mountain—or be thrown into a burn pit and incinerated. McKnight shipped to his mother's home in Tustin, California, some of the best artifacts, including prayer beads, a fancy dagger in a leather sheath, and a small Quran with a zipper.

"You have a Quran?" LaCroix asked. "Is it brown? Does it have a zipper?"

"How did you know?" McKnight said.

"Where do you have it?"

"In my footlocker," McKnight said. "In a closet somewhere."

"Dude, we need that!" LaCroix said, no longer containing his excitement.

"Why are you guys asking about this?" McKnight wondered. He didn't think he had done anything illegal by bringing the souvenirs home, but had he done something wrong? He had just started a new job working for the federal government. "Do I need a lawyer or something?"

"No, no," LaCroix said. "We don't care what you all took back. You're not in trouble. No one in the platoon is in trouble."

McKnight exhaled a bit, even if his heart kept pounding.

"Look," LaCroix said, "we're prosecuting this individual. We've been looking for that Quran. We need it."

"No," McKnight said.

"What? No?" LaCroix was taken aback.

"It can never be replaced," McKnight explained. "I'm never going back to Afghanistan." McKnight was proud of having fought in Afghanistan. Now someone who hadn't earned those items wanted them. These weren't just objects; to him, they represented his time in an ancient land in a war he fought for his country. He wasn't willing to just give them up. His uncle had given him a bayonet from a great-uncle who fought in France during World War I. His grandma had given him remnants of the antiaircraft fire, the flak, that her brother—who flew fifty missions over North Africa during World War II—had carved out of his B-17 bomber aircraft. His grandpa had served on the USS *Mertz* in the Pacific during that war as well and had gifted him Japanese money, and his cousin a Japanese machete he'd picked up along the way. Someday these artifacts from Afghanistan would belong to his children and his grandchildren, who would be able to look upon them—and remember Dwayne McKnight—with pride. And this cop wanted him to turn them over to the government? The same government that had sent him to get shot at in that scary, strange land that seemed stuck in the Stone Age?

"Look at it this way, McKnight," LaCroix said. "You are helping put away a guy who killed your friends." LaCroix then gently gave him the cold reality of the situation: "You can either give it to us willingly or we can subpoena you."

Oh boy, McKnight thought. *I don't need the FBI getting involved with my new job.* He wanted to tell LaCroix to fuck off. But he didn't. He had a family now. He had responsibilities.

But it wasn't easy keeping his cool. McKnight's new job at the prison was stressful enough, and his nights were full of tossing and turning as he relived Afghanistan and Iraq every night. He had recurring dreams of being killed—either overseas or inside the prison. Suppressing his trauma wasn't working; he would have dizzy spells and seek help at the local VA. And this jackass from New York was telling him to hand over these objects that meant the world to him? It brought all this hurt to the fore.

He exhaled.

"Okay," McKnight said, giving in.

LaCroix told him that he would make sure an FBI agent from the Victorville office would be in touch with him as soon as possible to arrange to pick up McKnight's battlefield souvenirs.

As inventoried by an FBI agent on October 29, 2012, 1:35 p.m. Pacific time, McKnight had given to the US government a knife in a black leather sheath, a green cloth ammunition pouch or "chest rack," one laminated topographical "patrol map," one pocket-sized leather-bound zippered book presumed to be a Quran, and one beaded necklace presumed to be prayer beads. McKnight was given a receipt for the items.

As the package made its way to Bert LaCroix in New York City, he prayed something could be tied directly to Spin Ghul himself. Physical evidence that could help prove Spin Ghul killed Jerod Dennis and Ray Losano. Physical evidence that would allow those who served alongside Jerod and Losano to help deliver justice to their fallen brothers.

CHAPTER TWENTY-ONE

KRISTEN GREEN

Islamabad, Pakistan

Barbara Jean McGuine had been raised on the island of Oahu in Hawaii. She joined the US Air Force shortly after graduating high school in 1980 and shipped off to Grand Forks Air Force Base in North Dakota. There she met Airman Bruce Wormsley. They were married in a trailer park in Emerado, by an Air Force veteran turned Pentecostal minister. It was 1983, and Barbara was twenty. Their daughter Kristen was born in 1984.

The marriage didn't take. Barbara met another airman, Sergeant Milton Green, who worked in computers, and they hit it off. Milton left the Air Force in 1987, and all three of them moved to Columbia, Maryland. He worked at Fort Meade. In 1989 he got a better job at the US State Department in Washington, DC. Soon an opportunity presented itself to work at the US mission in Bonn, Germany. Barbara and Milton married, moved abroad, and both were able to work at the US mission in Germany. Their son Zachary was born in 1992.

With both parents working for the US government, the Green

family was able to travel the world. They lived in and worked in other embassies in China and the Ivory Coast. In 2000, they moved to the US embassy in the capital of Pakistan, Islamabad.

After 9/11, there were many fears that Pakistan was dangerous. Families had been evacuated from the embassy not even a week afterward. Barbara temporarily moved to Ellicott City, Maryland, with Kristen and Zachary, where they attended local public schools. Five months later, the US ambassador to Pakistan decided that conditions were safe enough for the families to return to the US compound.

Barbara, Kristen, and Zachary returned to Islamabad. Their family reunited. They liked their lives. They had many Pakistani friends and loved learning about local culture. Barbara was preparing to join the foreign service. In March, Kristen, a high school senior at the International School of Islamabad, had been accepted to attend Florida State University in the fall. She organized a special field day on March 15 for her classmates, trying to raise school spirit.

That Sunday morning, March 17, the Greens went to the Protestant International Church, near the US embassy, as they did every Sunday. They sang the hymn "This Is Holy Ground."

This is holy ground
We're standing on holy ground

The modest hall was only about half full, with maybe sixty or so other worshippers there that day. A lot of embassy staffers and their families had still not returned to Islamabad after the post-9/11 exodus.

After the hymn finished, the minister began his sermon.

It was roughly 11 a.m.

Two men walked into the church, and started throwing grenades.

The windows of the church shattered. The church was covered

in blood. More than forty people were wounded, including ten Americans.

Five were killed. Including Barbara Green and seventeen-year-old Kristen.

Christopher Reimann picked up Dave Franco at the Islamabad Airport hours later.

Reimann was the senior FBI official—called the LEGAT or legal attaché—stationed in Pakistan since January 1999. Franco was one of the Bureau's best investigators and following the 9/11 attacks had volunteered to deploy for an overseas assignment to focus on counterterrorism. Reimann felt Franco's skills were needed in Pakistan and had requested his redeployment. They were classmates at the FBI academy and good friends.

"Hurry up," Reimann told Franco as they waited for his luggage. "Get your stuff, let's go."

Franco assumed that Reimann was worried because the chaotic Islamabad Airport was a target-rich environment, and the two FBI agents were now the prime targets.

In actuality, Reimann wasn't particularly worried about their safety, as the inside of the airport was past several security layers and was fairly secure. Reimann was hurrying because he'd made a deal with cafeteria workers to have them come in at 5 a.m. to make breakfast, the FBI agents keeping earlier hours than the diplomatic staff. Franco's plane had come in later than expected, and he wanted to get back to get some coffee and grub before their morning meeting.

It was 4 a.m. local time, and Franco was spent. The FBI agent had been in El Paso, Texas, when the call came in, shortly after Barbara and Kristen and two other innocents had been killed, and within hours he was on his way to Pakistan. Despite his superman reputation, Franco was only human. At the morning briefing at the embassy, he nodded off in the middle of the presentation. The assistant LEGAT, Jennifer Keenan, threw a plastic cup at him to wake him up.

For Westerners, Pakistan in 2002 was a terrifying place, and it was only getting scarier. The investigation into the 9/11 terrorist attacks of only six months before made it clear that the path for would-be jihadi fighters in Afghanistan ran through Pakistan as if it were Route 66. Pakistan itself was a hotbed of violent religious extremism. In January 2002, just weeks before Barbara and Kristen were killed at the Protestant International Church, a *Wall Street Journal* reporter named Daniel Pearl was kidnapped by Islamist terrorists on his way to interview a local cleric. Pearl, thirty-eight, had been exploring the cleric's ties to British citizen Richard Reid, the member of al Qaeda and would-be shoe bomber who unsuccessfully tried to blow up a plane flying from Paris to Miami on December 22, 2001. Pearl was beheaded in early February, and videotape of his dead body surfaced later that month. His murderers remained at large. Reimann had up to twenty FBI investigators who reported to him on these and many more cases all over the country.

The morning briefing covered all active cases, leads regarding suspects in the murder of Pearl and the church bombing—the crime scene of which was still being processed. The larger 9/11 investigation included anyone involved in the nexus of terrorism. One suspect thought to be nearby, a Palestinian called Abu Zubaydah, wasn't officially in al Qaeda, but he had a good relationship with the group as a facilitator who helped young jihadi recruits train and make connections across the border in Afghanistan. In exchange, al Qaeda provided Zubaydah with protection from anyone who might be seeking to do him harm—whether a rival faction, the Pakistani government, or anyone else.

The US had been trying to find Zubaydah for years. He was

thought to have played a major role in the 1998 embassy bombings and in April 2000 was one of twenty-eight extremists convicted by a Jordanian court in absentia of plotting to attack American and Israeli targets in Jordan.

The famous August 2001 Presidential Daily Brief titled "Bin Ladin [sic] Determined to Strike in US," which was made public in 2002 during the investigations into US intelligence failures leading up to 9/11, reported that "The millennium plotting in Canada in 1999 may have been part of Bin Ladin's first serious attempt to implement a terrorist strike in the US. Convicted plotter Ahmed Ressam has told the FBI that he conceived the idea to attack Los Angeles International Airport himself, but that Bin Ladin lieutenant Abu Zubaydah encouraged him and helped facilitate the operation. Ressam also said that in 1998 Abu Zubaydah was planning his own US attack."

The FBI was in a defensive crouch, in many ways. It was hard, bordering on impossible, to get justice in these cases. Scrambling in the face of a blooming threat, their goal was simply to prevent any more attacks. They didn't want any more 9/11s, no more Daniel Pearls, no more Kristen Wormsley Greens.

Abu Zubaydah, it was believed, had come to the region in February 2002, working with the local al Qaeda affiliate "Jaish-e-Muhammad," posing as a businessman and renting Shabaz cottage, in Faisal Town, attracting al Qaeda recruits and members from Saudi Arabia, Sudan, and Yemen. Not long afterward, his activities attracted notice, one neighbor wondering why the lights in his house never went out. Pakistanis, particularly those in more educated and affluent neighborhoods, were on alert.

One day, a soccer ball bounced into the wrong yard, and, according to rumor, a police constable driving by wondered why someone was yelling in Arabic in their Urdu-speaking town. Soon enough, the FBI was monitoring the house and the phone calls being made from it.

On March 27, 2002, Franco joined the other FBI investigators in their office in Lahore, where Reimann gave them a broad outline of their plan to arrest Abu Zubaydah that night.

It would be a joint operation with Pakistani law enforcement, who knew up to a dozen different safe house compounds in Faisalabad where Abu Zubaydah might be found. And since they didn't want anyone tipping him off, Reimann came up with the plan to form twelve teams and hit all twelve of them at the same time.

The Pakistanis would be taking the lead, FBI officials said. That was how it was meant to be perceived, given the politics at play.

"Be careful," Reimann told Franco when he learned he would be at "F3," or the third safe house in Faisalabad, Pakistan's third-largest city and its most industrialized. "A tall guy with a long beard could be in there," he said, meaning bin Laden, whose whereabouts were still unknown. "Yours is the primary location." It was the most likely site where the highest-value terrorist might be.

Reimann and Franco then drove with others from Lahore to Faisalabad. It was about a two-and-a-half-hour drive.

In Faisalabad, Franco wore a bulletproof FBI SWAT vest and a local outfit of sorts, a *shalwar kameez*—a shirt that hangs down to one's thighs, with matching elastic-waisted trousers. His Danner tactical boots were a US law enforcement giveaway for anyone really paying attention, but it was the best he could do. He also had a sidearm, a rifle, and a photograph of Abu Zubaydah. In the photo, with his short hair and glasses, Abu Zubaydah looked to Franco like a meek, nerdy little accountant.

It was the middle of the night as March 27 became March 28, and it was numbingly hot. As they waited, the only distraction from the heat was the mosquitos.

Finally, local police decided it was time to roll. Driving in a Toyota sedan, Franco followed Pakistani police to the safe house at location three. He parked a block down from the police, in a relatively affluent neighborhood.

The police approached the safe house, a large, two-story structure surrounded by a courtyard, cement brick walls, and a sturdy steel gate in the front of the complex. After an assault team cut the wires, hopped the fence, and took care of the guards, the Pakistani law enforcement officials got out of their vehicles, banged on the door, and announced in Punjab that they were there to gain entry.

The lights in the safe house turned on.

Then they turned off.

Then they turned on.

Then they turned off.

"This isn't good," Franco said.

The Pakistani police were yelling, and within seconds rounds started flying.

The situation quickly became chaotic.

Franco had been advised to "disengage"—to leave—if anything like this happened, so he retreated to the end of the block. Reimann was about a mile away and arrived at Franco's location quickly.

Inside, the Pakistani cops crashed the door and ran in as Abu Zubaydah and three others grabbed money and false identification and ran up the stairs to the roof. They jumped over the fencing and onto the adjacent roof of the villa next door, where four Pakistani policemen were waiting for them.

"You're not Muslims!" Abu Zubaydah yelled at his captors.

"Of course we are," said an officer.

"Well, you're American Muslims," he replied.

The conversation came to an end when Abu al-Hasnat, a Syrian fleeing along with Abu Zubaydah, tried to wrestle away a policeman's AK-47, a struggle that resulted in Abu Zubaydah being shot in his abdomen, leg, and groin. Al-Hasnat was shot and killed.

After the gunfire subsided, Franco and Reimann drove back to F3. Two blue pickup trucks belonging to Pakistani officials were parked in the street. A dead body was in the bed of one of them. Another individual, alive, sat in the back seat.

Franco approached the one in the back. The man was bleeding profusely. His face resembled the photograph of Abu Zubaydah that Franco had, but he was clean shaven, and even more jarringly, this man was much larger than Franco expected—at least six feet tall, maybe taller, and broad. He was pretty sure it was Abu Zubaydah, but over the radio, at some of the other locations, other agents made it clear they thought they had Abu Zubaydah in custody, too.

"This is Abu Zubaydah," Franco told Reimann definitively.

"How do you know?"

"Look at the picture," Franco said, holding the photograph up to the wounded man in the back of the pickup truck. "Look at the face."

Abu Zubaydah's head was hanging down, resting on his chest. Franco brought out his camera—he wanted to take a photograph to send it back to the FBI as soon as possible.

"Pick up your head so we can get a good picture of you," Franco told him.

The man mumbled something, Franco couldn't make it out, not that he spoke the language anyway.

"He said," a Pakistani cop explained, "that he just wants to die."

At that, Abu Zubaydah looked up at Franco, who could see his pain, desperation, and agony.

"We need to get him to a hospital," Franco said. They were not going to let Abu Zubaydah take the easy way out. He took his photograph and sent it to the FBI.

Minutes later, he and Reimann got word: That is definitely Abu Zubaydah. Do not lose him.

It was past 3 a.m. now. Before the police caravan could move out, before arrangements could be made to take Abu Zubaydah to the hospital, Franco ran into the safe house to scoop up as much potential evidence as he could while Reimann guarded the suspect.

The house was large, with multiple bedrooms, but it was decorated like a safe house—mattresses on the floor, very little furniture, eerily transient. Franco's goal was to collect any object that might contain evidence of an imminent attack against the US or its allies, or any information about the 9/11 attack. Into giant trash bags he scooped bombmaking materials, a soldering iron, wires, circuitry boards, computers, hard drives, notebooks, logs, registers, phone books, photographs, passports.

At an American crime scene with a secure perimeter, such a process in an FBI investigation would take hours and be conducted with methodical, fastidious precision. In Faisalabad that night, Franco pulled it all off in under fifteen minutes.

At the truck, Franco handed several bags of evidence over to Reimann, who in turn told Franco to accompany Abu Zubaydah to Faisal Hospital. Franco got into the back of the truck, the terrorist behind him.

The truck wouldn't start.

The driver cranked the engine and pumped the gas, but it wouldn't catch.

They waited outside the compound like sitting ducks, the churn of the hapless rev of the motor almost laughing at how preposterous and dangerous this all was.

Reimann asked the local Pakistani police if he could get his fellow cops to push the truck with their hands. It started to move, but slowly.

It was unclear to Franco how this impasse would resolve itself, when he suddenly felt the thrust of a second police pickup truck pushing into them from behind. Their driver released all resistance except for steering as the second truck essentially pushed them for the roughly one-mile journey to the hospital through the middle of one of the world's most dangerous spots as Dave Franco sat next to one of the world's most-wanted terrorists.

Doctors, nurses, and medical personnel came quickly to Abu Zubaydah as he was wheeled into the hospital.

"How's your officer?" Franco asked a Pakistani police commander once they arrived at the hospital.

"Who?" the commander answered.

"Your officer?" Franco said. "He was wounded in the raid?"

"Oh," the commander said. "Don't worry about him—we've got plenty of officers."

John Kiriakou, from the CIA, was with them all as well. A cell phone, presumably Abu Zubaydah's, kept ringing. But it was sealed in an evidence bag.

"Whose stupid idea was it to seal up the phone?" Kiriakou asked.

"It's evidence of a crime," said one of the FBI agents.

"No, it's a communication device," Kiriakou said. "The phone's not evidence of a crime. Everybody's got a phone."

"We can't open the evidence bag," said the agent. "It would break the chain of custody."

As they debated the phone, it quickly became clear to Dave Franco that his presence was not sufficient to keep Abu Zubaydah in US custody here in the middle of the night in Faisalabad. There were rumors of Islamic militants coming to rescue their compatriot at any moment. He called Reimann to make clear his vulnerability and need for reinforcements.

Reimann told him that additional FBI forces were already en route to help secure Zubaydah. When they arrived, Reimann told Franco that the driver would bring him back to the FBI staging location in Faisalabad.

The next day, March 29, Franco and Reimann returned to the hospital. A CIA operative approached Reimann. He was on his satellite phone with Langley. CIA director Tenet and his medical adviser wanted to know how Abu Zubaydah was doing and whether they should move him to another hospital.

Franco had been trained as a medic. Reimann sent him to Abu Zubaydah's room to assess conditions. Franco went and was not impressed. Abu Zubaydah looked awful, and the hygiene at the hospital was abysmal.

He was back on the call five minutes later. His basic take was that if Abu Zubaydah stayed in that hospital in Faisalabad, he would die from dysentery.

The CIA and Reimann agreed they would need to move Abu Zubaydah as soon as possible. The government of Pakistan sent a helicopter within minutes. A convoy soon left the hospital on the way to a government field that contained a helipad. The chopper that met them was monstrous, an old Soviet pile of junk, a relic.

"You gotta go with him," Reimann told Franco.

"No," said Franco.

"You gotta go," Reimann said again.

"I don't have my contact lens case," said Franco.

"You can buy a new one," Reimann said, starting to smile. Goddamn Franco.

"Is the government going to pay for it?" Franco asked.

"Just get in the damn chopper!" Reimann said.

Abu Zubyadah and another patient were put into the ancient helicopter, and Franco followed.

The helicopter wasn't able to take off.

Franco looked to the pilot, who gave a thumbs-down.

A mechanic climbed onto the top of the chopper and began whaling on the rotors. *Bang! Bang! Bang!* The entire mission to capture Zubaydah was starting to feel like a comedy sketch.

Bang bang bang—

The mechanic dropped down and started talking to the pilot, who tried to start the helicopter again.

No luck.

Another mechanic approached the bird, holding a giant battery and jumper cables.

Were they really about to jump a helicopter like a beat-up Toyota Corolla?

The mechanic with the cables signaled to the pilot, and the chopper began to sputter to life. The mechanic unhooked the cables and jumped down. The pilot punched a few buttons, and the rotors began spinning.

As the helicopter began rising not far from Faisal Hospital, Dave Franco looked down and saw Reimann hysterically laughing at him.

Franco's eyes were like balloons, almost popping out of their sockets. It reminded Reimann of the scene in *Caddyshack* when a fisherman is stunned to see Rodney Dangerfield's yacht barreling right toward him.

Against all odds, the helicopter ride was uneventful. At the Lahore hospital, a Pakistani doctor took one look at Abu Zubaydah and shook his head pessimistically at Kiriakou, the CIA agent, who met him there.

"Seriously, Doc, he's got to live," Kiriakou said. They needed the intel Abu Zubaydah could provide.

Kiriakou grabbed a sheet and began ripping it into strips. He tied Abu Zubaydah to the bed.

"What are you doing?" asked the doctor when he returned to the room.

"No offense, Doctor, but I don't know you and my orders are that this man cannot leave until we take him out of here," Kiriakou said.

"He's in no condition to leave," said the doctor. "He's in a coma."

Hours later, Abu Zubaydah awoke. Kiriakou approached him and asked him in Arabic what his name was.

"I will not speak to you in God's language," Abu Zubaydah replied, in perfect English.

After asking for wine, Abu Zubaydah was given another hit of Demerol and passed out again.

Then, hours later, Abu Zubaydah was weeping, begging for Kiriakou to kill him right there in the hospital. He knew what he had waiting for him.

The CIA told the FBI that the Agency was going to take it from here. They made plans to fly him out of Lahore, to parts unknown.

Reimann's deputy, Jennifer Keenan, would later say that FBI director Robert Mueller had given firm instructions: don't let him leave until you fingerprint him.

The CIA pilot was irritated, but the FBI fingerprinted Abu Zubaydah before the CIA could fly him away.

Franco went to a hotel and passed out.

Abu Zubaydah eventually healed from his bullet wounds. But later, at a black site in Thailand, he was tortured, slapped and slammed against a wall, prevented from sleeping for days on end, and waterboarded to the point of being "completely unresponsive, with bubbles rising through his open, full mouth," according to an investigation by the Senate Intelligence Committee. CIA officers were told his interrogation would take "precedence" over any medical treatment, despite the wounds from which he was still recovering. CIA officers discussed his remaining "incommunicado for the remainder of his life."

The capture of Abu Zubaydah—the CIA's first detainee subjected to "enhanced interrogation techniques"—would lead to one of the CIA's most notorious episodes.

His testimony, obtained from torturous treatment, would be unusable in trial and of questionable accuracy.

But what the FBI and Franco had done earlier that night adhered to protocols.

More than a decade after that fateful night, the team prosecuting Spin Ghul called on Chris Reimann, Jennifer Keenan, and Dave Franco to testify about their activities in Pakistan. Their detective work that evening helped prove that Spin Ghul was connected to Abu Zubaydah's and Osama bin Laden's vast terrorist network.

CHAPTER TWENTY-TWO

SUSAN KELLMAN FOR THE DEFENDANT

Brooklyn, New York

It was an overcast October morning when Susan Kellman strolled into the EDNY courthouse in Brooklyn to meet her newest client, an al Qaeda terrorist.

Kellman, sixty, had made a career out of representing some of the most notorious defendants in New York City—mobsters associated with John Gotti, international gangsters, captains of drug cartels, and financial fraudsters. But she didn't quite know what to expect upon meeting the al Qaeda fighter whom the FBI had just flown in from Italy.

At the courthouse, as she'd done a million times before, Kellman went through security, putting her bag and keys onto the X-ray conveyor belt, walking through the metal detector. It was almost silly at this point, but of course it was protocol. The guards—like everyone else in the machinery of "the system"—were just doing their jobs. Still, the notion that she would be carrying any kind of contraband was preposterous. Kellman had to undergo a vigorous background check to get the high-level security clearance she needed to even represent

Spin Ghul. A clearance that allowed her to fairly review the evidence, which could be viewed only in what national security folks refer to as a SCIF, or a sensitive compartmented information facility.

Every now and then, Susan Kellman would think about the bizarre journey that had brought her to this moment. In November 1972, she was a senior at State University of New York in Albany driving home to Brooklyn in the black Plymouth Belvedere she'd rebuilt over the summer at the garage where she worked. Stuck in traffic on Chambers Street in Lower Manhattan, a man in a three-piece suit asked her for a ride. She obliged, and he turned out to be a Democratic state legislator named Mel Miller. Previously preparing to be a teacher like her parents, her chance meeting with Miller instead set her on a course for law school and began her career in New York state government.

Until, again, a fateful interaction detoured Susan Kellman: a former college roommate phoned her, desperate. Her boyfriend had been arrested and was at the federal lockup in Manhattan, known as the MCC. It was a drug case. He'd flown from Colombia to JFK, gotten off a plane with some others, and subsequently drugs were found on board and the men were arrested. Could she help?

At that time, Kellman had been appointed to serve as special counsel to the New York City Schools chancellor. She didn't even know what the MCC—the Manhattan Correctional Center—was.

Her former roommate begged her. Please.

When Kellman walked into Judge Eugene Nickerson's courtroom on behalf of the California boyfriend of her former roommate, her intentions were to hand her client off to the first experienced defense attorney she saw. Upon arriving, she learned that her client was one of six defendants, and the other five were represented by defense attorney and civil rights activist William Kunstler, of the Chicago Seven trial fame. A man labeled in 1970 by the *New York Times* as "without doubt the country's most controversial and, perhaps, its best-known lawyer."

"I don't know what I'm doing," Kellman told her client. "I could barely find the courthouse. Just let me give your money to Kunstler and let Mr. Kunstler represent you."

But, in another turn of events, Kunstler was arranging a plea deal for his five, and her client did not want to acknowledge any guilt.

"No," he said. "I want to go to trial."

They did and, miraculously, Kellman pulled off a successful defense. Her client was acquitted. A few months later, her former client recommended her to a new defendant facing drug charges. Another acquittal. Kellman would later modestly credit these victories to sympathy if not outright pity: she suspected the jury sensed her terror at trying these cases with no formal training whatsoever. But the fates had spoken: Susan Kellman was a criminal defense attorney.

She came to see the role of the defense advocate as invaluable. The system was full of honorable men and women in robes, others with badges, some sitting at the prosecution's table, but the system was also stacked unfairly against defendants. People charged with the most serious crimes could cut a deal and end up walking free if they cooperated with the government. Undercover agents could sweet-talk some dumb kid into signing on to a half-baked conspiracy, and poof, there went fifteen years of the kid's life. Her role was that of an attorney defending not just a client but the integrity of the constitutional system. It falls to the defense attorneys to ensure that the government plays by the rules and that constitutional protections are not disregarded in the name of securing "safer streets" or simply adding more points to a prosecutor's scoreboard. English jurist Sir William Blackstone wrote in 1769 that "the law holds that it is better for ten guilty persons to escape, than that one innocent person suffer," and that became Susan Kellman's credo.

Thirty years later, in addition to becoming a single mother of a son and daughter and innumerable fostered rescue dogs, Kellman had been on the front lines defending some of the highest-profile cases in New

York City. This included doing seven months in the longest federal criminal trial at the time, the 1985–87 Pizza Connection prosecution of American and Sicilian mafiosi for heroin trafficking and money laundering. In that case, since the government failed to charge her client properly, the jury acquitted him of the drug charges—but convicted him of a money-laundering offense—which carried far less criminal exposure.

She had, pretty much on her own, built a practice as one of the more respected defense attorneys in the five boroughs. Now she was standing in the courthouse of the Eastern District of New York in Brooklyn, about to meet a potential al Qaeda terrorist.

Spin Ghul looked at Susan Kellman. His eyes were cold and mistrustful. He didn't seem to want to have anything to do with her. He didn't speak English, so she had an interpreter who spoke Hausa, but that didn't make him any more eager to open up. Spin Ghul was a religious extremist. Being a woman made the situation all the more challenging for Kellman.

On October 5, 2012, Spin Ghul appeared before US Magistrate Judge Marilyn D. Go at the US courthouse in Brooklyn for the prosecution in *The United States of America versus John Doe*. Spin Ghul's capture was still very much a secret being kept from the public. The US was represented by David Bitkower, Shreve Ariail, and Al Hamdani.

"Good afternoon, Your Honor. Susan Kellman for the defendant, and I'm assisted at counsel table by David Stern, my co-counsel, and we're also assisted by a Hausa interpreter."

Stern was another widely respected defense attorney who'd joined the team after Kellman. A former supervisor of the Legal Aid Society's Manhattan Office, where he defended some of the most difficult cases in New York, he had formed a private firm in 1992 with others from Legal Aid. His significant cases included defending one of the four convicted for the 1998 US embassy bombings. And he was no stranger to the team at the EDNY. The previous year, Stern had faced off against Shreve in his prosecution of Betim Kaziu, a man from Brooklyn who traveled overseas to attempt to kill Americans. In March 2012, Kaziu was sentenced to twenty-seven years in prison. Stern had also faced off against Bitkower in a capital murder case in 2008; the defendant was convicted and sentenced to life in prison.

The matter to be determined that October 2012 day was whether the proceeding should be closed to the public, with Spin Ghul referred to as "John Doe." The hearing was short; everyone agreed that for the sake of the ongoing investigation and to avoid a tainted jury pool, the arraignment should be discreet.

The defendant didn't speak to Kellman that day. Or the next.

It took several meetings, in fact, before Spin Ghul was even willing to look in her direction.

Eventually he began sharing a little. He was very hungry, he said through the interpreter. He didn't trust that the food being brought to him was halal—meaning adhering to Islamic dietary laws—despite the assurances from New York law enforcement that it was.

"I keep a kosher kitchen," Kellman told him, knowing that there are similarities between Jewish and Muslim dietary laws, both religions banning the consumption of pork and requiring that animals be killed in as humane and painless a way as possible.

His face lit up.

And that was how it came to be that Susan Kellman roasted a kosher Cornish hen for an accused al Qaeda terrorist.

His reaction when she brought in the meal—after the US marshals cleared the food—was moving. He tore into the bird as if he hadn't eaten in months, crying and eating, the salty tears mixing with the seasoning. It made Kellman want to cry herself—he was so pathetic and hopeless and hungry.

Kellman had read the transcript of the September 2011 deposition in Italy and knew there was a very good chance his confession would be deemed admissible. As a matter of course, she represented very few defendants who became cooperating witnesses, so she needed to figure out as much as she could to assess her options. Would he even consider turning and becoming a cooperating witness to help track down and prosecute other terrorists? She didn't know what to advise at this point—he was so physically fatigued and emotionally exhausted, so broken.

Kellman decided the first step was to get a psych evaluation. She needed to make sure he still had all his marbles. The defense team met with the government to hire an agreed-upon psychiatrist to assess his competence. Kellman and Stern also began looking into the law of armed conflict, governed by the Geneva Conventions.

These were attorneys who saw government excesses and overreach and were willing to call out the prosecutors or cops even if it didn't make them popular. They were intelligent, hardworking, and undeterred. It wasn't clear yet, in the fall of 2012, what tack Kellman and Stern would take to defend Spin Ghul or what arguments they would use against the US government. But it was clear that the two of them would do everything they could to give Spin Ghul the best advocacy to which every defendant in the US was entitled. They were defense attorneys for whom the principles of equal justice under the law were not just theoretical; they were principles they lived and breathed. These were also supremely competitive, ambitious attorneys motivated to excel for personal reasons as well. If they could find a weakness in the government's case, they would.

CHAPTER TWENTY-THREE

THE TEA

Brooklyn, New York

He reeked.

As FBI agent Raushaunah Muhammad sat with Spin Ghul in the back of the government sedan, Bert LaCroix driving them from the jail to the US courthouse, it was difficult for her to focus on the historical import of the moment because he just smelled so damn bad. He had refused to shower, and this protest of his had been going on for a while.

The two agents were escorting Spin Ghul to the US attorney's offices in Brooklyn. They arrived and walked him to a secure room, where David Bitkower and Shreve Ariail were waiting.

There sat the focus of their hard work over the past year and a half, their blood and sweat. Spin Ghul. In the flesh, and rather fragrant. As they remembered him from Agrigento. Short. Thin. Menacing.

Spin Ghul was joined by his attorney Susan Kellman, as well as two former NYPD detectives now on the JTTF: John Ross and his partner Bobby Losada, a.k.a. "Bobby Lo."

Ross and Losada were there for a "proffer," a process where suspects or defendants share knowledge about a case in the hopes of securing a cooperating agreement and the possibility of a less severe sentence. If the proffer goes south, the information can be used only in a very limited way at trial. In the best of circumstances, the defendant becomes a cooperating witness, agrees to testify about the information on the record, and enters into a deal with prosecutors.

Ross and Losada had a lot of experience taking bad guys and turning them into cooperating witnesses. Before they joined the effort with the US attorney's office as part of the Justice Department's unofficial post-9/11 recruitment effort to enlist NYPD veterans, they'd worked on various cases across different units with the NYPD. None perhaps was more pertinent to Spin Ghul's proffer process than the assassination of a local journalist in the early nineties.

On the evening of March 11, 1992, Manuel de Dios Unanue, a crusading anti-corruption and anti-cartel journalist, was shot twice in the head at point-blank range as he sat at the bar at the Mesón Asturias restaurant in Queens. The murder of de Dios, author of *Secrets of the Medellín Cartel* and former editor in chief of New York City's leading Spanish-language daily newspaper, *El Diario–La Prensa*, marked the first time the Cali cartel had murdered a journalist on American soil.

Ross and Losada worked with John Mena, who had arranged the murder of de Dios on behalf of the Cali cartel, turning him into a cooperating witness. Sentenced to eighteen years in prison, Mena saw five members of his family assassinated in Colombia as a result of his cooperation. With Mena's testimony, prosecutors saw de Dios's assassin sentenced to life in prison. The 1990s were a time of many kidnappings related to Asian and Colombian gangs, and Ross and Losada became expert at taking bad guys and flipping them.

At the beginning of the proffer process, Ross and Bobby Lo strategized. Their goal was to put Spin Ghul at ease and get him to divulge as much as possible. Both of them being older would help; in their experience, Islamist terrorists instinctively tended to respect older men. Ross had also traveled to Afghanistan, Niger, and nearly every other stop on Spin Ghul's journey of jihad, so as they began talking with the terrorist, he mentioned that part of the world with familiarity. Bobby Lo had a good sense of humor and was able to disarm Spin Ghul. They, too, would bring Spin Ghul halal food, as well as tea and cookies, all part of a well-orchestrated charm offensive.

"We'll never lie to you," Ross told Spin Ghul. "And we expect the same from you. We're going to ask you questions, and we want you to answer and tell the truth. If you don't want to answer a question, I'd rather you say that you're not going to tell me than to lie to me."

Ross's first impression was that Spin Ghul was extremely intelligent. He was also a true believer. Many terrorists, in Ross's and Bobby Lo's experience, were just thugs and criminals, nihilists or murderers, morons or psychos who just happened upon a lifestyle that landed them in the business of killing. Ross believed many were often faking zealotry, lying to their fellow jihadis, to law enforcement, and ultimately to themselves. But not Spin Ghul. During Ramadan, Spin Ghul took fasting to a new level, trying not to even swallow his saliva, regularly spitting into a paper cup. He was the real deal.

He also seemed quite dangerous. It wasn't that he was threatening while shackled and in custody, but Ross noticed the way his eyes desperately roamed the interrogation room: he was looking for ways to escape. Even a pencil was a potential weapon. One time, Ross escorted Spin Ghul into the men's room. Some construction was going on in the US attorney's office, mainly at night, and in the men's room the construction workers had left a ceiling tile open a few inches, right above the sinks. Ross saw Spin Ghul looking up into the gap.

"Even if you were to crawl up there, you can't get out," he cautioned the prisoner.

At one point Spin Ghul explained to Ross that in his view, "Jihad isn't just fighting. It's a struggle against you. Forever. Whatever I can do."

Spin Ghul's warning turned out not to be entirely true. At first, he was talking to them with ease, and the proffer sessions proved fruitful. Over the course of weeks, starting in October 2012, Spin Ghul once again told his entire story, from his rough childhood in Saudi Arabia to his path of jihad to Pakistan, Afghanistan, and Nigeria. He named names. He had a sense of humor and picked up English phrases pretty quickly. To Ross, sitting down and eating lunch with Spin Ghul became almost like grabbing a bite with a friend. A friend who would probably kill him if he could.

Raushaunah and LaCroix also got to know Spin Ghul pretty well, escorting him often from jail to the proffer sessions and back. Spin Ghul, very dark-skinned, would tease Raushaunah, who is rather fair-skinned, about her being "Black." Once in the back seat, he pointed to a dark brown mole on her left hand and said, "Oh! You Black!" which made both Raushaunah and LaCroix, who is also Black, laugh hysterically. Spin Ghul's interrogators weren't the only ones who could be disarming.

Despite his occasional friendliness, there was always a dark undercurrent lurking beneath the surface. In some moments, Spin Ghul's true menace would slip through. Raushaunah once escorted Spin Ghul to the restroom and from the hallway could hear him angrily cursing under his breath, talking to himself. Another time, when it was just her and John Ross in the interview room, Ross excused himself to get something from outside the secure area.

"You know what they say," Spin Ghul said to her, "whenever a man and woman are alone together there are three people present—the man, the woman, and *Alshaytan*," using the Arabic word for Satan.

Ross heard Spin Ghul's comment, stopped in his tracks, turned around, and picked up the phone to have someone replace him so that Raushaunah wasn't alone with Spin Ghul in the room for even a minute. Raushaunah didn't feel threatened, but she had no doubt that Spin Ghul, even unarmed, was every bit as determined to kill as he had been on the Afghan battlefield.

The proffer process continued throughout November and December. Full, long days, Monday through Friday. On occasion, Raushaunah would ask for a respite so she could record everything she had written down—no recording devices or professional transcribers were allowed in the room.

And then as 2012 drew to a close, Spin Ghul started to go off the rails.

Years later, accounts would differ as to what set him off, making him grow increasingly agitated, even more so than his worst outbursts on *The Excelsior* and in the Sicilian courtroom. Ross thought the tipping point came when he was served papers from Italy dealing with his extradition to the US, and Spin Ghul began insisting that he wanted to be tried by the International Criminal Court in the Hague, or at least by a military commission at Guantánamo Bay.

To Kellman, his defense attorney, the course of the case was altered by a box of tea.

One morning, out of the blue, Spin Ghul asked the group why the guards had given him a certain box of tea from the jail's commissary, which he insisted he did not order. Meeting after meeting, he asked about the tea. *The tea was somehow a trigger*, Kellman thought. It must have been the same tea he'd been given in Libya, where he'd been tortured for six years, which he'd talked about at length. In his memories, he'd spent most of the time in Libyan custody—from 2005 until 2011—hanging upside down from a rope, soiling himself when he had to go to the bathroom. On the occasions when he was given the chance to change his clothes, Libyan guards would sodomize him with soda bottles. The tea, she theorized, triggered these memories, and his mental condition began to deteriorate from there.

Eventually Spin Ghul stopped conversing. He became aggressive to the point that Ross and Losada felt the need to shackle him in place, with a metal attachment Ross bought at Home Depot and fastened to the floor of the interview room. In Spin Ghul's agitated state, Ross believed, Kellman's being Jewish also started to bother him. Ross stuck a piece of tape on the floor, beyond which Spin Ghul couldn't reach, and warned her to stay behind it.

Soon enough, the precautions didn't matter. Spin Ghul stopped cooperating completely.

Kellman and the other attorneys were back to square one, trying to figure out the best way to defend him, while the investigators resumed focus on building their case. They could use the information from the proffer to pursue leads, but this additional confession would not be introduced in trial. A setback, given that as of now they had no idea what the judge would allow to be introduced into evidence; it was always a possibility that the proceedings, with Spin Ghul's most incriminating on the record testimony from Italy, might not be permitted.

"Hey, Bert," Shreve said one day, toward the end of the proffer process. "What ever happened to the Quran?"

LaCroix took a second. Dwayne McKnight had followed instructions, handing over his battleground souvenirs to the FBI, and the package had arrived at his desk. The Quran included.

But the FBI's West Africa team was unfathomably busy. On the night of September 11, 2012, the Islamist terrorist group Ansar al-Sharia staged a coordinated attack against the US in Benghazi, Libya, killing Ambassador J. Christopher Stevens, Foreign Service Information Management Officer Sean Smith, and early on the morning of September 12 CIA contractors Glen Doherty and Tyrone Woods. The FBI launched a full criminal investigation; the political fallout was considerable, and the demand for the FBI to investigate and bring justice in this case overwhelming. (Charges would be filed against Ansar al-Sharia leader Ahmed Abu Khattala by August 2013, and he was captured by US Special Forces in June 2014.) This new additional pressure had caused LaCroix to momentarily forget the Quran.

"Crap," LaCroix admitted. "I never sent it to the lab."

He ran back to the office and immediately sent it down to the forensic lab at Quantico, seething at himself for forgetting.

In early 2013, a few weeks after Spin Ghul stopped cooperating, John Ross and Bobby Lo were picking up another cooperating witness at the cell block in the Brooklyn courthouse when they heard an obnoxious wailing.

"That's your guy in there," said one of the US marshals. And indeed, now that he mentioned it, John Ross and Bobby Lo could discern that the sounds were coming from Spin Ghul. "He ripped a stainless-steel bed off the wall," the marshal added.

Bobby Lo walked over to the cell where the sounds were coming from and slid open the steel window.

"Spin, what are you doing?" he asked.

Spin Ghul's face changed into a smile. "Bobby!" he said. "How are you?"

"Spin," Bobby said, "you can't do this. You're driving everybody crazy."

"My jihad is never over," he said. "I may not be able to attack, but I will always do things to create turmoil."

Their relationship with Spin Ghul became known in law enforcement circles. The Bureau of Prisons called upon Ross and Bobby Lo to swing by the MCC jail a couple of additional times to help calm Spin Ghul down. Once, they came upon him in an agitated state, wearing milk cartons he had saved up, peeled apart, soaked in his sink, and pasted together, molding them into makeshift armor. Another time he had been removed from his cell and taken to the medical unit, where he was so violently uncooperative the guards had shackled him to a chair that reminded Ross of the way Hannibal Lecter was locked up in *The Silence of the Lambs*. He just wouldn't stop struggling against the system. The word *jihad* means struggle, and, as he had promised Ross and Bobby he would, he was taking that definition literally.

Ross knew there was a method to this demonstrative madness, that Spin Ghul was far from insane. He couldn't fire a gun, he couldn't physically fight the guards, so this was what he did: create chaos. There was even a term for it among law enforcement—the Jihad of Annoyance. But the act was good; he had the commitment of a true believer, after all. It was so convincing that Ross knew someone just might fall for it.

CHAPTER TWENTY-FOUR

CROSSING JORDAN

Quantico, Virginia

Fingerprints—distinct and unique—form in the womb long before you're born. If you avoid scarring, your prints remain largely unchanged throughout your life. Zoom in close enough, and the lines that form your fingerprints resemble a mountain range. The protrusions are called "friction ridges" and the valleys "furrows." No two fingerprints, or "friction ridge arrangements," are the same. Of the hundreds of millions of fingerprints catalogued over the past hundred-plus years, no two have ever been shown to match.

In China, fingerprints were used to sign contracts and to prove one's identity, possibly as far back as 300 BC. A document titled "The Volume of Crime Scene Investigation—Burglary," traced to the Qin Dynasty between 221 and 206 BC, described the first known use of fingerprints as evidence.

During the course of an average day, any number of substances might come into contact with your "friction ridge arrangements," oil or dirt, ink or dye, even your own sweat, which travels from sweat glands in your dermal layer out of the pores in your skin. Any of those substances can coat the friction ridges and act as a means to transfer a reproduction of your friction ridge arrangement when you touch an object. The retention of the print is particularly robust if that object is porous. The residues of the oil, ink, or sweat are absorbed into the porous object, such as paper, leaving a fingerprint behind that can potentially be compared and matched with an official fingerprint record.

Nicole Bagley learned this basic information in her forensic and investigative science classes at West Virginia University. She took a "Tenprint" class—basics on what are called "known fingerprints," meaning, for example, those taken by cops when you're arrested. The prints a forensic investigator might find on a wineglass are called "latent prints," because they aren't visible to the naked eye, and she took a class in that, too. She also participated in a program that teamed up with the local medical school so students could take prints from cadavers. It's one thing to familiarize oneself with the loops, arches, and whorls of the Henry Fingerprint Classification System from the late nineteenth century. It's quite another to methodically match them. That could take a lifetime of study and practice. Nicole was hooked.

Growing up in Lancaster, Pennsylvania, Bagley had shown an aptitude for science. Originally, she'd planned to be a veterinarian, but during high school she worked at a local vet's office, and the sadness that came with animal care—putting down a dog, for instance—was too much for her to handle. She was watching TV one evening when NBC's *Crossing Jordan* came on, a police procedural about a renegade, gorgeous forensic examiner with a shady past and brash ways who breaks the rules and solves crimes.

"You could do that," Bagley's mom said.

"Yeah, I probably could," Bagley said.

The next year, she applied to West Virginia University because it had a respected forensics program. She graduated in 2008 and joined the FBI shortly thereafter, examining known prints at the FBI office in Clarksburg, West Virginia, and transferring two years later to the big lab in Quantico. There she began an approximately eighteen-month training program with the FBI Latent Print Operations Unit, consisting of lectures, oral boards, moot courts, classes such as the biology of friction ridge skin, and instructions on how to process evidence for the detection of latent prints.

The FBI lab in Virginia at first seemed buttoned-up and straight-laced. She had a tattoo, an intricate filigree design that ran down the right side of her neck, creeping all the way to the edge of her right shoulder blade.

"They let you in here with that thing on your neck?" an older examiner said to her one day.

"Phone interview," she said with a shrug.

Within a week, Bagley concluded that most folks in Quantico were just as weird as she was, each as unique as a fingerprint. She dyed her hair red, first by accident, then for fun. She wore a nose ring, which she took out when she testified so as not to alienate conservative jurors.

When she finished the training program with the Latent Print Operations Unit, making more than one hundred thousand comparisons of latent prints with official sets of fingerprints, she gifted herself a new tattoo: on her chest, a large anatomically correct rendering of a human heart wearing headphones and blasting music.

One of Bagley's mentors during training had been a woman who worked in the Terrorist Analysis Group, and as Bagley began her own career as an independent latent print analyst, she received an item to inspect. It arrived in a box with a desiccant pouch to help keep it preserved. It was a pocket Quran, with a leather cover and zipper. It was sent from a JTTF agent whose last name Bagley wasn't sure how to pronounce: Bert LaCroix.

Nicole Bagley put on her nitrile gloves and began to examine the evidence.

Perched on a chair in the Latent Prints Lab, she inspected the leather cover and inside pages of the holy book—using nothing more than normal ambient room light. A small percentage of people happen to have a natural fluorescence on their fingerprints, enhanced because of either diet or creams and oils.

Next would come "gluing" the cover; that's what forensics experts call the process of subjecting cyanoacrylate, or "superglue," to a high heat, turning the liquid chemical into a vapor. Sometimes that vapor can find and stick to latent residues on, say, a leather book cover, resulting in a visible hard plasticized print.

Both because this was a religious book and because he'd promised to return it to McKnight once all legal proceedings had concluded, LaCroix had requested that the forensic examination be conducted in the least destructive way possible. So Bagley would withhold the use of ninhydrin to treat the pages, since that chemical tints paper purple.

There was a less destructive chemical, shorthanded as DFO. Using a camel-hair brush, she carefully painted the DFO onto the first five pages in the book, then the last five pages, meticulously and methodically working her way in from the outer pages. She placed the Quran into a heated development chamber, accelerating the reaction of the DFO with the amino acids of any latent residues that might have been present. Using a laser light and protective goggles, she viewed those pages, seeing the hallmark fluorescence of the DFO reaction. Zeroing in on the fluorescence, she developed friction ridge detail enough to be photographically preserved. Further processing of the Quran was put on hold while Bagley analyzed the images.

She found a print.

Were these impressions left by the defendant himself?

She compared the print from the Quran with the "known print" card bearing the name Ibrahim S. Harun that the FBI laboratory gave her.

She studied the images.

They were not a match.

She double-checked.

It was a print, but it did not belong to Spin Ghul.

She did not know whom it belonged to.

Bagley continued.

She tried again, spraying the DFO on pages 6 to 10 of the Quran, as well as the pages that were tenth through sixth from the back of the book.

Nothing at all this time.

Bagley continued looking, working her way through the holy book at a deliberate pace. Next she would do pages 11 to 15, and the opposite in the back.

Frankly, it wasn't odd in fingerprint examinations—and she'd done more than ten thousand of them in her studies and professional life—to find absolutely nothing. No, it wasn't unusual at all.

CHAPTER TWENTY-FIVE

GOBSMACKED

Brooklyn, New York

Susan Kellman was trying to figure out what was going on in the brain of her client. The proffer talks had broken down in December 2012. He seemed to be getting less tethered to reality. Was it real? Was it an act? Of course, he was a self-professed al Qaeda terrorist, but he was also a man who had experienced horrific torture at the hands of the Libyan authorities. She was trying to represent him as best she could, but he wouldn't even talk to her anymore. Was that zealotry? Anger? Illness? Without a clear line of communication, all she knew for sure was that he was escalating his demonstrative behaviors. In May 2013, he had requested that the indictment be changed to use his real name but when the court offered to comply and it was suggested he would need to sign the form that would make that happen, he refused to sign anything.

Spin Ghul continued to demand that he be tried by the International Criminal Court or a military tribunal. "I don't have the power to decide whether you get tried in a military court," Judge Edward Korman explained, going into how the executive branch of government was headed by the president of the United States, trying to help Spin Ghul understand that a lowly judge had no power to send him to a military court.

"And I certainly have no power to send you to, you know, to a world court, assuming there is such a place that you could even be tried," the judge added. "So, what you're asking me for, I can't do."

Judge Korman praised Kellman as an excellent attorney and advised Spin Ghul to make the best of his situation.

"I don't care about her," Spin Ghul said. "Even if you put her in the same room with me, I will not speak with her."

The defendant had a lot of complaints, of various degrees of seriousness and accuracy.

"The Niger embassy did not come and tell me what's right and what's wrong to explain the system to me," he griped.

But that was not true, Kellman explained. She, Stern, and prosecutors had spoken with the Nigerien ambassador, met with him, and arranged for him to meet with Spin Ghul. The meeting lasted for hours, but Spin Ghul decided that the ambassador was an imposter. The ambassador presented his credentials, but Spin Ghul didn't buy it, accusing him of being an undercover CIA operative.

On June 28, 2013, they were back in court, and Spin Ghul worked himself up into an unhinged tirade that ended with him cursing at the judge and being removed from the courtroom.

"It doesn't appear to me that he's competent," observed Judge Korman. "Where is the report from this doctor?"

The hearing had begun with a cascade of grievance flowing from Spin Ghul.

He complained about the inadequate Quran he'd been given; he wanted the one he had a decade before, a special one with footnotes and commentary.

Kellman had visited almost every bookstore in Brooklyn that sells Arabic-language books, and as far as she could discern, the only Quran that met his requirements was an approximately thirty-volume hardcover set, which the prison system would not permit. She found softcover chapter-by-chapter pamphlets without the commentary.

Spin Ghul had stopped talking to Kellman, but he railed at her in court, mentioning an anecdote she'd shared with him about her having vodka in her office fridge decades before (it wasn't even hers). "A person who drinks alcohol . . . does not have the capacity to be a witness or a lawyer," he said. "A person who comes in front of a judge should be a clean person and should not have any—what's the word—vices."

"He's refused to talk to any civilian attorneys," Kellman reported. "He wants a military attorney. He wants to be tried in a military tribunal. He is probably the only person who wants to go to Guantánamo."

"I don't mind if I am killed," Spin Ghul had previously told Judge Korman. "I prefer that. It's best if I die."

"Well, just like I don't have any power to send you to a military court, I have no power to grant your wish to die," the judge had replied.

Shreve tried to give the court an update on the status of the case, with the prosecution providing evidence to the defense team on a rolling basis. But Spin Ghul began shouting and rambling.

"From 2005, I was in Libya," he said, interrupting the proceeding in a mix of Hausa and rudimentary English. "What happened in Libya? What happened? What CIA doing in Libya?"

It went on from there. "I am fight. Me no afraid America. . . . I kill him right now. It's my honor. . . ."

"I need you to be quiet, so I can finish listening to the assistant United States attorney," the judge said.

"It is no secret . . . kill me . . . why everything this information," he continued.

"Mr. Hausa?" Korman said, using one of Spin Ghul's many names. "If you don't—"

"You no God. You no Allah. You only judge. . . . This is no court."

"All right. Are you finished?"

"It is no court," Spin Ghul said. "Fuck you, Judge."

The marshals immediately hauled Spin Ghul out of the courtroom.

The modern insanity defense dates back to the afternoon of Friday, January 20, 1843, in the heart of London. At roughly 3:50 p.m., a Scottish carpenter named Daniel M'Naghten fired his pistol at point-blank range into the back of Edward Drummond, the secretary of Prime Minister Robert Peel.

The next day, while in custody, M'Naghten said, "The Tories in my native city have driven me to this," claiming that conservative politicians had been targeting him. "I can get no sleep from the system they pursue towards me; I believe I am driven into a consumption by them; they wish to murder me."

A doctor who interviewed him in prison testified, "I have not the remotest doubt of his insanity," and the jury ultimately acquitted him "NOT GUILTY, being insane," establishing legal precedent that stands in many parts of the US to this day.

The M'Naghten Rule stated: "To establish a defence on the ground of insanity it must be clearly proved, that, at the time of committing the act, the party accused was labouring under such a defect of reason from disease of the mind, as not to know the nature and quality of the act he was doing, or if he did know it, that he did not know that what he was doing was wrong."

The very notion that an al Qaeda operative such as Spin Ghul would carry out a suicide bombing or mass murder might seem to the average person to be evidence of insanity. Who would do such a thing other than a crazy person?

But the insanity defense isn't a medical standard, it's a legal one. The insanity defense requires a diagnosis of "true mental illness," which is only partially ascertained with the help of medical professionals. Under the law, a "true mental illness" is a condition that would have prevented the defendant from understanding at the time of the crime that what he was doing was wrong. This complex and difficult-to-prove standard means that successful insanity defenses are extremely rare—raised in fewer than 1 percent of court cases and successfully so only about 25 percent of the time according to a study across eight states.

No one thought Spin Ghul lacked the ability to understand "the nature and quality" of his attacks on US troops or conspiracy to blow up the embassy while he was engaged in those crimes. He was whip smart, decisive, clear-eyed.

What Judge Korman was asking about was not Spin Ghul's sanity at the time of the alleged crimes but his "competency to stand trial." This is a different question—whether the defendant understands what's going on during the court case. Does he know he's on trial—and for a crime he's accused of committing? Does he grasp the basics of the roles of everyone involved—judge, prosecutor, defense attorney? Is he able to cooperate with his attorneys and assist in his defense?

A finding that a defendant is incompetent to stand trial doesn't serve as a defense—rather, he or she would be sent for treatment at a federal prison facility in the hope that the defendant could be restored to competence, at which point the case would resume.

The assessment of Spin Ghul's competence had started under the care of the Italian government. One mental health professional judged Spin Ghul to be normal; another deemed him psychotic and prescribed medications—an antipsychotic called haloperidol and a type of benzodiazepine such as Xanax to sedate him. After Spin Ghul's outburst in the courtroom in June 2013, Judge Korman wanted to know more.

"Is it your view, Ms. Kellman, is there an issue of his competence?" the judge asked. "I mean, he seems to me to be totally irrational."

"Your Honor, when he's competent, he's very competent and when he's not, he's not," Kellman said. She explained that the forensic psychiatrist the defense team had recruited, Dr. Mark Mills, was in the midst of examining Spin Ghul, but he hadn't yet submitted a report, though they expected one shortly. "My expectation is that we may see a report that says a good deal of this is manipulative," she said, "because when he was competent, he was extraordinarily right and extraordinarily coherent and extraordinarily competent. I'm not a psychiatrist but that was Dr. Mills' initial response as well, and when he doesn't get his way, he gets volatile and irrational."

Shreve agreed, but the judge had his doubts.

"It doesn't appear to me that he's competent," he said. "Where is the report from this doctor?"

"We're waiting for it," Kellman said again. Her expectation was always that court-appointed psychiatrists thought the defendants were sane and competent, faking their behaviors for the sake of being difficult or the chance of acquittal. She, however, wasn't so sure.

Dr. Mills's first visit with Spin Ghul had been four months before, at the end of February. Spin Ghul spent much of the time yelling at the government-provided interpreter, who was confused and more than a little humiliated by the experience. Mills thought Spin Ghul paranoid and potentially psychotic, but he wanted to see him again. On his second visit, on April 26, 2013, Spin Ghul still seemed paranoid, irrational, intermittently angry, and given to frequent complaints. Dr. Mills again suspected Spin Ghul was suffering from a psychotic disorder.

But on Dr. Mills's third visit with Spin Ghul, on May 3, 2013—exactly eight weeks before the hearing where he was ejected—the doctor had a revelation.

At this third session, Spin Ghul seemed calm and responsive. He was respectful, thoughtful, and in a most forthcoming way provided detailed answers to Dr. Mills's questions.

It was night and day.

The transformation of Spin from acting out to calm "gobsmacked" Dr. Mills.

And in that epiphany, in what Mills would later call a light bulb moment, the doctor came to a conclusion about what Spin Ghul was up to.

The term *malinger* in psychiatry means either "to falsify" or "exaggerate one's illness for an end." Maybe you're pretending your trauma necessitates excess sick days. Maybe you're trying to score some narcotics that you don't need. Or maybe you want to be found incompetent to stand trial—or to be found insane—because however rough a federal mental institution might be, it sure beats Supermax prison.

Mills concluded that Spin Ghul was malingering, but not for any of those more predictable reasons. No, Mills concluded that Spin Ghul was acting out and being as difficult as he could be because he wanted to "get back at" the US court system, the American justice system, or the US in general. This was now part of Spin Ghul's lifelong jihad.

The big question for Shreve and the prosecutors, however, was whether Dr. Mills's conclusion would be accepted by the courts. Would the judge find Spin Ghul—wildly inappropriate, bizarrely self-destructive, increasingly profane, decreasingly stable—not competent to stand trial? Might he permit a jury to consider whether Spin Ghul was not guilty by reason of insanity? Unbeknownst to the prosecution team from EDNY and the FBI, the defense team would ultimately claim Dr. Mills's testimony was corrupted and untrue. They would go on to find a different expert, who would argue that Spin Ghul was not competent to stand trial, which, if the judge agreed, would put the entire case in jeopardy.

CHAPTER TWENTY-SIX

MIND IF I HAVE ONE OF THOSE?

Brooklyn, New York

Dave Bitkower was in pain.

On Sunday, March 17, 2013, he'd been rushed to the hospital and given an emergency appendectomy. Five days later, he stood in court.

Prosecuting Spin Ghul had already been an intense experience. A labyrinthian challenge of jurisdictions across the world, classified information, and national security ramifications that went beyond one man. Along with a defendant so violent and erratic that it made it difficult to even get him to trial. Bitkower and Shreve had built the case for almost two years. They also had a new judge to replace Judge Korman, who was nearing retirement. Brian Cogan had been appointed to the bench in 2006 by President George W. Bush.

In addition to the physical pain Bitkower was enduring, there was also an emotional strain. This would be the last time Bitkower would be the primary prosecutor in the Spin Ghul case. He was moving to Washington, DC.

A few days before, Bitkower had popped by Shreve's office.

"Hey," he said. "I've got some news."

Bitkower's wife, Jodie, had accepted a job with the Securities and Exchange Commission in DC, so he had discreetly started looking into job opportunities there as well. At the US Justice Department in September 2012, Deputy Assistant Attorney General Jason Weinstein had taken the fall and resigned amid the "Fast and Furious" scandal. Assistant Attorney General for the Criminal Division Lanny Breuer was looking for a replacement. Bitkower had wowed the Justice Department team, so by the time he met with Breuer, all that needed to be said was "You're a Mets fan? You're hired."

It was a considerable promotion. Bitkower would go from supervising a dozen attorneys at the US attorney's office in Brooklyn to supervising 125 attorneys in three sections at the Main Justice building in DC.

But even with a promotion, it was tough to walk away from the Spin Ghul case. He had been working on putting Spin Ghul away from the very first minute the US attorney's office was notified that the Italians had picked up the al Qaeda operative. He had flown to Italy to hear Spin Ghul's testimony. He had talked to the soldiers who had been in the battle. He wanted to deliver justice.

Bitkower's only solace was that Shreve would take his place as lead prosecutor. They were good friends, saw each other socially, knew each other's wives. Shreve, of course, had been working it from the *second* minute. He would get the right outcome; Bitkower never doubted that.

But Shreve was tremendously disappointed. Bitkower had been an incredible colleague, supersmart, highly strategic, with a wicked, dry sense of humor. He was also a friend and the leader of their division. Bitkower gave his team latitude and authority. The office had a rare energy that most would look back on and remember fondly. Everyone worked with a fierce dedication toward the same goal. The intensity Bitkower displayed, like showing up in court a few days after being sliced open, was a big reason why.

Even as Bitkower planned his departure, there remained a lot of work to do before trial. He was fully committed until the last second of the last day he held the role of lead prosecutor. The case was not yet where it needed to be, and the prosecutors had to plan for a number of contingencies based on how the judge ruled. The defense team would no doubt push to have Spin Ghul ruled incompetent. The odds were also strong that they would try to suggest that what happened outside Firebase Shkin was within the laws of war—meaning immunity for Spin Ghul for the charges of killing Dennis and Losano.

They had spent thousands of hours on the case, because in the eyes of the law it took an enormous amount of work to prove the simplest of facts. But what their case boiled down to at this point was far from conclusive: they had a confession from a man of questionable credibility and, as of then, a nickname in a dead jihadi's journal. They needed to interview more soldiers to verify with trustworthy sources the picture Spin Ghul had painted of that day. Simultaneously, the prosecution team needed to go to Nigeria to work on proving Spin Ghul's conspiracy to blow up the US embassy. If they could prove this grandiose plot wasn't just in Spin Ghul's imagination, it could make his other confessions more believable, make everything else click into place. But most of all what they lacked was physical evidence, the kinds of bells and whistles the public was familiar with from TV shows such as *CSI* that juries ate up. Prosecutors were constantly on the hunt for the stuff that took a case across the bridge of reasonable doubt: irrefutable physical evidence.

Trials in real life are not as they are on television, from murder to conviction in forty-two minutes plus ads. Actual courtroom trials take months, if not years, and a case as complex as Spin Ghul's doubly so. Much of the next two years, 2014 and 2015, was spent with the prosecution and defense teams building their cases, preparing for the big day. The new judge needed to familiarize himself with the case and the relevant law, which caused even more delays. It had become clear to Judge Korman, a senior judge who was turning seventy-one, that the case was going to last years, so he had asked Judge Cogan, twelve years his junior, if he might be interested in taking it on. Korman had helped Cogan get onto the bench, and they had been friends for decades. Moreover, the Spin Ghul case was the kind of job Cogan liked.

"Give me your hard cases," Cogan would tell his colleagues. "That's why I took this job!"

The judge was also intrigued because the defense and prosecution teams contained attorneys of such high quality. He knew the case would test him, and he was excited.

Shreve, promoted in 2013 to deputy chief of the General Crimes Division, then again in 2016 to chief of Organized Crime and Gangs, continued to handle the Spin Ghul case and thus needed help, especially in the void Bitkower left behind. He found it with a new EDNY hire in his division, a young prosecutor named Matt Jacobs, thirty-two, a UCLA and NYU law grad from Thousand Oaks, California. Shreve first noticed Jacobs during the sentencing phase for defendant Alvaun Thompson, a pimp who sexually trafficked minors as young as thirteen. Unsurprisingly, most of the victims were terrified and uncooperative, so Jacobs listened to hundreds of recorded prison phone calls and was able to introduce evidence ahead of sentencing showing that Thompson had murdered a rival Brooklyn pimp. Shreve was impressed by Jacobs's work ethic and creativity.

Jacobs had once wanted to join the foreign service, so when Shreve told him about Spin Ghul, he was immediately sold. The Spin Ghul case for Jacobs was like inviting a Trekkie to the bridge of the Starship *Enterprise*. The case had Niger, Saudi Arabia, Pakistan, Afghanistan,

Italy, Nigeria, and Libya. It had foreign diplomats and intelligence agencies. It had al Qaeda cells and mid-level operatives who became senior leaders. And in the middle of it all was the cypher known as Spin Ghul.

They also considered bringing on another new assistant US attorney, Melody Wells, who worked in national security and cybercrimes and helped the team convict a citizen of Mali for the murder of a US diplomat in Niger in 2000.

"Why don't you chat up the case a little bit with her—but don't offer anything," Shreve told Jacobs. "See how she responds."

In the SCIF one day, Jacobs spun the tale, starting with Spin Ghul asking the Italian soldier for water on the deck of *The Excelsior*. Wells, thirty-four, was immediately hooked. Soon enough, she was on the team.

By 2016, as the trial date neared, Shreve, Jacobs, and the prosecution team reengaged with the soldiers from Firebase Shkin to figure out who would be the best witnesses. In some instances, it had been years since Raushaunah and LaCroix had first spoken to them. Some were easy to find and talk to, others not so much.

In the latter category were two men: Staff Sergeant Michiru Brown, who was shot and grievously wounded during the battle, and Victor Keith Graf, the staff sergeant and MP who found Jerod Dennis as he bled out. Part of the trial was telling the story, sharing that this person was killed, that this individual who was loved was no longer with us. Another part was making sure that it was clear that Spin Ghul was involved in this particular battle, and there could have been no other ambush that he participated in, no reasonable doubt that Spin Ghul had imagined the battle or was confusing it with another one.

Staff Sergeant Brown had been nearly impossible to reach. Eventually, Jacobs, Wells, Paciorek, and NYPD detective Ivan Rosado traveled to rural Arizona to a secluded area, where they essentially forced Brown into an interview. He obviously had been traumatized by the battle. The mere act of discussing it was painful, even excruciating.

It brought Jacobs back to a moment when he interviewed with US attorney Loretta Lynch for the job. She posed a hypothetical to him: What if a sweet old granny had witnessed a gang murder but was reluctant to testify because she knew the perps and was trying to protect them? What would you do? she asked Jacobs. The correct answer, Jacobs knew, was you compel her to testify. The hypothetical then evolved: What if she was reluctant to testify because she feared for her life? The right answer: You compel her to testify. You appeal to her civic duty, you beg and plead. If that didn't work, then by subpoena. But what if she refused to comply with your subpoena? Would you send the marshals to arrest her and bring her to court? Would you prosecute her for contempt of court? What about seeking jail time? Every prosecutor has his or her own line.

Jacobs contemplated all this as he spoke with Brown, the single most reluctant witness he'd ever met, including cooperating coconspirators. In the car after the interview, Paciorek and Rosado were adamant: do not call him as a witness. They were concerned it would be too traumatic for this soldier.

For Jacobs and Wells, it wasn't so simple. Spin Ghul had described Brown specifically: "a Black . . . very large individual." They all agreed that it would be difficult for him. But what if other witnesses fell through? What if his testimony was necessary for conviction? The value would have to be outweighed by the harm it would cause him.

Then there was former MP Victor Graf.

When the investigators phoned Graf, his outgoing voicemail message said "hello" and then paused, so it sounded as though he maybe had answered the phone. That feeling of being left hanging, unsure of what was going on, characterized Graf's lack of interest in talking, as did Jacobs's many failed attempts to reach him. They called him repeatedly at his home in North Carolina, leaving messages, never hearing back from him. His testimony would be crucial. They couldn't give up.

Before they traveled to southeastern Virginia to interview Trahan, Jacobs left another message for Graf:

"Hey, Staff Sergeant Graf," he said, "I'm going to be in your neck of the woods. I would love to talk to you. I will try you then."

Jacobs was amazed when he tried him next, from Virginia, and Graf answered. He said yes and gave Jacobs his address. The whole call lasted maybe forty seconds.

The drive was six hours.

Jacobs found himself on an unlit sand-and-gravel road that night, rural and sparsely populated, a mile off the highway, half expecting a pit bull to jump out at any second.

Graf was a broad, gruff-looking guy, almost six-two, a member of a biker club for law enforcement and veterans called Nam Knights of America. His body was festooned with tattoos. Among them: beneath his right shoulder was written the Pashto phrase for "warrior born from the sky," since there is no Pashto word for paratrooper. Underneath that was written "FW1FWA"—"fuck with one, fuck with all." On his right forearm was a horseshoe, in honor of his daughter who loved horses, along with the Mobius symbol, representing his son's neurodiversity. There were crosses on both biceps and the national SWAT symbol on his inner left forearm, which he himself drew with equipment he purchased.

Graf opened the door, and Jacobs went to shake his hand—then saw that Graf's right hand was covered in a black leather glove. Graf offered him his left instead, which Jacobs gripped and shook in the friendliest and manliest way he could.

Graf was draining a can of Miller Lite, listening to the anchors from Fox on his huge flat-screen TV. Jacobs was a Republican, but he felt a bit out of place, especially in his suit. He wanted to break the ice.

"I've been in the car for six hours," he said, pointing to the Miller Lite. "Mind if I have one of those?"

"Sure," said Graf, getting him a beer.

"What happened to your hand?" Jacobs asked.

"Motorcycle accident," Graf said. Which gave Jacobs an opportunity to talk to him about disability pay for veterans and how to make sure he got what he was entitled to through the VA.

"Want another one?" Graf asked after they'd downed the beers. Jacobs said yes.

"Have a seat," Graf finally said.

They sat at a table, and Jacobs tried to broach the topic gently, knowing how tough it could be for veterans to talk about what they experienced in combat.

"I would love to hear about what happened that day," Jacobs said. "From your perspective. As much as you know about finding Dennis."

Graf shared what he remembered. Jacobs was reminded of the character of Mike Ehrmantraut from the TV show *Breaking Bad*, the laconic cop-turned-criminal who never offered an unnecessary word. More beer came, then more memories. Graf was honest, including about faking having radio trouble with command so he could search for Jerod without permission. The story was compelling. Jacobs told him that the government might need him to retell it again in Brooklyn, in front of a jury. Graf was reluctant but ultimately said, "If you need me, I'll be there."

Afterward, Graf offered him a cigarette. Jacobs didn't smoke, but he said sure and smoked one anyway.

CHAPTER TWENTY-SEVEN

BLACKOUT

Abuja, Nigeria

Before boarding her connecting flight from Paris to Abuja, Nigeria, Melody Wells struck up a conversation with a middle-aged woman in line for the secondary passport check. To Wells, everyone else in line seemed likely to be Nigerian except for her fellow assistant US attorney from EDNY, Matt Jacobs, and this woman.

"You're American?" Wells asked her. "Headed to Abuja?"

She nodded and smiled. "Yes." She seemed excited.

"What brings you there?" Wells asked.

"I'm meeting my boyfriend," she said.

"Have you been to Abuja before? What's it like?"

"No, I've never been," the woman said. "This is my first trip. I've never even been outside the US before!"

She paused, and Wells took in the dynamics of what was going on here. "I'm really excited!" she said. "I can't wait to meet him!"

Uh-oh, thought Wells, figuring this was a romance scam. The poor woman. Wells smiled and tried to hide her suspicions about the disappointment that was likely waiting for this woman at the end of her journey.

Wells and Jacobs had flown on a Delta red-eye from New York to France, then on to Nigeria. They sat coach, back near the bathrooms—the unofficial US government class of seats, Wells joked—and struggled to sleep. It was Saturday, September 24, 2016. They were just a few months away from going to trial.

Wells and Jacobs had also been to Italy over the summer, before they headed to Nigeria. Jacobs worked in the organized crime division, so he and Shreve were already planning to head to Palermo for an annual conference recognizing the prosecutorial work done to combat organized crime. Wells was in the national security division of EDNY, so she wouldn't join them—but Dave Bitkower would. In his new position at the US Justice Department, he supervised the Organized Crime and Gang section of the Criminal Division, so when they got to Rome, Bitkower joined Shreve, Jacobs, and Wells for witness prep, meeting with the Italian soldiers from *The Excelsior*. They spoke with Assistant Warrant Officer Francesco Morgese, whom Spin Ghul had first approached for water. They talked to then-Lieutenant Riccardo Rosi, who was on *The Excelsior* when the Italian authorities placed Spin Ghul under arrest. And they spoke with Deputy Commissioner of the Italian State Police Guglielmo Battisti, who helped interrogate Spin Ghul before he started spiraling violently and had to be sedated. All three men would be called to testify in Brooklyn, and the prosecutors wanted to make sure everyone was prepared and memories refreshed.

In his new role at DOJ, Bitkower was mostly a bureaucrat and never got to do interviews anymore. Sitting with the team, he found himself continually interrupting Jacobs to ask follow-ups. Then he realized he was taking an opportunity away from a junior prosecutor on a big case, so he clammed up and moved his chair to the back of the room. Shreve laughed at him.

Later they all had dinner and wine, and Bitkower felt comfortable that the torch had safely been passed. On the trip to Nigeria, however, Wells and Jacobs went alone, without Bitkower or Shreve, although they were fortunate to be following up on Shreve's work from years before.

Before flying to Nigeria in February 2012, Shreve had reviewed Spin Ghul's confession to determine what evidence he needed to corroborate Ghul's story.

In 2003, Spin Ghul was training under al Qaeda operative Hamza Rabia in Lahore, Pakistan. Inspired by Osama bin Laden, who released a tape listing Nigeria as one of six countries to be liberated from enslavement to America, Spin Ghul flew to Lagos and then on to Kano. There he met with some of Hamza Rabia's contacts, among them a man named Muhammed Ashafa, who was also a member of an extremist Islamist group that would come to be known as Boko Haram.

Spin Ghul and Ashafa then drove to the capital of Abuja, hoping to carry out an attack similar to one that al Qaeda had perpetrated against the American embassies in Dar es Salaam and Nairobi in 1998, suicide bombings that killed more than two hundred and wounded more than four thousand innocent people, but they couldn't find the US embassy.

Spin Ghul tried to acquire explosives and sent Ashafa to Pakistan to secure enough money for a bribe. Ashafa was arrested by Pakistani authorities on his way back to Nigeria, and Hamza Rabia, who ran the safe house back in Lahore, called Spin Ghul and told him to flee, which was ultimately how Spin Ghul ended up captured and imprisoned in Libya.

As Shreve prepared to meet with Nigeria's Ministry of Justice, he thought about the various ways to prove Spin Ghul's story and that his plan to bomb the US embassy was true. He already had two built-in limitations: Ashafa's testimony would no doubt be inadmissible—the Nigerian intelligence agency was notorious for using physical coercion on its prisoners. And Hamza Rabia was dead, killed in Pakistan in December 2005 by a US Predator drone.

Shreve would need documentation, he knew. Perhaps travel documents showing that Ashafa went to Pakistan and back. Or evidence that Spin Ghul fled Nigeria shortly after Ashafa was arrested. Whatever pocket litter might have been on Ashafa at the time of the arrest. Physical evidence could be untainted, as opposed to whatever the Nigerians extracted from Ashafa under duress.

As Shreve flew to Abuja along with Bert LaCroix and FBI special agent Sussana Iljazi, he hoped the Nigerian agencies would be cooperative. It was certainly in their interest to work closely with the US, Nigeria's shaky history as a US ally notwithstanding. Boko Haram had in recent years emerged as a real domestic terrorist threat, killing more than 1,500 people in northern and central Nigeria from 2009 to 2012. Their targets were not just law enforcement and other government buildings, but newspaper offices, beer halls, schools, Christians worshipping in church, and Muslims who dared to work with the government. In August 2011, at the United Nations compound in Abuja, a vehicle bomb attack killed twenty-three people, including eleven UN employees, and injured more than eighty. When Shreve landed in Abuja, security was intense.

There was only really one option for him in terms of secure lodging in Abuja, the heavily fortified Transcorp Hilton, an immense facility with meticulously landscaped gardens, an outdoor pool, dining, a casino, and a handicraft market, located near the National Assembly and National Mosque. A tank was positioned at the front entrance, its muzzle pointed at entering vehicles.

Shreve was stunned and amused when he walked into the piano bar of the hotel, which reminded him of the Wild West, with spies, Arab sheikhs, mercenaries and soldiers of fortune, government officials from all over the globe, prostitutes, arms salesmen, and opportunists of every stripe. It embodied all clichés about a notorious developing world scene: a plush hotel bar where money meets grift meets intel meets terrorism meets hookers.

But the Nigerian government kept pushing off his requests to meet, so in their free time, Shreve and another EDNY assistant US attorney, there for a separate case, decided to visit the United Nations House, the site of the bloody August 2011 bombing by Boko Haram. Many of their friends from back in New York, including Greg Paciorek and other members of the West Africa team, were working on the case, and they wanted to pay their respects to the almost two dozen killed and more than eighty wounded. They borrowed an embassy employee and made the roughly fifteen-minute journey through traffic.

Months had passed since the attack, but as Shreve's car pulled up he was stunned to see the extensive damage, the lower three stories of the building decimated by the car bomb, debris remaining on the street. It was unnerving, all the more so when Nigerian guards, young men, quickly approached and banged on their car windows with the muzzles of their machine guns, reaching to open the doors of the car. Shreve assumed this was an aggressive shakedown for money.

"Get out of the car!" they yelled. "Get out of the car!"

Shreve thought to himself that this was it, he was going to be killed, this was how his life would end, but then the embassy employee hopped out of the car and began yelling at the guards. *This is fucking absurd*, Shreve thought. *We're here as Americans paying respects to the victims of a terrorist attack and two young guards with machine guns are about to shoot us.*

"Do you know who I am?" their embassy escort shouted at them, holding up his US embassy credential. "Do you know who I work for? I'm going to get your badge numbers."

Realizing their error, the guards, shamed and clearly worried about being fired, apologized profusely. Eventually they all shook hands, the embassy employee returned behind the wheel of the car, and they turned around back to the Hilton.

"What the fuck was that?" Shreve asked.

The employee explained, not without a note of sympathy, that the government hadn't paid the guards in weeks, and they needed some cash to take their girlfriends out to dinner.

Eventually Shreve and his team were beckoned to meet with the Nigerian government. They were screened through security, their phones confiscated, then walked past individuals handcuffed to doors, presumably waiting for arraignment. After sitting on a wooden bench for an hour, they were escorted to the second floor, to a nondescript government room. An hour after that, their escort led them to the fifth floor. It went like this for eight hours, taken from room to room, promised meetings and given none. They drove back to the Transcorp Hilton that evening, frustrated, miserable, and exhausted.

They spent a few more days waiting at the hotel, phoning back to EDNY, calling the Nigerian government and the US embassy. Beckoned back to the government building, they again pinballed from room to room, trapped in a satire of inefficient, corrupt bureaucracy.

Finally, Shreve, the other EDNY assistant US attorney, and the US embassy's assistant legal attaché, or ALAT, were brought to the basement of the building, to an office where two metal folding chairs stood in the center of a circle of plastic desks. A herd of six burly men barreled into the room and sat at all but one of the desks, encircling the Americans. Shreve had no idea what was going on, but it certainly was intimidating. Then the boss came in and sat in front of them.

For twenty minutes, this head bureaucrat berated the Americans for their allegedly arrogant avarice, for taking and taking and demanding from their developing nation while giving nothing in return. It was classic anti-imperialist dogma, and in the middle of this tirade the power went out. Shreve, the ALAT, and the government men were all sitting in pitch darkness.

Oh my god, Shreve said to himself. *What the fuck is happening?*

There was an awkward silence.

And then Shreve heard a loud baritone laugh from the man in charge, which echoed off the walls of the room. The man started joking about the lights going off, then they came back on, revealing sweat on his forehead and a grin plastered across his face.

"Okay, okay," he said, changing moods with the flicker of the lights. "What is it that I can give you?"

"We just want the files on Mohammed Ashafa," Shreve explained.

Shreve didn't need to explain who Mohammed Ashafa was. He'd been charged half a decade before by the Nigerian government for a litany of crimes involving Boko Haram and al Qaeda, including for having "contracted, sponsored and ferried" eighteen others "to receive combat training on terrorism from an Algerian Terrorist network known as Salafist Group for Combat and Preaching."

The man dispatched an aide to retrieve the Ashafa documents, and Shreve and the ALAT inspected them when they arrived. They were travel documents showing Mohammed Ashafa's emergency traveling certificate, allowing him to travel from Pakistan to Nigeria without a passport—proof of his deportation.

"Can we take these?" Shreve asked.

"Go with my secretary," the man said. "You can make copies."

There remained much work to do to ensure the documents' admissibility in court. What seemed a great score in 2012 as they reconstructed

Spin Ghul's narrative was less so in 2016 when they were prepping for trial. The documents Shreve secured of Mohammed Ashafa's passport and visa looked to Melody Wells more like something somebody's half-crazy aunt photocopied in 1985. Their admissibility was far from certain.

Evidence from foreign countries requires testimony or at least official documentation explaining its provenance. Wells submitted a request through the Mutual Legal Assistance treaty, transmitting through diplomatic channels, following all procedures for stamps, signatures, certifications. In the best-case scenario with a close ally and an efficient bureaucracy, it usually takes months, even years, before the admissible evidence arrives back on one's desk. Nigeria was another matter.

"Can anything be done about this?" Wells asked officials at the US embassy in Abuja. This request had been sitting in the Nigerian foreign office for literally years.

"Nope," she was told. "Nigeria doesn't respond to these requests usually."

But they needed this evidence. The Nigerian part of the case was important because it showed that Spin Ghul sought to commit a spectacular act of terrorism far from the battlefield, that he posed a clear threat to Americans around the world. Wells did not want to lose the case because just this one part of it was relatively weak, with a confession and no decent corroborating evidence. If the defense were to sow doubt about Spin Ghul's Nigerian plot, it might speak to his unreliability and chip away at other aspects of their case as well.

So as Wells and Jacobs touched down in Abuja, they had three goals in mind. First, to get a certified official version of Mohammed Ashafa's travel documentation, with perhaps a witness who could come to Brooklyn to testify as to its authenticity.

Second—and for this reason FBI agent Greg Paciorek and another investigator, Ivan Rosado, would meet them in Nigeria—they would try to corroborate what Spin Ghul had said about trying and failing to find the US embassy. As of now, that mystery was troubling and a potential problem for the prosecution. A terrorist mastermind who couldn't locate the US embassy?

Lastly, Wells and Jacobs wanted to visit Kano to see if they could find the construction company near "the only tall building" there where Ashafa sought to purchase the explosives for the crime.

There were, as always, security concerns, but in 2016 the US embassy and FBI seemed more worried about Wells and Jacobs being kidnapped for a ransom than being killed by terrorists. The FBI brought doorstops so that their hotel doors would be impossible to open while they slept. Jacobs assumed he was being watched at every moment, even in his hotel bathroom.

They didn't have to wear flak jackets, but they also weren't allowed to travel much. They joined the embassy staff on a five-mile run, but the FBI agents weren't happy about it.

Most of their time was spent at the hotel waiting for an appointment with the Nigerian government. They, too, were taken aback by the Transcorp Hilton piano bar, which reminded Jacobs of Mos Eisley's Cantina from *Star Wars: A New Hope.* And the similarities to Shreve's visit didn't end there, with meetings with the Nigerian authorities resulting in myriad runarounds.

"Thank you for coming, it was so nice to meet you, come back tomorrow." Lather, rinse, repeat.

After meeting with them several times, Wells and Jacobs acquired a collection of Ashafa's travel documents that were in moderately better condition than the copies Shreve secured in 2012. They didn't obtain mint-condition certified copies, but what they got was passable: a Federal Republic of Nigeria emergency certificate allowing Mr. Muhammad Ashafa Suleiman to travel to Nigeria from Pakistan within the period of one week starting on December 9, 2004, as well as a document dated

December 10, 2004, signed by a high-ranking Nigerian official, deporting Ashafa because he "is alleged to be a low/middle level Al-Qaeda operative."

The documents would be delivered via diplomatic pouch to establish a chain of custody, but Wells and Jacobs pleaded with Nigerian government officials, to no avail, for them to sign the certification that these copies of documents were official ones from their government. The Nigerians were just reluctant to help that way. When the prosecutors returned to the US, they would have to figure out how to fix that problem.

Wells and Jacobs were told that they could not travel to Kano to see if the details about the failed explosives purchase—the rock quarry, the streets, the only tall building, as Spin Ghul told the story—checked out. Both the legal attaché and the assistant legal attaché feared the conditions up north were too dangerous.

Wells and Jacobs were disappointed; they knew the testimony, wanted to retrace the steps themselves. They pushed. The LEGAT and ALAT pushed back. Someone from the embassy would travel to Kano and take whatever pictures EDNY needed. Two sets of attorneys had made trips across the globe over nearly five years to obtain the concrete proof of Spin Ghul's time plotting a terrorist attack in Nigeria. Wells and Jacobs hoped that what they were returning home with would be good enough.

CHAPTER TWENTY-EIGHT

FREUD

Detroit, Michigan

When Spin Ghul's attorney David Stern needed someone to examine his client, Jess Ghannam was on a short list of experts who had dealt with and evaluated the psychology of some of the most extreme terrorists in the world.

Ghannam's journey to his profession began in the early 1970s. A Palestinian American kid growing up in Detroit, Michigan, he was assigned Sigmund Freud in a class at Bentley High School. It blew his mind.

In their company town of Detroit, Ghannam's dad was an engineer for the Ford Motor Company, but the son became fascinated by the workings of the human mind. How are brains capable of brilliance and evil? Freud's explanation that the unconscious mind had power and control over us—"The ego is not master in its own house"—fascinated him.

A bachelor's in psychology from the University of Michigan was followed by an MA in psychology and a PhD in clinical psychology from UC Berkeley. He did his postdoc at Stanford and became a clinical professor of psychiatry in the School of Medicine at the University of California San Francisco. Ghannam's work focused on the impact of war and armed conflict on children and refugees.

Perhaps unsurprisingly for the son of Palestinian refugees who left Ramallah for Detroit in the late 1940s, he was also active when it came to Arab American civil rights. He spoke Arabic, had a cultural understanding of many variants of Islam, and was recruited by lawyers defending detainees being held at Guantánamo Bay. As an expert in the many cases of Guantánamo detainees, Ghannam got a security clearance from the US government in 2012. Many former detainees had been tortured by the CIA at a black site in Afghanistan called the Salt Pit. Based on this work, Ghannam knew intimately the conditions of confinement and was able to analyze the impact on a person's psychological functioning.

The competency hearing for Spin Ghul would be held on February 21, 2017, and in the lead-up he was acting out.

Back in April 2014, Kellman tried to explain to Judge Korman—the previous judge on the case—that Spin Ghul had been having "a tantrum," but the clerk interrupted to note that "for the record, counsel came out and advised me that the defendant threatened to kill not only his own counsel, but you, Judge."

"Where did I say that?" Spin Ghul asked. "When did I say that? When did I say that to my lawyer, too? . . . I am not ready to kill anybody here."

"Okay," said Judge Korman.

"That's an improvement," Kellman observed.

Judge Korman ordered Spin Ghul to the United States Medical Center for Federal Prisoners in Springfield, Missouri, for examination by a psychiatrist on whether he was competent.

"I suggest that it's one of two things, Mr. Harun, either you're playing crazy or you are crazy—and I use the word *crazy* in the sense that laymen use it, and I can't proceed without being certain that you're not crazy and that you're competent . . . to go to trial and assist in your defense at this time."

But in September 2014, the case had been reassigned to Judge Brian Cogan, who was much more skeptical of Spin Ghul's outbursts.

Cogan didn't buy the argument that Spin Ghul's refusal to cooperate in his own defense was because of any underlying medical issue. "Narcissism is not mental incompetence," he said in March 2015. "He is clearly able to assist in his defense if he wants to do so. He has his own agenda. . . . I find him to be quite calculating and aware of how to get where he wants, even if it's a place that none of us think he ought to be."

Spin Ghul's frequent absences from hearings troubled Cogan so much that he ordered him brought to the court on May 13, 2016. Spin Ghul resisted—violently. The marshals had to use force to bring him out of his cell. They put him into the van but became so concerned he was going to kick out the windows that they restrained his hands and feet with shackles. Spin Ghul then tore off his clothes, arriving in court wearing nothing but his prison-issued underwear. The marshals told the judge they could outfit him with a shirt, but they were reluctant to unshackle his legs to put on a new pair of pants. As had become standard by this point in his court docket, Spin Ghul was put into a room where he could watch the proceedings via TV monitor with a translator. He spent the time screaming incoherently at the top of his lungs.

In some sense, Spin Ghul's tactics were effective even if the new judge assigned to the case didn't buy the act. Cogan was confused about what to do. "I need to do everything possible to give him an understanding of what's going on," he told the court. "But keep in mind we've had extensive mental health evaluations, and I have made the finding already that this is a defendant who, with a resolution that I have not seen in any other defendant, absolutely refused to acknowledge or participate or have any interest in these proceedings in any way and whose desire is simply to obstruct them as much as possible and shield himself from any knowledge."

Short of sedating him with drugs, which no one was suggesting, Cogan was at a loss as to how to keep Spin Ghul informed about the status of his case, including the date of his trial.

David Stern told the judge he didn't think it would be a good idea for anyone to go back there to talk to his client. "He is in his underwear exposing himself," Stern said.

On November 15, 2016, Kellman told the court that the defense would be presenting another expert on Spin Ghul's competence.

"I've met with my client a number of times, and I don't know if he's on this world," Stern told Dr. Jess Ghannam. "He's not talking to me. He won't talk to me. Can you help me?"

Stern had first heard of Ghannam from Joshua Dratel, who joined the defense team in November 2015. Dratel established his career defending terrorists long before 9/11, defending Wadih El Hage, an early bin Laden associate convicted in the 1998 US embassy bombings for being part of the formative al Qaeda conspiracy to kill Americans.

The Harvard Law graduate was keenly focused on defending his clients. In 2001, Dratel had been brushing his teeth in his Battery Park City apartment just blocks from the World Trade Center when the first plane hit. He knew it was terrorism and called his cocounsel on the El Hage case, Sam Schmidt, who had a better view of the towers. "Sam, what are they doing?" Dratel asked. "Do they not know we have a sentencing in two weeks? We are going to get life now." Next he called his nine-year-old daughter's school to make sure she was okay.

A past president of the New York State Association of Criminal Defense Lawyers and an officer of the National Association of Criminal Defense Lawyers, Dratel soon made it his mission to provide a counterpoint to the US government's methods fighting the "war on terror," having defended the radical, even infamous defense lawyer Lynne Stewart herself. The coeditor of *The Torture Papers: The Legal Road to Abu Ghraib*, Dratel was the first civilian lawyer at Gitmo, where he defended Australia's David Hicks, who fought alongside the Taliban.

Dratel had met Ghannam through the small universe of those working to defend Gitmo detainees, and he'd told Stern about him.

After a month of waiting for clearance, Ghannam flew to New York and on Monday, November 14, 2016, visited Spin Ghul at the MCC. He had to proceed through three security checkpoints before finally making it to the inner sanctum where Spin Ghul was held. Spin Ghul's individual cell was extraordinarily spare and bleak: a concrete slab with a mattress, a showerhead, and a toilet. Some natural light came from a window with thick frosted glass. The walls were bare. Spin was completely naked. He was, as always, on suicide watch. Guards told Ghannam that he tore apart his mattress fairly regularly. *The conditions were worse than those at Guantánamo Bay*, Ghannam thought. There was so much sensory deprivation that three years later, when Ghannam heard Jeffrey Epstein committed suicide in that same space, he wasn't surprised.

In that meeting, and in other ones that followed over the next few weeks, Spin Ghul would demonstrate signs of paranoia.

"Do you hear that?" he asked the doctor.

"What?"

Ghannam didn't hear anything. It was so quiet, he could hear himself breathing.

"What do you hear?" he asked the prisoner.

"That drone out there is listening to everything we're speaking about," Spin Ghul said.

They initially met for roughly two hours. Spin Ghul would intermix three or four different languages—Hausa, English, French, and Arabic. He mixed words and phrases. Ghannam told the defense team—which now also included Joshua Dratel—that he did not have enough information to assess whether Spin Ghul was competent. He needed details about how the Libyans treated Spin Ghul while in custody and why mental health professionals in Italy treated Spin Ghul with antipsychotic meds. He also wanted to talk to people who knew Spin Ghul before that fateful day on *The Excelsior*—people currently in US custody at Gitmo. Hadi. Faraj. Abu Zubaydah.

Was Spin Ghul unhinged to begin with? Perhaps. In Ghannam's experience, some of those who joined al Qaeda and similar groups already had psychiatric illnesses; the dogma and mission of the group offered them a way to organize their disordered thinking into a system. But either way, Spin Ghul's adherence to Islamist ideology convinced Ghannam that he had become untethered. There are literally al Qaeda playbooks for handling being captured or arrested, and in none of them are adherents told to fake insanity. Spin Ghul's other actions involving nudity, defecation, even masturbation in front of others suggested to Ghannam that he had lost touch with reality—no pious and austere holy warrior would ever think of doing such things. Nor was Ghannam convinced that all this was for show; guards told the doctor that Spin Ghul laughed to himself, talked to himself, in the middle of the night when no one else was near him.

Ghannam's conclusion at the end of the interviews and months of research was the same as his initial impression: Spin Ghul was the most psychologically disturbed individual he'd ever interviewed.

CHAPTER TWENTY-NINE

LOVE AND WAR

Oklahoma City, Oklahoma

It was as if Melody Wells herself had traveled back in time to the morning of April 19, 1995, right before the bomb went off.

It was now March 31, 2016. Twenty-one years earlier, lawyers in an office across the street from the Alfred P. Murrah Building had been taking and recording a deposition that went on before, during, and after the bombing. For visitors to the Oklahoma City National Memorial & Museum, including Melody Wells, listening to that recording two decades later, the sound of the explosion was upsetting and even surprising.

Tim McVeigh and Terry Nichols killed 168 people, including nineteen babies and children at a daycare center, wounding more than eight hundred others. Their act of unspeakable cruelty traumatized countless Americans forever and stands to this day as the worst act of domestic terrorism in the country's history.

The museum had been created to make sure Americans would never forget the tragedy, and Wells, Jacobs, and Shreve made time to walk through it, passing the some-three-hundred-foot-long reflecting pool, the elm tree that had withstood the blast, now called the Survivor Tree, and the Field of Empty Chairs, each one representing someone murdered, chairs placed in nine rows for each floor of the federal building where the field is now located. All three prosecutors had young children at home and were particularly moved by the section of the park memorializing those killed in the daycare center.

This, of course, was what an attack might have looked like, had Spin Ghul been successful in Abuja. Regardless of ideology—McVeigh's and Nichols's deranged antigovernment ramblings or the perversion of Islam preached by al Qaeda—it was all mass murder fueled by hatred.

Wells, Jacobs, and Shreve were in Oklahoma City to meet with the family of Jerod Dennis. FBI agent Raushaunah Muhammad and NYPD detective Ivan Rosado came with them. The law office where Jerod's little brother Renley worked as an intern while he attended law school opened a conference room for them.

The prosecutors wanted Jerod's family to feel comfortable with the team. Shreve, who'd been working the longest on the case, took the lead in the meeting. Spin Ghul's trial would take place on March 6, 2017, at 9:30 a.m., in Courtroom 8D South at the federal courthouse in Brooklyn, NY. The family needed to be ready for what they would hear.

Most Gold Star families are given little information about how their loved ones' lives ended. The details can be torturous—whether because of the pain the servicemembers suffered, the disastrous mission they'd been assigned, or the error that led to such grave consequences.

This visit was an important one. Previously, on March 15, Shreve, Jacobs, and Raushaunah Muhammad had flown to Arizona to meet with the family of Ray Losano—his widow Sarah, daughters Alorah and Lillian, sister Melinda, and parents, Roberto and Oralia Losano. They met in a room at the federal courthouse in downtown Tucson. That meeting was much like this one, with Shreve bracing the Dennis family for unpleasant accounts of Jerod's final minutes.

The Spin Ghul case would assuredly be covered by the press, and witnesses would testify about what happened to Jerod. The prosecution would be as sensitive as they could—not being too graphic or descriptive about what Jerod had gone through if they could help it. But they were also trying to convict Spin Ghul for murder, so painful facts would need to be aired. This would be the first time family members heard about Jerod's death in this level of detail. The prosecutors wanted them to understand the reason why they were unearthing these painful moments—the US attorney's office needed to prove that Spin Ghul's story matched with the facts on the ground, so they would provide for the judge and jury a blow-by-blow account of the battle.

Did the Dennis family want to attend? If they did, there was funding and assistance to bring them from Antlers to Brooklyn.

"I want to be there," said Jane Nelson, Jerod's mom, a comment that made Shreve tear up.

The team also walked them through the other components of the trial, the conspiracy to blow up the US embassy in Nigeria. The prosecutors also let them know that if Spin Ghul was found guilty, they would have the right, as family members of one of his victims, to speak to the court during the sentencing part of the trial.

Jane Nelson found herself back in the fog of grief, of shock and disbelief, that descended upon her in 2003 when she first learned Jerod was gone.

The Dennis family had a lot of questions. At one point, Jillian, Jerod's sister, expressed a more existential query.

"Why is this illegal?" she asked. "Why is this a crime? Isn't everything fair in war?"

It was something Jane didn't quite get either. Her son and the al Qaeda operatives had been in battle in a foreign land. They'd been fighting each other. It never even occurred to her that the man who killed her son could be prosecuted in an American court.

Melody Wells was concerned about that very argument. And Spin Ghul's defense team was also quite focused on it, especially Dratel. From his work at Gitmo, Dratel also knew and consulted with Lieutenant Colonel David Frakt, a JAG with the US Air Force Reserves, who had been able to get one Gitmo detainee released back to his family.

Frakt thought Spin Ghul's actions in Afghanistan should be protected by the laws of war. In 2012, Frakt had written an award-winning legal paper exploring the appropriate treatment of "Direct Participants in Hostilities"—individuals who fight who aren't part of a uniformed military for a state.

Frakt told Ghul's defense team that their client's actions in firing upon the servicemembers who served at Firebase Shkin were in full compliance with the laws of armed conflict. Spin Ghul used lawful weapons. He fired against lawful targets. He was in a declared theater of armed conflict. *At least four of the six charges the US government was prosecuting Spin Ghul for should be thrown out altogether on this basis alone*, Frakt thought.

By this point in his legal career, Frakt had represented two detainees at Gitmo, one of whom he successfully got released back to Afghanistan. The son of a law school professor and dean, Frakt had been at Harvard Law School in 1992 when he went to see a military courtroom drama that changed his life. *A Few Good Men* starred Tom Cruise as a Harvard Law School graduate and JAG standing up for underdogs—in this case two US Marines at the base at Guantánamo Bay. Cruise's character, Lieutenant Dan Kaffee, has a famous showdown with a monstrous Colonel, Nathan Jessup, played by Jack Nicholson, whom he goads into admitting on the stand that he'd been lying and was culpable for another Marine's death.

"That's what I want to do," Frakt said to himself, excited about the prospect of both serving his country and being an attorney. And within a couple decades, he, too, found himself at Gitmo pressing a senior military officer, trying to get him to admit to lying on the stand. It was an altogether different set of circumstances, but in this case it was real.

In November 2001, when President Bush first announced his administration's plans to prosecute detainees at Guantánamo Bay, Frakt was excited to volunteer to prosecute the bad guys. He thought it would be his generation's version of the Nuremberg Trials after World War II—a contrasting model for the rule of law and civilization, something to be proud of.

But Bush decided not to classify the defendants—non-US citizens fighting for al Qaeda or otherwise involved in terrorism against the US—as prisoners of war, which would provide them with protections under the Geneva Conventions. Instead, they were classified as "unlawful enemy combatants." In Frakt's view, the mistreatment of detainees followed naturally from that decision. He came to think of the original military commissions and the treatment of detainees by the US generally as an embarrassment, a blight.

The military commission prosecution of Salim Ahmed Hamdan, Osama bin Laden's driver, did nothing to disabuse Frakt of his disappointment. The case ultimately led to the US Supreme Court ruling in 2006 that the military commissions were unconstitutional: Congress had to have created them, not George Bush with the stroke of a pen. But that wasn't the only problem Frakt saw. He also wondered just what the hell the US was doing pursuing small game like a terrorist's chauffeur.

Another high-profile commission prosecution was of Omar Ahmed Said Khadr, a Canadian whose father had taken him along as he joined al Qaeda in his homeland of Afghanistan. Khadr was accused of throwing a grenade that killed an American soldier, Sergeant First Class Christopher Speer. Khadr was fifteen years old at the time.

"These commissions were supposed to be about 9/11 and serious terrorists," Frakt would remark to colleagues. "And we're using them to prosecute drivers and kids."

His own personal role models, other than Tom Cruise in *A Few Good Men*, had the courage to take unpopular positions. His father had been a civil rights attorney in the 1960s. And a former boss of his whom he had clerked for the year before joining the military was a judge who, after the Oklahoma City bombing, had admonished people not to jump to conclusions that Islamist terror groups had been behind the attack. Through their examples, and his studies of history, Frakt knew that US history was not a linear path of America always doing the right thing. Rather, it's a narrative of halting progress interspersed with episodes of shameful treatment of various minority groups.

"We don't always live up to our ideals," Frakt would say to his law students, whether at Duke, Georgetown, or Pitt law schools. "But in our finest moments we do."

In February 2008, aspiring to be part of that tradition, Frakt volunteered to defend a different Gitmo detainee, Mohamed Jawad, who at the age of fifteen or so was accused of throwing a grenade at and wounding two US troops and an Afghan interpreter in Kabul. Afghan security forces arrested Jawad and told him they would kill him or a member of his family if he didn't confess, which he did, after which he was delivered to the Americans. At a US base outside Kabul, he was subjected to "highly coercive" interrogation techniques that led to another supposed confession, albeit one that was quite different from his first one. His mistreatment continued at Bagram, then Gitmo, where during one period of time he was repeatedly woken up and transferred from cell to cell to deprive him of sleep in what guards called the "frequent-flier program." The confessions were obviously tainted, the evidence flimsy, the conditions under which Jawad was being kept horrific. Frakt initially didn't understand why this case was even being prosecuted.

A possible solution to the mystery was offered when an accusation surfaced that a legal adviser to the Military Commission Convening Authority had been seeking gripping cases for prosecution to capture the imagination of the public. Since Jawad's alleged victims were still alive and would be able to testify against him, a trial against Jawad would fit the bill, went this theory. Frakt successfully filed a motion against the adviser, alleging "unlawful command interference," and he was eventually removed from authority. The military judge ultimately found Jawad's statements inadmissible since they'd been "obtained by physical intimidation and threats of death which, under the circumstances, constitute torture." Jawad was ordered released and returned to Afghanistan in August 2009. The outcome wasn't Jack Nicholson admitting angrily, "You're goddamn right" he ordered the code red, but it was a win for American ideals, Frakt felt.

After familiarizing himself with the case, Frakt flew to Brooklyn. Kellman picked him up outside his hotel and took him to the SCIF, the sensitive compartmented information facility, in the courthouse, to review the materials. Then he met with the whole defense team and offered his conclusions.

Frakt started with the basics: There's a doctrine called combatant immunity where a professional soldier or member of a national armed force in uniform fighting on behalf of a country that is complying with the laws of war has the right to engage in combat. That means the soldier cannot be charged with a crime for maiming or killing people, attempting to maim or kill people, or destroying property in the line of combat.

However, Spin Ghul was not entitled to combatant immunity, Frakt said. He did not meet the criteria. He didn't fight in uniform or for a sovereign state or national military force. You could make an argument that the Taliban would have fit such a definition, as both the ruling government and national army of Afghanistan before the US arrived. That was not the case with al Qaeda, a terrorist organization spread over many countries, tied to no particular government.

But, he went on, that didn't mean the law of war was irrelevant. In fact, he thought it could be utilized to dismiss four of the six counts in the indictment.

First, however much Americans might detest al Qaeda, Frakt said, Spin Ghul's military actions against US forces were fully compliant with the laws of armed conflict.

Some weapons—antipersonnel mines, booby traps, incendiary weapons, blinding laser weapons—are banned in war, but Spin Ghul had used firearms and conventional explosives such as grenades, which were lawful weapons. He used these weapons against lawful targets—not civilians. He fired his guns and detonated his explosives in a clear war zone, in a declared theater of armed conflict. He didn't embed himself among local Afghan civilians. He didn't use civilians as a shield. Killing Americans in Afghanistan, Spin Ghul, Frakt believed, could be prosecuted in Afghanistan, under that country's criminal justice system. But prosecuting a Nigerien in the US for fighting in Afghanistan made no sense according to international law.

Second, as a member of al Qaeda, an armed non-state actor organization, Spin Ghul was a civilian who was directly participating in hostilities. A "DPH," under the law of war. Something of a gray area in international law.

Frakt wanted to testify. He wanted to argue that Spin Ghul fighting on the battlefield did not constitute a conspiracy to murder Americans abroad in violation of federal law. The indictment argued that the killings of Jerod and Losano "would have constituted murder as defined in Title 18, United States Code, Section 1111(a)." But the law of war and the domestic law where the fighting occurs, not American criminal law, determines whether a killing on the battlefield is unlawful, Frakt explained. Just because the trigger was pulled by someone the Bush administration deemed an "unlawful combatant" didn't make the killing unlawful, too.

Frakt also believed the context of Spin Ghul's attacks in 2003 from the perspective of 2016 mattered as well. For an al Qaeda fighter in Afghanistan in 2003, the choices for Spin Ghul were to: (a) surrender, be taken to a black site, and be possibly tortured, then taken to a kangaroo court military commission; (b) fight the Americans and risk being captured and experiencing the same. Spin Ghul's decision to fight wasn't surprising given this context.

As a military officer, Frakt told the defense attorneys, he of course mourned the loss of Jerod Dennis and Ray Losano and any US servicemember. But he found nothing disturbing in Spin Ghul's conduct in that battle. Indeed, however offensive it might seem to some in a different context, within the confines of a legal argument about the laws of warfare, he would go so far as to say that Spin Ghul fought fairly, bravely, and honorably against vastly superior US forces.

Yes, at other times, certainly in Nigeria when planning to blow up the US embassy in Abuja, Spin Ghul was planning to engage in acts of terrorism. But on this day, he was simply a fighter engaging in warfare.

It was, in fact, unprecedented for the US attorney's office to charge Spin Ghul with engaging in a battle on a battlefield in Afghanistan. Beyond that, the US government was arguing that in the Global War on Terrorism, the US could declare someone to be a hostile force, meaning it was open season on them: American forces could kill them anywhere, anytime, anyplace. But the US was also saying to them: You can't fight back. You can't defend yourself. And if you try, it's a crime. So much so that we can reach out across the world and grab you and bring you back here to try you for something you attempted abroad. Even if it was on a battlefield.

The entire defense team was excited. This was a powerful argument made by an expert, and if the judge were to accept this line of reasoning, they could beat the prosecution before their case got off the ground.

CHAPTER THIRTY

MISS YOU SO MUCH

Brooklyn, New York

Terrorism prosecutions rely upon classified information, and Spin Ghul's case was no different. But it isn't as if Brooklynites called at random to report to jury duty can be vetted and given national security clearances.

When classified information is introduced in a criminal proceeding, there are rules and regulations for how to bring the information forward, detailed in the Classified Information Procedures Act, or CIPA,[1] signed into law in 1980.

In the late 1970s, several criminal defendants in cases involving classified materials escaped the harshest penalties because prosecutors feared the disclosure of those materials in trial. Perhaps the most notorious example was the grand jury investigating whether former CIA director Richard Helms had lied to Congress about the CIA's role in the assassination of Chilean president Salvador Allende.

As conservative columnists Rowland Evans and Robert Novak

---

[1] Pronounced SEE-pah.

warned, such a prosecution might mean that "in his defense, Helms would be compelled to reveal the most secret Oval Office and National Security Council deliberations. This unquestionably would involve former presidents in what the CIA's critics call the seamy, squalid side of the intelligence game. Helms would be relieved from protecting sources and directions given to him, even by a President, if forced to defend himself in a public trial."

Not exactly subtle, but effective. Helms escaped by pleading no contest to two misdemeanor charges of giving incomplete information to Congress.

President Carter's assistant attorney general, Philip Heymann, noted the Catch-22 in a hearing before one House subcommittee. "In the past, the government has foregone prosecution of conduct it believed to violate criminal laws in order to avoid compromising national security information," creating an impression if not the reality that those "with access to military or technological secrets have a broad de facto immunity from prosecution for a variety of crimes."

Concluded the subcommittee in 1978: "enforcement of laws intended to protect national security information often requires disclosure of the very information the laws seek to protect."

CIPA aimed to put an end to this by allowing a private hearing of that evidence before trial, away from the jury and the public, even away from the defendants.

Thus in 2001, for example, Josh Dratel, who had a security clearance, participated in a CIPA hearing and was privy to evidence against Wadih El-Hage, his client, in the case against those accused of participating in the 1998 embassy bombings. But El-Hage, the accused, was not brought into the loop.

It would be a similar situation in Judge Cogan's court with Spin Ghul.

Courtroom 8D South was emptied of everyone except those cleared to hear the classified information—the prosecution, the defense, the judge, a special law enforcement officer, and a special court reporter employed by the courts for CIPA hearings. Other than Joe Kaster joining the prosecution from the National Security Division of the US Justice Department, the tenor of the hearing was exclusionary. Phones were confiscated. The room was locked.

Even if Spin Ghul had changed his mind and decided to participate in his trial, he would not have been allowed in the CIPA hearing. This was a safe place for both the prosecution and defense to discuss classified information. In theory, CIPA worked for both sides. If the prosecution had classified information that could be exculpatory for the defendant or could help impugn a prosecutorial witness, they were no less obligated to turn it over. Likewise, if they had anything damning, they could do so.

Sometimes the prosecution could appeal to the relevant agency—say, the CIA—to declassify the evidence. Other times, the court would agree to allow a "substitution"—an official document that omitted the part of the evidence—say, how it was obtained—that the agency in question needed kept secret. Sometimes there would be no agreement and the evidence would simply not be used, or perhaps the court would just dismiss the charges if the classified information suggested the defendant was not guilty.

The defense was arguing vociferously that none of the information in the CIPA hearing be introduced in trial. As a general matter, Dratel had been arguing for years that CIPA was unconstitutional, denying any defendant his or her rights under the Fifth Amendment to the US Constitution to testify in his own defense and to present a defense; and his Sixth Amendment right to assistance of counsel, to confront evidence and witnesses against him, to be present at critical proceedings in his case, and to assist in the preparation and presentation of his defense.

But before he could make a decision, Judge Cogan had to hear exactly what this classified evidence was—and where it came from.

FBI special agent Sussana Iljazi had worked on the West Africa team with Raushaunah and LaCroix and had been involved in the Spin Ghul case from the beginning. Born in the Bronx to immigrant parents from the former Yugoslavia, Iljazi, forty-two, first started working for the Bureau as a contract linguist because she spoke Albanian, Bosnian, Macedonian, and Serbo-Croatian. As a Muslim with deep knowledge of the Quran, she not only bonded with Raushaunah, but she also felt she had a deeper understanding than most of how exactly terrorists twisted the sacred teachings.

From her time at the FBI, Iljazi knew that a vital part of any investigation into al Qaeda needed to focus on the whole network, every single tentacle that wrapped around the globe. She wanted to dive into the intelligence—not just FBI files but those of OGAs, Other Government Agencies, the code for the alphabet soup of spy agencies such as the CIA, DIA, NSA, and more. With Spin Ghul's confession detailing his journey from Saudi Arabia to Pakistan to Afghanistan to Nigeria, she had a good background of where to look, conducting database queries and analysis beyond his testimony and into anything having to do with al Qaeda in that era.

She spent months accumulating it all, finding myriad avenues to explore. She searched names and kunyas, noms de guerre, email accounts, and phone numbers. She called her connections at the Pentagon, tracked down case agents, read everything she could about raids of al Qaeda operatives, examined every cable for items of evidentiary value. Of the trove of leads she found, two in particular proved relevant, both of which were the subject of the CIPA hearing.

One was from the evidence thrown into trash bags by Dave Franco during the FBI's raid on Abu Zubaydah's house in Pakistan fifteen years before. Evidence from that 2002 bust would be used in trial, and the court needed to have the facts of the arrest and acquisition of the evidence established.

Shreve and the prosecution wanted Chris Reimann, Jennifer Keenan, and Dave Franco to testify.

Judge Cogan needed to sign off on what they had to say as well as establish parameters about what they could discuss.

The other evidence Iljazi tracked down was related to Ahmed Ghailani—the man found not guilty of 284 of 285 charges for his role in providing the explosives for the 1998 US embassy bombing in Tanzania. Ghailani had been arrested in Gujrat, Pakistan, in 2004 during a raid in which the Pakistani police also seized a computer hard drive.

Iljazi read in the detailed cables that the email addresses and passwords Spin Ghul used to communicate with Hamza Rabia were linked to the hard drive, which also contained a letter from Hamza Rabia to Spin Ghul.

She read the letter.

In it, Hamza Rabia was giving Spin Ghul clear orders and instructions as to his mission in Nigeria.

The two had communicated using email accounts created in Pakistan on the morning of Saturday, August 9, 2003. As Spin Ghul told the Italian court in 2011, one was ususts@Yahoo.co.uk, the other was slslglgl@yahoo.co.uk; password A-S-A-S-1-2-3. That data—those messages—were included on that hard drive.

"We weren't sending messages to one another," Spin Ghul had explained to the Italian court. "I would open the same email and write and then he would come in later and open the same email and also write."

The purpose of the CIPA hearing was to establish the authenticity and origins of the material. How they got to the Pentagon, where Iljazi had tracked down the hard drive.

Melody Wells would be reading from the letter in her summation, and there was a trove of information in there.

The messages from Hamza Rabia to Spin Ghul were not only religious, they were also affectionate as well. "Dear brother, we miss you so much, and we would love to see you for all the love that we have for you in our hearts," one began.

He shared how other associates of theirs were doing, chitchat about fellow jihadis being taken off the battlefield.

"Some of the brothers who were killed are . . . Abu Ayman, who was killed while engaged in a combat with a group of American Intelligence riding ordinary vehicles and guarded by some devious individuals," one message read. "At least three persons from the American Intelligence were killed." Another brother was killed "in a suicide operation in Kabul." Some Uzbek brothers were killed by the Pakistani army in Waziristan, some others were captured, including Dhia', who helped Spin Ghul during his travel, and a few others.

The letters offered some big-brotherly advice as well. Spin Ghul had asked Hamza Rabia if he should get married. "[Y]ou are the one who should answer this question," he advised, though he could tell him from experience, "a single brother is more giving than a married one, especially if he is devoted to the work."

Beyond that, the messages were full of specific instructions from Hamza Rabia—calling himself "Tom"—to Spin Ghul on how to be an undercover operative on a mission to kill Americans and Jews in Abuja.

Don't always use "one specific internet café" when emailing, "Tom" said. Mix it up, and "don't stay at the café for more than ten minutes. You view the message and leave promptly." If you want to read the news, do that at a different café. Moreover, don't "read the message at the internet café, but rather copy it to a small disk and take it home with you."

Read it on your personal computer at your home, he said. Write the response there, too. Keep your time online in an internet café communicating with us to a bare minimum.

For that matter, "Never converse in an obvious manner or in clear language over the internet or over the phone. Always use a code or a cipher in your conversation." He sent him a cipher—a sheet of code words to use—separately.

And don't use your phone in Nigeria for international calls—use a special phone for talking to us, and keep it turned off at your house.

Now to the job at hand.

"The Americans are utilizing Nigeria as their own base to control the West African region," Hamza Rabia as "Tom" wrote in one message. "We thank Allah for the presence of jihad awakening in this region. You know very well the importance of targeting the Jews and the Americans during this stage. They represent the head of the snake, and they are the devils who kill Muslims in many Islamic countries."

Other advice was the kind that any mentor might give to a protégé, only it was for the purpose of better killing innocent people: Focus on the mission. The details. Collaborate. Plan. Be methodical. Be patient. Do the job well.

His mission was to prepare for a "military action."

So "Tom" advised that Spin Ghul recruit more help. "The number of personnel who are available right now is very low." He would need "two or three decent young men with good morals. They must be smart, as well as being devoted to jihad and martyrdom. The most important thing is that those young men should be seeking jihad, not us forcing them to do so." He recommended unmarried men, with knowledge of Arabic and English. Recruit them, send them to him in Pakistan for a five- or six-month-long training—though don't tell them it will take that long. If they can fund their own travel, great; if not, "Tom" said they could pay for it and even reserve the tickets.

Make sure the recruits are suitable, though, because there was no room for error and bad recruits could be dangerous. As to the mission itself, Spin Ghul needed to "start searching to purchase genuine explosives in the country that you are in, and also in Niger." The "Algerian brothers" might have some ideas on how to get the explosives as well; "we are in need for at least one ton." Find a place to store the material securely, maybe in the ground, perhaps on property disguised as a farm.

The target should be anywhere Americans congregate, he advised—embassies, military bases, hotels, amusement centers, clubs, large companies.

"Tom" wanted Spin Ghul to be careful not to pick just any victims: "We mean the Americans, the British, and the Jews," he specified, "not the whites or the Europeans in general." Too many jihadis don't understand the difference, he cautioned, so "as soon as they notice a group of tourists or people with European features, they say that those are Americans. This is not true, and there is a difference."

Prepare for the worst, "Tom" advised. Have "a contingency plan (such as spare passports with names, which you will mostly use; and explore itineraries to flee the country) in the event that something happens, God forbid. . . ."

Above all, take your time, Hamza Rabia said to Spin Ghul. "Please do not rush to perform your work; always slow down and show restraint because in this war we are not too concerned about promptness and speed. It is a long war."

Melody Wells was frustrated by what she saw as a lot of eleventh-hour filings by the opposing counsel defending Spin Ghul. They were aggressive and excellent defense attorneys, and she had no qualms with their tactics, but it was pretty unusual still to be waiting for experts' disclosures—they were still waiting for Dr. Ghannam's ultimate diagnosis, for example—so close to the trial.

The defense had been busy filing motions in the last few weeks before the trial. They all dealt with three major issues. The first was this CIPA hearing and whether the selected information from the Abu Zubaydah arrest and the Ahmed Ghailani raid would be permitted to be introduced in court. None of this should be introduced in trial, Dratel and the defense team contested. Prosecutors, he argued, were unfairly using their "unfettered discretion" to selectively declassify certain evidence while hiding communications that contained "invaluable exculpatory information that is material to his defense." It was "cherry-picking," which clearly deprived him of the basic discovery that Spin Ghul was entitled to under Federal Rules of Criminal Procedure.

The second batch of motions concerned whether Lieutenant Colonel Frakt would be permitted to testify and introduce the laws of war in Spin Ghul's defense. And finally, the third set dealt with whether Spin Ghul was competent to stand trial. Before Shreve, Melody Wells, and Matt Jacobs were able to go to court to try Spin Ghul and seek justice for his victims, they had to clear these three hurdles.

In January 2017, they cleared the first one. Judge Cogan outright rejected the defense's arguments that the introduction of the classified material was unconstitutional. CIPA's constitutionality was long established. That still left two more rulings to go before trial. If either decision went the wrong way, it could be bad for Shreve and his team. If a jury heard from Frakt and saw the logic in his argument, there would be no justice for the families of Jerod Dennis or Ray Losano. And if Spin Ghul was found incompetent to stand trial, he would be whisked away to a comfortable facility for a decade or so, after which who knew what could happen? The evidence might vanish, the witnesses might die, the Justice Department might lose its taste for another trial. Spin Ghul might even end up a free man, plotting and carrying out the evil of which he was more than capable.

CHAPTER THIRTY-ONE

LOUISIANA

Brooklyn, New York

Matt Jacobs had one task on February 21, 2017, and that was to destroy Dr. Jess Ghannam on the stand.

That day was the scheduled hearing on Spin Ghul's competency. Ghannam was arguing that Spin Ghul was psychotic and not only was not competent to stand trial but also likely would never be. If Judge Cogan believed Ghannam, Spin Ghul would be sent to a federal psychiatric facility for the rest of his life. Losing the competency motion would be tantamount to losing the case—no trial, no justice for the Dennis or Losano families or any of the wounded soldiers, years of investigative and prosecutorial work down the drain.

Spin Ghul being treated kindly and sensitively by doctors and nurses for the rest of his life was not Matt Jacobs's aim. Punishment and locking him away forever was. And right at that moment, Dr. Jess Ghannam—who came across as smart, caring, and serious—posed a threat to that outcome.

Jacobs had spent many weeks preparing. With his paralegal Olivia, he searched for any evidence that would call into question not only Ghannam's objectivity in this case but also his credibility altogether. Jacobs had come to believe Ghannam was an agenda-driven activist masquerading as an intellectual, one harboring a deep hatred for the US. He wanted to end Ghannam's side career as an expert witness.

That was not the perspective of the defense team, of course. They believed Ghannam was able to see Spin Ghul as a human being, someone who had had a mental breakdown, and that the other medical experts were tainted and had been leaned on by the all-powerful US government to shade the reality of Spin Ghul's mental disintegration.

Jacobs started by asking Ghannam about a previous case in which he'd testified, a terrorism prosecution in Toronto, Canada. Raed Jaser was a Palestinian living in Canada found guilty by a jury on three terrorism-related charges for conspiring various attacks, with a codefendant, including plotting—unsuccessfully—to derail a passenger train between New York and Toronto so that it would fall off a bridge, killing innocent people. Ghannam was brought in for the sentencing proceedings to assess Jaser's intention, motivation, and state of mind, specifically, as Ghannam put it, "the charges and allegations of being a radical Muslim extremist engaging in terrorism."

Ghannam didn't buy the government's case, testifying that Jaser's "primary identity was that of a substance abuser," not a terrorist. Jaser's role as an extremist who wanted to commit violence was an act. "This is an individual who is quite broken, psychologically," Ghannam told the Canadian court. "Con men are really good at becoming what they need to become in order to con people."

Not only did the judge not agree with Ghannam's analysis, but he also rejected him harshly. "Ghannam's opinion that Jaser was profoundly addicted to drugs and/or alcohol at the time of the present offences was contradicted by a convincing body of contrary evidence" the prosecution submitted, the judge wrote. Wiretaps of Jaser talking to an FBI agent, when he was supposedly high, "contain no suggestion of impairment due to drugs or alcohol." The judge also rejected Ghannam's opinion that Jaser "was not sincerely committed to an extremist Jihadist interpretation of Islam," which he also felt was significantly undermined by the wiretaps, "replete with lengthy passionate speeches on this subject."

The court compared Ghannam's notes from his meetings with Jaser to his conclusions about the defendant and found inconsistencies. The judge said he could "overlook a few of these inconsistencies, as simply reflecting cryptic note-taking, but the number and gravity of the inconsistencies and their repeated bias towards supporting Jaser's story suggested [a] lack of objectivity. Most importantly, Dr. Ghannam's explanations for the inconsistencies were not credible and he eventually resorted to evasion and argument... until I had to stop him."

The judge ruled that he couldn't accept Ghannam's testimony or his report. "It is completely inadmissible in certain respects and it lacks credibility and reliability in other respects. It is entitled to little or no weight."

Jacobs reviewed the Canadian judge's conclusions. "Do you believe that your testimony in that case was objective?" he asked Ghannam.

"To the best of my ability at that time, I do believe that," Ghannam said, adding that he had an even "higher level of confidence" in the case of Spin Ghul.

"You testified Jaser was not a jihadist, correct?" Jacobs asked.

"Correct."

"That he was a con man, correct?"

"Correct."

"And then Nabil, the brother of Jaser, testified," Jacobs went on. "And he controverted your testimony, correct?"

"I didn't hear his testimony," Ghannam said.

This line of questioning wasn't a surprise to Ghannam; three days before, Jacobs had disclosed to the court that he had found the records of this Canadian case. Kellman, Stern, and Dratel were not happy to hear the news. That they had first heard of it from Jacobs, not Ghannam, was a particularly bitter pill to swallow.

"When did you disclose this finding to the defense attorneys that hired you for this case?" Jacobs asked the doctor.

"Approximately three days ago," Ghannam said, after the defense attorneys "brought it to my attention."

"So you never disclosed it to them?" Jacobs asked.

"That's correct."

"Why did you hide it?"

"I didn't hide it," Ghannam said. "I wasn't aware of it actually."

Jacobs turned to part of Ghannam's analysis of Spin Ghul, noting how filthy he was. During both visits, Spin Ghul, he noted, was "disheveled, unkempt, and exhibited poor self-care and poor hygiene. Poor even by standards of correctional facilities." Ghannam concluded that Spin Ghul was "finding it difficult, if not impossible, to bathe himself," though Jacobs noted that a different doctor said Spin Ghul was intentionally refusing to bathe. Specifically, in a December report, according to a Dr. Chiedu Okafor, "patient states that he is not bathing due to the fact that he does not want to make the prison's job any easier in taking care of him or being around him."

Is that what the Canadian judge "meant by selective analysis of evidence, cherry-picking evidence?" Jacobs asked.

"Objection, Your Honor," said Kellman.

"Sustained," said Judge Cogan.

Jacobs was trying to paint a picture of an expert whose biases were so strong he refused to even acknowledge countervailing evidence.

"Dr. Ghannam, you are an activist, right?" he asked.

"Can you define 'activist'?"

Jacobs introduced a video clip from *Arab Stories: Bay Area*, a 2014 PBS/KQED feature about the president of the board of the Arab Film

Festival—Ghannam—saying he was "born into politics" and that though he was a UCSF professor during the day, "when the lights go down I put on my other hat which is community activist."

End of clip.

"So I want to go back to my question," Jacobs continued, "do you consider yourself an activist, Dr. Ghannam?"

"A community activist," Ghannam said.

Jacobs walked through what this meant: Ghannam cofounded in 2009 the US Campaign for the Academic and Cultural Boycott of Israel. He was a member of the International Executive Committee of Al-Awda, working for Palestinian refugees and their descendants to return to their previous homes in Israel or the West Bank. He had been a member of the Muslim Legal Fund of America as well as president of the San Francisco chapter of the American Arab Antidiscrimination Committee. He also hosted a weekly radio show called *Arab Talk*.

"You're a political activist too, right?" Jacobs asked.

"I prefer human rights activist," Ghannam said.

Jacobs showed clip number two: Ghannam speaking in Berkeley, California, at a 2004 rally for independent presidential candidate Ralph Nader, then challenging President George W. Bush and Democratic nominee Senator John Kerry.

Ghannam said he was there on behalf of "citizens who want to challenge the imperial wet dreams that George Bush and John Kerry have."

He told a story about visiting Rafah, in Gaza, which had "been brutally devastated by the 'Israeli Destruction Forces,'" and where he ran into a young boy named Ahmed, who asked him where he was from.

"Unfortunately," Ghannam said he told the boy, "I had to say, 'I'm from The Empire.' I was very apologetic about it, but he understood."

Ghannam also told the Berkeley crowd that Bush and Kerry "both believe that the destruction, the co-optation, the removal of constitutional protections for people of color, specifically Arab Americans and Muslim Americans, should be foregone in the interest of national security. And I can tell you that they have already built the internment camps."

"Do you regret saying that?" Jacobs asked Ghannam.

"No, I don't," he said.

"Where are the internment camps?"

"They were in Louisiana."

It's unlikely that many in the courtroom had any idea what Ghannam was talking about, but his assertion concerned a Reagan-era internal discussion within the Immigration and Naturalization Service about how to deal with noncitizens in the country "likely to be supportive of terrorist activity within the United States." Part of the internal memo, titled "Alien Terrorists and Undesirables: A Contingency Plan," recommended the construction in Oakdale, Louisiana, of a camp to "house and isolate" up to five thousand alien residents from selected countries. The contingency plan was never carried out; such a camp was never constructed.

Jacobs had no idea what Ghannam was referring to, and he figured the allegation was bizarre enough to let it stand on its own.

"You're aware that the entity that you refer to as 'The Empire' is one of two parties in this criminal matter, correct?" Jacobs asked. "But is it your testimony that that doesn't affect your ability to offer objective expert testimony?"

"Absolutely, Counsel," Ghannam said.

Jacobs kept going. Retweets. Contributing a chapter to a book that called suicide bombers "Suicide Warriors." Signing a joint 2003 letter to the editor of the *Journal of the American Medical Association* objecting to an overly broad definition of terrorism because "One person's terrorist is another person's freedom fighter." A 2012 video clip in which Ghannam accused the US of a war crime in Iraq, the immediate "catastrophic collapse of the health care system because there was no power and electricity. This was in my opinion deliberate."

To suggest that there was a direct line between Ghannam's political views and his diagnoses, Jacobs asked about Noor Uthman Muhammed. Noor was a Sudanese citizen who was arrested during the 2002 raid that captured Abu Zubaydah, and he was charged years later at Gitmo for working at a terrorist training camp before 9/11. Ghannam conducted a preliminary analysis suggesting that Noor Muhammed possibly suffered from undiagnosed and untreated post-traumatic stress disorder as well as depression, even though Ghannam had never met the detainee. The defense never asked him to conduct a final report. In 2011, Muhammed pleaded guilty to terrorism charges; he was repatriated to Sudan in 2013.

Ghannam, Jacobs noted, submitted other documents to the military commission advocating that Noor would be a good candidate for release and reintegration into civil society.

"That's similar to your opinion that Raed Jaser was not a jihadist?" Jacobs asked.

"I don't see the connection at all," Ghannam said.

"But for both of those individuals, these convicted terrorists, you thought they could live in society without hurting people?" Jacobs offered.

"Objection," said Kellman.

The prosecution's implication was clear: Ghannam sympathized with terrorists—Jaser, Noor, and now Spin Ghul—for political reasons, and this affected his judgment. Under questioning, Ghannam suggested that he had concerns about whether two other doctors who had diagnosed Spin Ghul—Dr. Mark Mills and Dr. Richard DeMier—violated the ethical rules of their profession by assessing Spin Ghul's health status. He also said he had concerns about whether they were qualified to offer their views, given that they lacked the "linguistic sophistication, linguistic competence, or cultural competence" to truly understand Spin Ghul's psychosis.

And with that, Jacobs rested.

In his redirect, defense counsel David Stern tried to refocus the judge's attention on some of the reasoning behind Ghannam's conclusions. Spin Ghul's revolting lack of hygiene was evidence that he wasn't thinking rationally or in accordance with extremist jihadi beliefs. Spin Ghul, after all, "grew up and was a devout Muslim," Ghannam explained, "and the bathing practices within that culture and within the Islamic tradition and cultural habits are very well prescribed. They are very well-identified and it is extraordinarily rare to forego bathing habits in any context for a Muslim."

That was one of the aspects of the other doctors' lack of "cultural competence" that he was referring to, he explained. Same with reports of Spin Ghul masturbating in front of other people, and with reports of him defecating in front of someone else.

"It is beyond the pale," Ghannam explained, "for anybody who is a devout Muslim." Of the hundreds of devout Muslims he'd evaluated, he had never seen anyone else so violate "the normative cleanliness rituals of Islam."

To Ghannam, there was no logic to the prosecution's argument.

No devout Muslim would ever do these things in the name of jihad, in the name of resistance.

He wasn't surprised that Jacobs had gone after him and his political views; he was used to being attacked on the stand. "They have to come after me ad hominem," he would later say. "They have nothing else. My report was solid." It wasn't as if he wanted Spin Ghul released into the public. He was essentially asking for something more: that Spin Ghul be sent to a federal psychiatric facility, where he would receive accommodations that even many Americans with mental illness weren't afforded.

Jacobs felt dazed. He knew he had made his points adequately; Judge Cogan at one point told him he was "getting to a saturation level" during one section on Ghannam feeling the US was complicit in alleged Israeli crimes. Did he go overboard? Cogan was a big believer in free speech. It was always possible that by going so hard after Ghannam's political views, Jacobs's strategy had backfired. As he returned to the prosecution's table, Shreve and Melody Wells whispered "great job" to him.

But did the judge agree? Had Jacobs adequately made the case that Ghannam's views on US foreign policy were so radical that his expertise was compromised?

Judge Cogan retreated to his chambers to make his decision about whether Spin Ghul was competent to stand trial.

CHAPTER THIRTY-TWO

STORYTELLERS

Brooklyn, NY

Matt Jacobs ran to his computer as soon as the email alert came in: Judge Cogan had made his ruling. Even Jacobs couldn't quite believe how harsh it was. Not about Spin Ghul so much as Dr. Jess Ghannam.

"Dr. Ghannam's credibility is severely compromised," Cogan wrote, pointing out areas where Ghannam didn't seem to acknowledge facts that contradicted his theory.

Regarding Spin Ghul's "lack of hygienic self-care," for example, the defendant had "previously stated that he chooses to keep himself unkempt and unclean to make it more difficult." Moreover, Judge Cogan had been on the case since 2013 and "time and time again" personally observed that Spin Ghul "chooses when to be respectful and cooperative." The last time that Judge Cogan saw him, he noted, was for a court conference on a video link from his cell, and Spin Ghul "could not have been clearer and more deliberate in demonstrating his contempt for me, if not personally, then as a symbol of an institution he detests."

The judge rejected the notion that "Dr. Ghannam's ability to speak to him in Arabic . . . prompted cooperation one day and agitation the next; it is the game that he plays." And even when the defendant was being difficult, Cogan observed that Spin Ghul understood the judge's role. Spin Ghul's lack of respect for the judge and his rejection of the trial "does not demonstrate his incapability of assisting in his defense. Rather, they demonstrate that he has volitionally refused to assist in his defense in the same way that he has volitionally refused to bathe himself." But beyond Cogan disagreeing with Ghannam's conclusions, Cogan did not respect Ghannam as an authority. "Dr. Ghannam's opinion is fundamentally unreliable because Dr. Ghannam is not credible," Cogan concluded. Jacobs had repeatedly impeached the doctor "with evidence demonstrating his bias against the US such that the value of his opinion was discredited almost entirely." Ghannam had every right to espouse his views, Jacobs had said. But in this case, those "beliefs, which he has publicly stated on radio shows, in documentaries, at rallies, at protests, and in writings, bespeak an individual whose bias is so significant that, in cases like this, his credibility is irrevocably compromised." Cogan seemed particularly offended by Ghannam calling the US "an imperial juggernaut" that keeps countries in the Arab world "under [its] boot and thumb." That, combined with Ghannam's observation in a letter to the editor of *JAMA* that "One person's terrorist is another person's freedom fighter," proved to Cogan that Ghannam was incapable of "objectively analyzing the psychological condition of an alleged al Qaeda terrorist being tried in the United States."

"His opinion cannot be divorced from his bias," Cogan said.

For Judge Cogan, it was not a tough call. The psychiatrists who had previously examined Spin Ghul—Dr. Mills and Dr. DeMier—had had a difficult time diagnosing the defendant because he was so uncooperative. But ultimately, Cogan agreed with their conclusion that it's much easier for a sane person to pretend he's insane than for an insane person to feign sanity. Cogan viewed Spin Ghul's refusal to cooperate as deliberate.

Cogan took Ghannam's arguments and qualifications seriously. His political beliefs were not necessarily relevant—but in this case, as Judge Cogan reviewed it, those sympathies did seem to impact his judgment and credibility. Ghannam excluded information that contradicted his narrative, Cogan believed. He had an agenda.

Spin Ghul was fully capable of standing trial, Judge Cogan ruled. Matt Jacobs was excited to read the news. Melody Wells breathed a deep sigh of relief: a competency hearing so close to trial was unusual, and she had been worried. Obviously, there was, theoretically, an argument to make that he was insane. But it wouldn't be made inside Judge Cogan's courtroom before the jury hearing the case of Spin Ghul.

Dr. Ghannam was not surprised when he heard the news. "It's fricking New York City," he would later say. Even if the trial was taking place more than fifteen years after 9/11, the courtroom was still just blocks from Ground Zero, the site of the former World Trade Center. There was part of Ghannam that thought it didn't matter what he said, the pressure—culturally and politically—to lock up Spin Ghul for the rest of his life was intense, and no judge would ever leave his fingerprints on a decision that would conclude otherwise. *The deck was thus stacked against anyone playing a part in any sort of defense*, he thought. "No one was asking for Spin Ghul to be released," he later observed. "He did a lot of bad things. But what do we do in the world when people who do bad things also have severe mental illness? I still feel we have an obligation to give people the best possible defense that we can." By denying his analysis entirely, the judge did not allow Spin Ghul to have that defense, Ghannam believed.

The stage was set for the trial. Spin Ghul was considered competent and would face the prosecution in US criminal court with all the rights afforded to American citizens.

Melody Wells came from a rich tradition of storytelling. Back home in Houma, Louisiana, her handyman dad was also a raconteur who regaled the family every night with his adventures, which occasionally involved a baby alligator or some such critter. Her uncle Ken was an award-winning newspaper writer and editor whose novels prompted no less than Tom Wolfe to call him "the Cajun Carl Hiaasen."

Though she was a line prosecutor, Melody saw her job before the judge and jury very much in the same storytelling tradition. She had to weave a compelling narrative while carefully embroidering evidence into it. She spent her time on the case making a storyboard of sorts, a PowerPoint that helped her keep track of the story. The prosecution would get only one shot to have the judge and jury understand what they had spent years preparing. The jury would be hearing this wild tale for the first time, and they would hear it only once. It had to be presented in a way that was clear, compelling, and easily understandable.

Melody, Shreve, and the rest of the prosecution team labored for hours on this task in the tiny conference room near Shreve's office on the fifth floor.

The most obvious way to tell the tale of Spin Ghul would be chronologically. To start with the crime—with the Slayers outside Firebase Shkin, getting fired upon in an al Qaeda ambush. She and the team tried that, starting theoretically with testimony from soldiers and ending with his confession on *The Excelsior* and then again in the Italian court. But it didn't seem to work. You have compelling stories from the soldiers, but where was the perp? None of them would be able to identify him in a lineup or anything; it was a violent, chaotic battle.

They tried to reorder the presentation.

Melody grew frustrated. They were having difficulty keeping it all packaged into one cohesive story.

They brainstormed. They needed to grab the jurors by the lapels and immerse them in the narrative. The jurors needed to care about the case and pay attention to the details.

Eventually the team arrived at a place where, though it would be unusual, they started with Spin Ghul on the deck of *The Excelsior* asking Morgese for water.

Because Spin Ghul was, after all, the one who told this story. It was an evil story, but it was a clear one. They would start with Spin Ghul confessing on *The Excelsior* and then, in Italy, telling the story of his life.

Amid all of this, the email alert came in on Judge Cogan's ruling on whether Lieutenant Colonel Frakt could testify that the Firebase Shkin part of the case was protected by the laws of war.

Shreve and his team had argued that Spin wasn't entitled to "lawful combatant immunity" under the Geneva Convention relative to the treatment of prisoners of war because al Qaeda did not meet all four criteria as an organization whose members could qualify for prisoner-of-war status. An example: the organization's members must have a fixed distinctive emblem or uniform recognizable at a distance. That certainly did not describe al Qaeda.

Cogan concluded: the prosecution was right.

First, there was no need for a legal expert, Cogan said. That was the judge's job. And, he wrote, "I have already ruled that al Qaeda does not adhere to the law of war."

Melody Wells was so relieved—this was the defense's best argument, and it had just been completely shanked.

The prosecution had cleared the hurdles of the pretrial motions.

They remained nervous.

It was a must-win trial.

If Spin Ghul was acquitted, would he end up essentially walking out the door and into Brooklyn? What about the victims who were relying on Shreve's team? Everyone felt prepared, but they all keenly remembered the 284 counts dismissed in the Ghailani case because of a single miscalculation by the prosecution. One mistake or unfavorable decision could still bring their case tumbling down.

CHAPTER THIRTY-THREE

LADIES AND GENTLEMEN OF THE JURY

Brooklyn, New York

On Monday, March 6, 2017, Shreve's iPhone alarm—the particularly irritating one called "radar"—began its high-pitched nag at 5:30 a.m.

It was still dark outside his third-floor Brooklyn walk-up. Trying not to further awaken his wife or disturb his three-year-old daughter or infant son, he crept into the kitchen to brew the darkest, richest coffee he could. After shaving and showering, he put on his blue suit and one of the navy ties his mom had bought him—with the little rhinos. Shreve grabbed his overcoat and the scarf his wife was always reminding him to wear before heading out into the cold.

The US attorney's office was roughly a mile away, but this morning he took a quick detour, heading first to the subway stop across from Clark's Diner, where he sat for a shoeshine, a pretrial good-luck tradition. He grabbed another cup of coffee near the office, then headed in. The trial was set to start at 9:30 that morning.

The whole team had been at the office until late the night before, and as Shreve walked in—along with Matt Jacobs, Melody Wells, Joe

Kaster, and others—no one felt completely settled. It wasn't that they were unprepared, but more that they felt like jugglers with fifteen balls in the air. Witnesses were flying in from as far east as Italy and as far west as California. John Ross, Bobby Lo, and the FBI agents were making sure witnesses were showing up on time and preparing for testimony. Melody and Matt were coordinating the testimonies to make sure the narratives aligned and that there were no gaps. Physical evidence had been tagged and labeled and was being shuttled to the courtroom in a cart pushed by Wells. Other evidence was secured in a safe on the second floor of EDNY headquarters and in Shreve's office; still more was stored in an evidence locker at the courthouse.

Much had changed in the world of politics and counterterrorism in the previous few months. The surprise election victory of Donald Trump ushered in an era when the Overton window of what was acceptable discourse regarding the war on terror had opened up considerably. Including killing the families of terrorists, banning Muslims from entering the US, and assuming control of Iraqi oil fields. That morning, President Trump would sign an executive order blocking from entry into the US the citizens of six predominantly Muslim countries.

The strategy of prosecuting foreign terrorists apprehended abroad in US criminal courts almost immediately ran into a buzzsaw named Jefferson Beauregard Sessions. In 2017, the brand-new attorney general was irritated when Toscas and FBI deputy director Andrew McCabe raised the matter of extraditing Abu Khaybar—a Sudanese citizen being held by the UAE in Yemen—for criminal prosecution in Brooklyn. In fact he was not just irked, McCabe would later write in his memoir without naming Abu Khaybar, Sessions "was volcanically offended that we had even proposed it . . . he berated us for treating terrorists like criminals. For giving constitutional rights to enemy combatants." The attorney general didn't seem to care that anything could happen to Abu Khaybar if the US didn't try him. After all, the war in Yemen was unpredictable, and who knew what the Emiratis would end up doing with him if the Trump administration didn't prosecute him.

In an attempt at reassurance, Toscas shared with Sessions the story of Spin Ghul, a success story as both the FBI and Justice Department saw it. If the US hadn't built a case against him, Spin Ghul would have been released into Western Europe, just a flight from Manhattan. But Sessions didn't seem to care. Giving Spin Ghul or Abu Khaybar any constitutional rights made little sense to him. The attorney general wouldn't intrude on Spin Ghul's trial, but the message from the new administration was clear: no one should expect the Spin Ghul template to be replicated anytime soon.

Not that anyone on the prosecution team had even a moment to consider the political tides, which had shifted back and forth with the force of a tsunami during the nearly two decades of the war on terror. Trial lawyers did their best to ignore such matters, in order to focus entirely on their craft. It can be tough on marriages and families—attorneys joke that going to trial while having young kids is like playing basketball on roller skates—and for the most part Shreve tuned out his personal life and the world at large. In these closing weeks, he barely interacted with his wife other than to kiss her good night and hug her goodbye in the morning. His focus was singular: put Spin Ghul away for life.

Shreve labored mightily not to appear nervous, but of course he was. He knew the case was solid, but crazy shit happens in a trial. There is so much that a lawyer is responsible for, thousands of details and an insanely dramatic pace in which you must keep them all straight. One misstep could cause a judge to lose their cool and yell at you in front of the jury. If one key witness fails to show up or one testimony goes south, it's all on you.

Spin Ghul did not stand up when the deputy of the court told those assembled, "All rise." That morning the prisoner had been taken from his cell to a secure room where a feed of the proceedings was being transmitted. An interpreter was with him, one who spoke Hausa, but it wasn't even clear if the defendant was paying attention.

Jane Nelson sure was. She had flown from Oklahoma to Brooklyn to watch the trial, along with her ex-husband Jerry, daughter Jillian, and son Renley. Jerod had been taken from this world fourteen years before, but for a mother the pain felt new and raw.

The prosecution sat on the left side of the room, if you were looking at the judge. Shreve, Melody Wells, Matt Jacobs, Joe Kaster, Greg Paciorek.

The defense sat on the right. Susan Kellman, Joshua Dratel, David Stern.

It had grown tense between the two sides. Shreve wanted to make sure the defense didn't plan on using Spin Ghul's absence as an avenue for appeal.

"Judge, if we're going to ask for every single thing we think the other side shouldn't do, we would be here forever," Stern had countered.

The jury—twelve ordinary citizens in Brooklyn, men and women, there for the unusual task of judging the criminality of actions in Afghanistan and Nigeria—entered at 10:19 a.m. The prosecution had moved for them to remain anonymous. This was, after all, a case against a man from al Qaeda.

Matt Jacobs was up first, giving the opening statement for the prosecution. He'd committed the roughly twenty-minute open to memory, rehearsing it during his early morning forty-five-minute commute on the subway. When his fellow commuters began changing seats, moving away from him, he realized he was audibly muttering to himself.

But now it was time to say it aloud.

"The defendant is an al-Qaeda terrorist whose mission was to kill Americans," Jacobs told the jury. "He went to Afghanistan just before 9/11 where he swore allegiance to Osama bin Laden and trained in al-Qaeda's terror camps. Then, he put his terrorist training to use."

The prosecution began its narrative on the deck of *The Excelsior*. After Spin Ghul's confession on the boat, prosecutors then detailed his second testimony in the courthouse in Agrigento. The prosecution's investigative work across the globe would trace Spin Ghul's journey into the world of al Qaeda in Pakistan, to his ambush against the Americans outside Firebase Shkin, to his plans with Hamza Rabia to blow up the US embassy in Abuja, Nigeria.

For Susan Kellman and the defense team, the goal was to portray Spin Ghul as unstable and his confession as unreliable. Yes, she acknowledged, the defendant "pledged his allegiance to al Qaeda, and al Qaeda is a designated foreign terrorist organization," she said. "Mr. Harun may not share your world view, but is that enough to convict him?"

The first witness was called. Italian Green Beret Francesco Morgese of the Guardia di Finanza took the stand, telling the tale of the al Qaeda terrorist who just happened upon them, describing his behavior and his claims about where he had been and his role in al Qaeda. Along with his detailed testimony about that day came Government Exhibit 17T, the confession written on the ship, which began: "I, the so-called, Adnan Ibrahim Harun Adam. Nom de guerre: 'Espingol.' I am a member of Al Qaeda organization in West Africa."

Morgese's colleagues from the ship, Guglielmo Battisti and Riccardo Rosi, followed. The jury seemed engrossed with their stories, but by the end of the first day, Judge Cogan had a warning for the prosecution: pick it up.

"Please go through your case in detail and eliminate any purely cumulative witnesses," the judge instructed. "The three people we heard today all said the same thing, which is okay if there is some hotly disputed point on which the credibility is challenged, but I don't think there is much dispute over what happened on that boat. So I'm not sure we needed these three witnesses; and I don't want to repeat that expenditure of time again."

The prosecution had planned for six weeks of trial, but Judge Cogan wasn't having it. Testimonies were shortened. Duplicative witnesses canceled. All fat was trimmed. As Judge Cogan saw it, the evidence in the case was so overwhelming, there was no need for the government to engage in overkill. Nine days after opening statements, having heard from witness after witness, the judge announced it was time for closings. After almost nine full years of effort by dozens of investigators—including complications requiring fraught diplomacy with the governments of Italy and Nigeria, decisions made at the highest levels of the US government, thirty witnesses testifying and countless others interviewed—the lofty pursuit of justice for the families of Jerod Dennis and Ray Losano and the servicemembers of Firebase Shkin was about to come to a stunningly truncated close.

Melody Wells awoke in her small Brooklyn Heights apartment at the crack of dawn on March 15, the day of closing arguments, replaying the scene Shreve had acted out less than two weeks earlier. She was nervous, and she was also holding on to a secret: she was eleven weeks' pregnant. This meant she was forgoing her normal cups of coffee.

Finishing her bowl of Cheerios, Melody put on her go-to, a blue skirt suit with a low-key white blouse. She walked the ten minutes to EDNY, nervous and foggy from the caffeine deprivation. But she also felt good about the closing. It was strong.

After years of successful sleuthing, the prosecutors had been able to accumulate a great deal of evidence. But would the jury buy it? None of it was direct eyewitness testimony of someone who saw Spin Ghul pull a trigger or throw a grenade. There was no video of Spin Ghul in Afghanistan, Pakistan, or Nigeria. No witnesses from among the al Qaeda coconspirators, given the precluding of testimony born from torture.

Melody Wells stood before the jury, looking into the eyes of those twelve men and women.

"'I want to give you a history of how I entered into terrorism.' Those are the defendant's words, and this is the defendant," she began, pointing to a photograph of Spin Ghul. "For three days in a courtroom in Italy in front of a judge and with his lawyers, the defendant proudly confessed his terrorist life story."

Wells then proceeded to tell that life story, in detail, but she knew his words were not enough. Every claim, every boast, every anecdote needed to be backed up by proof that it happened.

Spin Ghul's origin story of terror began weeks before September 11, 2001, when he traveled to Pakistan and trained at Camp al Farouq. Tony Graziano, formerly a special agent assigned to the US Army Criminal Investigation Division, now retired, had been called to testify. Graziano had been sent to visit al Farouq to ensure that what intelligence officials had concluded about the training camp and what Spin Ghul had claimed matched up with reality. Terrorism expert Evan Kohlmann further testified that recruits were instructed in explosives and small arms, just as Spin Ghul had said.

The soldiers from Firebase Shkin who had traveled to Brooklyn to share their painful memories also shared the ugly results of Spin Ghul's expertise: Konrad Reed, Scott Trahan, and David Cyr, who were right near where Spin Ghul was firing from; Lee Marvin Blackwell, who had been with Ray Losano when he was fatally wounded; "Doc" Simmons, who had tended to those shot and blown up; Victor Keith Graf, who found Jerod Dennis; Brian Severino, who ran the casualty collection point; and Dwayne McKnight, who helped look for Jerod Dennis.

The prosecution had reviewed the testimony with each of the servicemembers. On the stand, Konrad Reed thought he recognized Spin Ghul from the battle, but when he told Matt Jacobs of that after his testimony, Jacobs told him that it was better for his credibility to have just stuck with what he had been consistently saying for years. No need to overtorque what was already a solid case with a years-later, 20/20 hindsight identification. This was a criminal court, after all, and though an eyewitness testimony would be strongest, there were just too many questions about Reed's memory, too many opportunities for the defense to poke holes in his testimony, to take the risk. Everything else had been solid to the comma.

Spin Ghul's role in the al Qaeda web was an important part of the case. He was no leader, but he wasn't just a guy who happened into terrorism. Kohlmann described the men whom Melody referred to as a "who's who" of al Qaeda leaders, operatives, and other terrorists from 2002 to 2003 with whom Spin Ghul associated. They were, she said, "his mentors, his bosses, his associates, his inspirations." Spin Ghul testified, for instance, that a man named Khabab al-Masri trained him in how to use "chemical components for a bomb—like hydrogen peroxide" and instructed him in how to use "the poisons that kill: ricin, cyanide, potassium." Kohlmann's testimony matched exactly with what counterterrorism officials knew about al-Masri, believed to have been killed in Waziristan by a US drone strike in July 2008.

And then there was Abu Zubaydah, whom Spin Ghul had also claimed to have met during that time period. Captured by the FBI in 2002, allegedly tortured by the CIA, and held at Gitmo to this day.

"And so you're wondering," Melody asked, "is it true that the defendant met this high-ranking jihadist, Abu Zubaydah?"

She reminded the jury of the testimony of Dave Franco and Chris Reimann, the FBI agents involved in the March 2002 raid in Faisalabad, Pakistan, when Abu Zubaydah was captured. Franco had testified about the evidence they'd gathered at the Faisalabad safe house then brought to Lahore, where they recorded it all on an FD-192 evidence log form. One of those items was a small leather notebook with notes scribbled inside it, including a phone number, 027425777.

Melody played FBI special agent Greg Paciorek a clip of an interview with the defendant in which he mentioned a phone number ending in 777. She asked him if he recognized that phone number.

"It was mentioned multiple times" during his testimony in Agrigento, Paciorek said. "It was his"—Spin Ghul's—"home telephone number in Saudi Arabia."

Melody had handed Paciorek a piece of paper from that testimony and asked him if he recognized it.

"This is the sheet of paper that the defendant wrote down the 777 number upon," he said.

The classic 1950 Japanese movie *Rashomon*, directed by legendary filmmaker Akira Kurosawa, retells the story of a samurai murdered in a forest from four different contradictory perspectives, a drama that highlights how subjective we all are about the events we witness and how inclined we all are to share the details that make us look the best. Melody Wells's closing arguments aimed to be the opposite of *Rashomon*, showing remarkable cohesion and similarities when it came to the narratives from an al Qaeda terrorist and his targets.

Spin Ghul's description of the ambush fit exactly with that of the servicemembers from Firebase Shkin. Trahan and Spin Ghul both placed Angoor Ada, the town where the al Qaeda safe house was located, across the border from Firebase Shkin. Trahan and Reed confirmed Spin Ghul's account of their rocket attacks, Reed and Severino confirmed they were Katyusha rockets, which Spin Ghul said he was in charge of firing personally. Dwayne McKnight's map of the area aligned with Spin Ghul's geographic recollections.

Then, of course, came the details about the ambush itself. Melody walked through memories Spin Ghul had of the event that pinpointed it on April 25, 2003—the Friday call to prayer heard over the Shkin loudspeaker, the planned Rumsfeld visit to the region just days after the attack. Severino and Trahan remembered Apaches hunting for the fighters who had been reported crossing the border and not finding them, which squared with Spin Ghul's testimony that the helicopters didn't get low enough to see any members of his crew.

Both Spin Ghul and the American soldiers spoke about how the al Qaeda fighters were able to hide in the low ground. When the fighters began firing on the Americans, Spin Ghul had recalled, they first hit "a Black individual and his body type is the body type of a commando. He's very thick, thick-built." This of course was Staff Sergeant Michiru Brown, as Trahan described him, "a large man. Looks like a middle linebacker, Black, bald." Spin Ghul recalled Brown yelling for backup. Cyr recalled him calling for help.

The battle continued to unfold as Melody stitched together the defendant's confession and witnesses on the stand. The Kalashnikovs fired, the grenades thrown. Then Konrad Reed tried to call in mortars from the firebase, but those rounds missed their target. Lee Marvin Blackwell called in both jets and helicopters to the area. The details from the missed mortars to the planes flying overhead unable to locate their targets all matched what Spin Ghul had said nearly five years ago in Agrigento to David Bitkower and Shreve Ariail in Italian court.

The defense had objected to the soldiers testifying in full dress uniform "stock full of decorations," which Dratel argued was prejudicial and added a layer of theater to the case. The defense team also made sure that none of the testimony about what had happened to Ray Losano and Jerod Dennis was too bloody.

"There are certain parts of the testimony, in particular, Blackwell's testimony with respect to very graphic testimony about the injuries suffered by Mr. Losano, and we don't think that's necessary to prove anything in the case," Dratel said. "This is not a civil case with pain and suffering or any emotional aspect of the events."

Judge Cogan agreed, but that didn't mean there weren't moments of true pathos. Recalling the moment after Ray Losano was hit, Lee Marvin Blackwell refrained from the graphic details, but no one spoke as he recalled it.

"I picked him up," he said. "I kept screaming for the medic. Ray is pulling at me, clawing at me, and I told Ray I love him, I was proud of him. I told him his family loves him. I told him to hang in there, told him to calm down."

Air Force Airman 1st Class Raymond Losano (1979–2003)
PHOTO COURTESY OF LEE MARVIN BLACKWELL

He added: "He was losing a lot of blood."

The attack on Jerod Dennis came later in the battle. This was not Spin Ghul's group but rather a group of al Qaeda fighters carrying mortars. "The mortar group also had an encounter with the Americans," Spin Ghul had said. "There was a pickup that arrived, and I think there were four individuals."

They were Eddie Camacho, John Setzer, an Afghan fighter, and Jerod Dennis.

Graf found Jerod and brought him to safety, but by then it was too late.

Jerod's mom, dad, brother, and sister hung on every word Graf offered in court. They knew so little about Jerod's final moments.

"I called the command post," Graf said about his search for the missing private. "And when they called me—or called me back, they asked me to sit tight. There was an infantry group on foot coming to us."

"And when they said sit tight," Matt Jacobs asked, "do you mean sit—don't go out and look for Dennis right away?"

"Yes, sir," Graf replied.

"And how did you respond to that?" Jacobs asked.

"I didn't want to wait, so I chose to act like my radio wasn't working well and went ahead and proceeded up the hill," Graf said. Soon he came across Jerod Dennis.

"I rolled him towards me a little bit and pulled him from underneath the tree," Graf said. "He was . . . he was real lethargic, he was moving slowly on his own. He wasn't saying anything to me. I just looked at him, and I said, 'Buddy, we found you. We're going to get you out of here.'"

His testimony was the first time anyone in Jerod's family had heard of how their beloved son and brother had spent his last conscious moments.

Melody Wells looked at the jury one last time as she stood before them: "So, ladies and gentlemen, that is the testimony of the soldiers who survived the attack and you have seen and you've heard all the ways that what they described completely confirms the defendant's account of the attack that he participated in. They're describing the same events, the same day, the same place."

But there was more than witness testimony, she noted.

Spin Ghul, after all, had seen one of his fellow al Qaeda fighters lying on the ground, dead, the bottom half of his leg jutting outwards at a right angle from his body. Doc Simmons and Severino had described that man as well, and Government Exhibit 280 was the photograph of the corpse, Abu Walid.

Abu Walid, of course, was a notetaker, and his journal detailed the same basic journey within Pakistan and to the Angoor Ada safe house that Spin Ghul had described, mentioning many of the same fighters Spin Ghul had—Abu Khalid, Abu Hamza al-Australi—and even mentioning Spin Ghul by a different alias, or kunya, "Abu Tamim."

That journal was among the battlefield evidence collected by Severino and others, Melody Wells noted, as was a certain "pocket-sized Quran, leather-bound, with a zipper, with a gold emblem on the front." When the FBI asked Dwayne McKnight for the Quran, he handed it over, and it soon ended up being analyzed at Quantico by Nicole Bagley.

Bagley had testified first thing in the morning on Thursday, March 9, 2017, her nose ring removed, her neck tats hidden as best she could by a professional suit and blouse.

After explaining her craft and expertise, she recognized the government's exhibit, the "known fingerprint card" bearing Spin Ghul's given name, Ibrahim S. Harun, submitted to her at the FBI laboratory.

Those prints, she testified, matched the four latent prints she found on the Quran in her lab in late April 2013—exactly one decade since the ambush.

On April 25, 2013, ten years to the day after the attack, Bert LaCroix had been at his desk when he received a technical email from Nicole Bagley that he couldn't understand at all.

He emailed her back. "Do you have ten minutes to explain what this means?" he asked.

"Sure, no problem," Bagley responded. "Call me."

He did, and she explained: we found your subject's fingerprint in the Quran.

LaCroix jumped up out of his chair. "Yes!" he cried. "Yes! Yes! Yes!"

Soon word spread—Shreve in a SCIF at the US attorney's office, Bitkower poring over information on the Boston Marathon bombing at the National Security Division of the Justice Department. It was a real moment of jubilation. Juries love that *CSI* data, Shreve knew. This was huge.

In April 2016, Bagley had conducted a second examination of the Quran and found five other fingerprints, Melody Wells told the jury.

"After all of those years and all of those miles, the defendant's fingerprints are in the Quran that Dwayne McKnight dug out of that cardboard box that Sergeant Severino photographed in the TOC and that the defendant was reading in the moments before the attack," Wells said.

It wasn't a bloody knife, but it was Spin Ghul's fingerprint at the scene of the crime. Physical evidence. Unlike Kurosawa, Melody Wells didn't have sound or images to tell her story, but the story she told was expertly delivered and so movingly re-created that one juror was even crying when Melody mentioned Jerod Dennis and Ray Losano one last time. If her slate of witnesses weren't enough, the proof Spin Ghul had been there was undeniable.

Next came the story of Spin Ghul's plot to replicate the 1998 US embassy bombings in Nigeria. The plots were laid out in the email between he and Hamza Rabia, admitted during the CIPA hearing and introduced into evidence for the jury to read in full.

The plot failed because he and Mohammed Ashafa drove around the neighborhoods where the embassies were located and, as he testified, "We weren't able to find it. We saw some other Western embassies."

Their story checked out when the prosecutors explained the historical context. Nigerian leaders had decided to move their capital from coastal Lagos to more central Abuja, and the US embassy happened to be caught in the limbo of transferring locations when Spin Ghul planned his attack. Jerry Barnes, a former diplomatic security special agent, testified that the US embassy at the time of Spin Ghul's evil plot was temporarily located on Mambilla Street, tucked between a golf club and the state security services headquarters, with no signage or markers directing people to it. It was no wonder Spin Ghul couldn't find it.

That didn't stop Spin Ghul from continuing his conspiracy, seeking to purchase explosives. "I sent Maradone, one of the accomplices, to the headquarters of that company located on Zaria Road, Zaria Road in the city of Kano," he had testified. "On Zaria Road there's a very tall building, I think it's the only tall [building] in Kano. Behind that building there's a roundabout and that roundabout area is called Hausawa. Between the roundabout and the tall building there are some shops and their shop is among those shops."

The embassy wouldn't let Melody Wells and Matt Jacobs go to Kano to verify these details during their visit in 2016; an FBI agent based in Abuja at the time carried out the assignment. He recognized the tall building as Spin Ghul had described it.

The final part of the prosecutor's presentation was Mohammad Ashafa, the accomplice whom Spin Ghul described sending to Pakistan to communicate with Hamza Rabia in 2004. Ashafa's visa and arrest records were also introduced into evidence.

Matt Jacobs holding up a photo of Spin Ghul with Judge Cogan on the bench presiding. At the prosecution table (left to right): Greg Paciorek, Joe Kaster, Shreve Ariail, Melody Wells; the defense team sits behind them.
COURTROOM ART BY AND PUBLISHED WITH PERMISSION OF JANE ROSENBERG

"Ladies and gentlemen, later today, the judge is going to instruct you on the law; and what the judge says governs the case," Melody Wells concluded. "You must follow his instructions. Before that, I want to briefly discuss the charges and highlight a few things for you to consider when you deliberate later today.

"Here are the counts: conspiracy to murder United States nationals," she continued. "What I expect is that the judge will tell you that a conspiracy is simply an agreement and that United States nationals simply means US citizens. So the defendant is charged with agreeing with others to murder US citizens, and in order for you to find that, you have to find that the defendant acted with malice and forethought. And, ladies and gentlemen, make no mistake. Shooting Kalashnikovs and throwing grenades at US soldiers is malice. Plotting to blow up an embassy with the goal of killing everyone inside is malice."

The next count, she noted, was conspiracy to bomb a US government facility, which simply means an agreement to try to do so. "The evidence has shown beyond a reasonable doubt that that is exactly what the defendant's intent was" as well as the fact that "he worked with others to try to accomplish this goal."

Spin Ghul was also charged with conspiracy to provide material support to al Qaeda. Not only had Spin Ghul obviously joined the jihad to fight with that group; he'd also joined and become active with full knowledge and appreciation of its attacks on the US embassies in 1998, on the USS *Cole* in 2000, and of course September 11, 2001.

"Over the last two weeks, we have provided you with an immense amount of information and evidence, and we have appreciated your patience and your attention and your diligence throughout the trial," she said. She asked them to consider all the evidence—the confession, the testimony, the documents, the Quran, the al Qaeda journal, the communication between Spin Ghul and Hamza Rabia.

"And I submit the evidence has shown beyond a reasonable doubt that the defendant and other al Qaeda fighters attacked American soldiers, murdering Ray Losano and Jerod Dennis, injured Captain Trahan, Sergeant Reed, and others, and that after that, the defendant conspired to blow up an American Embassy with the goal of killing everyone inside. The evidence has shown beyond a reasonable doubt that the defendant is guilty of all of the crimes charged. We ask that you convict him."

Then it was time for the defense to speak.

Shreve braced himself for the expected onslaught from Susan Kellman. He presumed she would argue that Spin Ghul's boasts were exaggerations. There were, after all, zero eyewitnesses called—and it's not as if a Black al Qaeda fighter wouldn't stand out. She would no doubt argue this was a circumstantial case, about a man who was arguably an enemy fighter on the field of battle. And even though they kept Dr. Ghannam from testifying, there was always the possibility that one of the jurors shared his worldview of American imperialism and thought al Qaeda fighters killing American soldiers in Afghanistan was justifiable resistance. *This was not over—not by a long shot*, Shreve thought.

But then David Stern spoke.

"We are not going to make a closing statement," he said. "We want to go directly to charge."

The prosecution was stunned. Shreve in particular was worried that the defense refusing to even make a closing statement could open up the case to an appeals claim of ineffective counsel. He'd never seen anything like it.

It wasn't as if the defense team hadn't been engaged during the trial, pointing out that photos from Kano, Nigeria, in 2016 did not necessarily resemble Kano in 2004, and that Dave Franco did not know which room Abu Zubaydah occupied in the Pakistani safe house to definitively place the address book in his room.

The defense's refusal to offer a closing argument was odd, Shreve argued to Judge Cogan after the jury had left the courtroom. Shreve was worried that this was going to be used by the defense on appeal as a due process violation, as a basis for a claim of deficient legal representation. He wanted time to research what Kellman was doing and its ramifications. At the very least, he argued, the defense team should have to tell their client that they weren't going to offer a closing argument.

Stern told Judge Cogan they opposed that.

"We didn't tell him every single time we didn't cross-examine. We have made a strategic decision. It's not one of those decisions reserved to a defendant, specifically. And to highlight this to him—as to all the other things we have or haven't done—is inappropriate."

Susan Kellman, for her part, was amused, knowing how disappointed Shreve must have been to have not been allowed to give his rebuttal statement. No doubt he had prepared for it for months, if not years. His moment in the sun. And now he wouldn't get it. Well, too bad. Sometimes the strongest defense was to convey to the jury that the government had simply not proven its case.

After all, in Judge Cogan's instructions, the jury would be told that Spin Ghul had pleaded not guilty and the burden was on Shreve and his team to prove guilt beyond a reasonable doubt—the burden was not on Spin Ghul or Susan Kellman.

Spin Ghul, a Nigerien raised in Saudi Arabia, an al Qaeda terrorist, a man who would clearly kill as many Americans as he could if given the chance, was bestowed with the same rights in the American system as any law-abiding American citizen. Judge Cogan instructed the jury that the man who gleefully, proudly, fired at US troops on patrol thousands of miles away "is to be considered innocent." Never before in American history had a foreign combatant like this one been afforded this sacred privilege.

And what did that mean? "This presumption of innocence alone is sufficient to acquit the defendant, unless you as jurors are unanimously convinced beyond a reasonable doubt of the defendant's guilt after a careful and impartial consideration of all the evidence in the case," the judge explained. "That presumption was with the defendant when the case began. It remains with the defendant even now, as I speak to you. And it will continue with the defendant into your deliberations—again, unless and until you are convinced that the Government has proven his guilt beyond a reasonable doubt. If the Government fails to sustain that burden, you must find the defendant not guilty."

Judge Cogan gave the twelve men and women those instructions and sent them to the jury room at 1:40 p.m. ET.

The jury hadn't even deliberated for two hours when the lawyers were beckoned back.

The jurors had reached a verdict.

Shreve intellectually took that to be a good sign—the shorter the deliberation, the more likely a conviction, he believed. But he wasn't going to be able to exhale until he heard the words themselves.

They came at 4:05 p.m.

"Be seated, please," Judge Cogan said, holding a piece of paper. "Ladies and gentlemen, we have your note that says, 'We have reached a unanimous decision,' signed by Juror Number 1. Juror Number 1, is it correct that you have reached a unanimous decision?"

"Yes, it is," Juror Number 1 said.

"Would you please hand the verdict form to Ms. Clarke?" Cogan asked. "Ladies and gentlemen, what I'm going to do now is read the verdict sheet aloud. It's very important that you listen carefully because I'm then going to ask each one of you if it represents your true and accurate verdict. All right?"

The prosecutors held their breath.

"On the verdict sheet, on Count 1, the jury found the defendant guilty," read Judge Cogan. "On Count 2, the jury found the defendant guilty. On Count 3, the jury found the defendant guilty. On Count 4, the jury found the defendant guilty. And on Count 5, the jury found the defendant guilty."

The trial had been emotional for the Dennis family. They had cried a lot. They hated how rude Spin Ghul was to the court, to the soldiers, to the judge, to the judicial system. Jillian Dennis, for one, wasn't happy that the Italians had insisted the death penalty be off the table.

It had been a horror, from that grim day in April 2003 until now, sleepless nights and uncontrollable weeping and the devastating weight of grief. Fourteen years of it, almost to the day.

But they had been in New York only for the first week of the trial, after which they returned home. They had jobs; Jillian and Renley had families. And to be honest, it was a lot.

When the call came from Matt Jacobs informing them that the jury had found Spin Ghul guilty on all counts, Jane Nelson felt some peace knowing Spin Ghul would never see the light of day again, never carry out any plots against Americans again. And she knew the Dennis family was fortunate in the twisted sense that one of those responsible for the death of their beloved Jerod was captured and brought to justice. It reminded her of what Jerod stood for, what he was proud to have been a part of, and what he ultimately died for. But her heart ached for him.

Which was how Renley Dennis felt, too. Intellectually, he could see the importance of what happened. But it was still just sad. He didn't have his brother.

CHAPTER THIRTY-FOUR

YOU WILL NOT HAVE MY HATE

Paris, France

Antoine Leiris sat at home with his seventeen-month-old son Melvil while his wife, Hélène, took a well-deserved night off. She and a friend had gone to a sold-out show to hear an American band at a nightclub. Despite their name, the Eagles of Death Metal were something of a mix of grunge and bluegrass.

After lullabies and hugs, Antoine put Melvil to sleep and retreated to his bedroom where he read a novel.

It was Friday, November 13, 2015.

Then text messages started coming in. Perplexing ones.

Why are people asking me if I'm safe? He rushed to the living room to turn on the news. A terrorist attack had been foiled at the Stade de France, in the suburbs north of Paris.

Antoine thought of texting Hélène to suggest she take a taxi home, but before he could do so he noticed people on his TV screen watching their TV screens, staring at a different channel from the one he was watching, wearing faces that suggested horror.

Then the news came across on the ticker at the bottom of Antoine's own screen: TERRORIST ATTACK AT THE BATACLAN.

The Bataclan. The nightclub where Hélène had gone.

Desperately, Antoine rang his wife. It went to voicemail. He tried again. And again. And again.

Hélène Muyal-Leiris and eighty-nine other innocents were slaughtered by three terrorists with ISIS. The three fired into the crowd of 1,500, then either died by suicide vests or in the subsequent shoot-out with police.

Two nights later, Antoine, a journalist, took to Facebook and wrote an open letter to the terrorists.

"I don't know who you are and I don't want to know, you are dead souls," he wrote. "If this God for whom you kill blindly made us in his image, every bullet in the body of my wife is a wound in his heart."

Antoine wrote that he would not give the terrorists "the satisfaction of hating you. You want it, but to respond to hatred with anger would be to give in to the same ignorance that made you what you are."

"I saw her this morning," he wrote. "At last, after nights and days of waiting. She was as beautiful as when she left on Friday evening, as beautiful as when I fell head over heels in love with her more than 12 years ago.

"On Friday evening you stole the life of an exceptional person, the love of my life, the mother of my son, but you will not have my hate."

Antoine's Facebook post became a media sensation, then one year later it became a book, an international bestseller. One that made its way to the Barnes & Noble in Norman, Oklahoma, where Renley Dennis was in law school. The title—*You Will Not Have My Hate*—jumped from the cover and stopped Renley in his tracks. He purchased the thin hardback, took it home, and couldn't put it down.

Antoine's book spelunked into the depths of his despair, the hollows of his grief. In his beautiful memoir, Antoine recalled that just four days after his wife had been slaughtered, he answered the doorbell to their apartment.

"I've come to read the electric meter," the man said.

Hélène had stuck the reminder of the pending visit to the refrigerator, but Antoine had forgotten. "I thought that if the moon ever disappeared, the sea would retreat so no one could see it crying," Antoine wrote. "I thought the winds would stop dancing. That the sun would not want to rise again. Nothing of the kind. The world continues to turn, and meters must be read."

As pledged, the book does not give the terrorists the gift of his ire. Melvil and Hélène and the chasm in their lives without her are his focus. ISIS is not mentioned.

Renley reread the book on his flight from Oklahoma City to New York, in February 2018. He thought about Antoine's message and how it contrasted with an experience of his father, who, one Memorial Day not long after Jerod's death, was invited to a church service where the minister talked about the need to carpet-bomb Muslim countries. "Bomb them all," he'd said. The anecdote had horrified Renley when his dad told him about it. It was the last thing Jerod would have wanted.

Renley, his sister Jillian, and mother Jane were heading to Brooklyn for Judge Cogan's sentencing of Spin Ghul. Matt Jacobs had told the family that under the Crime Victims' Rights Act, passed in 2004, they and the servicemembers who served alongside Jerod had the right to be heard and to submit statements during sentencing. Renley wasn't sure whether he would speak or whether his mom and sister wanted to. But he was sure that he didn't want Jerod to have anything to do with hate.

He thought about Jerod's letters home. This kid who grew up running around in the Kiamichi wilderness north of their town of Antlers, Oklahoma, would write to Renley about how similar the Afghans were to the Okie ranchers they grew up with. Instead of branding, the Afghans dyed the chickens pink and the goats yellow.

Renley thought deeply about all this on his flight. Not about the GLOBAL WAR ON TERRORISM, all caps, but about the microcosm of Jerod Dennis and Spin Ghul. Renley wondered if the only difference between him and Spin Ghul was that he was born in the US and Spin Ghul was born in Saudi Arabia. Would he have turned out like Spin Ghul had he been forced to live that life?

He thought about it all when he sat down in the hotel with his work laptop and began writing his victim's statement. He decided he wanted to say something on behalf of his older brother. The court needed to at least understand who Jerod was.

On the morning of February 16, 2018, US marshals came to Spin Ghul's cell to escort him to Judge Cogan's courtroom for sentencing.

"This is not my court," Spin Ghul told them. "That is not my judge."

He refused to budge.

Marshals advised the court that they couldn't get Spin Ghul onto the bus to come to the court for sentencing without sedating him, and Judge Cogan didn't want to sedate him. So, as was now standard, Spin watched the proceedings on a TV monitor from a secure facility at the prison.

Was there anything the defendant wanted to say? the judge asked him.

"Fuck you, Judge," Spin Ghul said, extending both middle fingers toward the camera. "Fuck you."

"Well, I'm glad to see Mr. Hausa has learned a little bit about our language while he's been with us," Cogan quipped.

The hostility further underlined to the judge that Spin Ghul's behavior was entirely voluntary. He was showing the court his disdain not because he was insane, but because he hated America.

As always, Kellman, Stern, and Dratel were there to represent him when the proceedings began at 10 a.m.

Across the aisle, Matt Jacobs sat in the first seat for the prosecution. Shreve was there, having been teaching national security law at UVA during a sabbatical, so he sat second chair, next to Kaster, and then came Paciorek. Melody Wells was gone, having taken a job with the US attorney's office for the Northern District of Illinois in Chicago.

Bitkower was there, too. Having left the Justice Department as the Trump administration began, he was now in private practice and had come up to support the team and see the conclusion of the case that had started with a phone call almost seven years before. It was bittersweet to observe from behind the bar in the courtroom.

It was similar for Raushaunah Muhammad, who sat in the courtroom as well. She had tried to make it from DC, where she now worked, for the verdict, but the closing arguments and jury decisions went so quickly, she couldn't make it to Brooklyn in time. She made sure to be there now. She had opened the investigation into Spin Ghul and arrested him. She was certainly going to be there to see the sentencing.

There was housekeeping to be done before the victim statements, Judge Cogan noted, referring to disputes the defense and prosecution continued to have over the Presentence Investigation Report. One of them, for instance, being that the defense objected to the ridgeline incident being called a terrorist attack, pushing for it to be changed to something more like a military engagement.

"I'm going to deny that request," Cogan said.

The defense also argued that the defendant was a "mere soldier."

Cogan took issue with both of those words. "Putting aside the dispute over whether he should be considered a soldier, I don't think there was anything mere about this defendant. It seems to me he is at least middle management and maybe upper middle management in al Qaeda." Spin Ghul "had a meaningful relationship with senior terrorists within the organization" in a way privates do not have with generals, and he "served as an envoy between al Qaeda and other terrorist groups."

With that, Judge Cogan opened the proceedings. Matt Jacobs restated the basic facts of the case and noted the names of those killed in action: nineteen-year-old Private First Class Jerod Dennis of Antlers, Oklahoma, and twenty-four-year-old Airman First Class Raymond Losano of Del Rio, Texas.

"Significantly, Judge, the killing of servicemen in Afghanistan didn't satisfy this defendant," Jacobs reminded the court. "He had bigger ambitions. After the ambush in 2003, he went to al-Qaeda leaders and he told them he wanted to carry out what can only be described as mass murder terror attacks against Americans elsewhere in the world; specifically attacks like the embassy bombing in East Africa."

Moreover, Spin Ghul remained "firmly committed to jihad today," having stated in open court, "I'm a warrior and the war is not over, our terrorism is not over."

Renley suspected his remarks would be quite different from those of the servicemembers, so out of deference to their experiences, he chose to speak last. First was Command Sergeant Major Brian Severino, who'd flown up from Fort Bragg, North Carolina. Severino was about to retire after thirty years and was recovering from shoulder surgery. He seemed upset, even angry.

The thirty-year career soldier had deployed multiple times to Afghanistan and Iraq and had been exposed to combat often since April 25, 2003. But, he noted, that day had a profoundly horrible impact on him. Since then, he told the court, he had lost the ability to experience simple pleasures, stopped participating in family events, and "disassociated myself from my family, removed myself from my family it had such an impact on me."

He wanted the court to understand that all the Severinos suffered because of Spin Ghul. "It's just not myself that was suffering from this event," Severino said, "but my family suffered. Eventually, I lost my family, and I got divorced after nineteen years of marriage."

The roots of his pain were simple, he explained. "I feel like I was not there to take care of my duties and protect the soldiers. I let down Jerod and Ray Losano. I failed them and their families by not protecting them and bringing them home like I was supposed to as a leader." Parents looked to men like him and entrusted them with those they hold dearest, their children. "They trust us to take care of them and protect them, and on this day I failed, and it has weighed on me."

David Cyr spoke next, noting April would mark fifteen years since the deadly ambush, though it felt like yesterday. "Not one second, minute, hour or day goes by where the tragic events of that fateful morning is not at the forefront on my thoughts," he said.

He debated what to talk about today, Cyr said.

In these moments, Cyr said, he becomes overwhelmed by a guilt-ridden depression. Maybe, he observed, he should discuss how it wasn't until 2009 that his sisters Jenna and Nancy admitted they feared their own brother, so worried that his anger would cause him to lose his sanity and kill someone. Or his bilateral hearing loss from the grenades? Or his post-traumatic stress disorder? Ultimately Cyr wanted Spin Ghul to know that he found the strength and courage to seek professional counseling four years before, characteristic of the strength he had because "no matter what atrocity you commit against me, I am, and forever will be, a United States Army soldier at heart, mind, body, and soul, and you cannot defeat that."

He would continue his fight, Cyr said. "It is my mission to live as long as it takes to be there for my family, my former comrades, my brothers in arms, and myself to see your isolation from society for the rest of your life."

Perhaps Spin Ghul thought he had won a moral victory of some sort, but, Cyr said, "today you will forever endure the loss of not successfully taking my life. And I stand here in victory over you, and you will never take away from me my will to fight, live, and the love I have for my brothers and my country."

Renley was nervous as he stepped to the front of the courtroom. But as the moment drew close, he began to feel a profound sense of peace. He sensed Jerod was there with him.

"In July of 1987, Jerod Rhoton Dennis became a leader," Renley told the court. Because that was the moment that Renley was born and three-year-old Jerod Dennis became his big brother. "Jerod would translate his new brother's cries and grunts for the adults so they can warm the milk and change the diaper." His older brother gave him lessons in basketball and fishing and showered him with the gift of love and laughter.

Private Jerod Rhoton Dennis (1983–2003)

Renley then addressed Spin Ghul.

At some point before April 25, 2003, Spin Ghul obviously "felt the pain of the world, a pain we've all encountered; loss of something or someone, and you chose to react to that pain with anger and rage." An anger and rage that deprived the world of Jerod Dennis.

"Since that day, I have not stopped looking for him everywhere I go and in every face I encounter," Renley said of his older brother "since those first hellish moments in this new reality. I have every right to hate you, to curse you. I have every right to be angry, to use my tongue like a dagger in an attempt to get even, and no one would blame me."

Channeling Antoine Leiris, Renley told Spin Ghul: "You, your anger, your rage, your malicious intent, your weapon of my hero's destruction, your guns, your violence, your bullets, your tools of harm, all of that is just background noise to the true tragedy here. Jerod's absence. Our loss."

But "Jerod lives on more than ever," Renley said. "My sister, my mother, and father, my family and friends see him in me and I see him in them. It is in our lives you will see Jerod's legacy of love, laughter, and caring." That legacy, Renley asserted, lives on, stronger than Spin Ghul's few seconds of destroying it.

"I will not join you in your cyclical hatred," Renley said. "I will not give in to your systemic terrorism with hatred and anger. You may have caused my pain, but Jerod caused my forgiveness. Because of Jerod, I say to you that I hold no ill will towards you.

"Jerod is only concerned with those he loves now and I know that. So I will do what I have done since July of 1987: follow his lead. You and your few seconds are not my concern. My family, friends, Jerod's memory and legacy are. Those are the people and things that carry me forward. Everywhere I am present, there will always be at least two, my brother and me. As for you, I hope you let go of your anger and rage and find peace in your life."

Renley Dennis folded up his paper, which Melody Wells had kindly printed out for him, and walked back to his seat, between his mother on his left and sister on his right. Jane Nelson patted his leg, grabbed his hand, and squeezed.

"I'm very proud of you," she whispered.

Jillian leaned over and gave him a kiss.

Judge Cogan, affected by Renley's testimony, asked for a brief recess. It was one of the most powerful victim's statements that Judge Cogan had ever heard. To make sure he didn't demonstrate any emotion from the bench—trials were not about judges, he felt deeply—he adjourned to his chambers to collect his thoughts and balance all the factors dispassionately, away from the spotlight.

When he returned to the courtroom, he sentenced Spin Ghul to life in prison.

AFTERWORD

JUSTICE IN THE WAR ON TERROR

Two hours and twenty minutes south of Denver, off of Highway 67, sits the immense correctional compound USP Florence ADMAX, the United States Penitentiary Florence Administrative Maximum Facility. The Florence Supermax, as it's more commonly known, is home to fewer than four hundred prisoners. They are the worst of the worst. Judge Cogan's sentence of life in prison essentially means Spin Ghul will live here until his death.

He's in appropriate company. If you've heard of a notorious murderer from the modern era, the odds are he has been through here.

El Chapo. Timothy McVeigh. Ted Kaczynski, until shortly before his death in 2023.

The Bureau of Prisons discloses very little about the Florence Supermax, but a *San Francisco Chronicle* story from 1998 describes new prisoners spending virtually all their time in their twelve-foot-by-seven-foot cells, with concrete beds and desks, a sink and a toilet. A spokesman for Florence

Supermax says prisoners also have televisions in addition to a shared dining room and recreation yard.

Spin Ghul, like every inmate, is responsible for making his bed daily, in accordance with posted regulations, and for keeping his cell floor clean. Florence Supermax gives him his clothes—khaki pants and khaki shirt—as well as toothbrush and toothpaste, soap, comb, and razor. Every day, Florence Supermax conducts at least five official inmate counts, so Spin Ghul must stand by his bed at various points throughout the day.

This is now Spin Ghul's home. He is with many others from al Qaeda, including Abu Hamza al-Masri, the former radical cleric from the Finsbury Park Mosque in the UK, convicted on eleven terrorism-related counts including a deadly 1998 hostage-taking in Yemen, sending a follower to train and fight in Afghanistan in 2000, and trying to set up a terrorist training camp in Oregon.

At Florence Supermax are domestic terrorists you may have heard of by name or description, including the so-called twentieth 9/11 hijacker Zacarias Moussaoui, would-be shoe-bomber Richard Reid, attempted underwear bomber Umar Abdulmutallab, attempted Times Square bomber Faisal Shahzad, Boston Marathon bomber Dzhokhar Tsarnaev, and 2017 New York City truck attacker Sayfullo Saipov.

There are those whose crimes preceded those of Spin Ghul, 1993 World Trade Center bombing conspirators Ramzi Yousef and Mahmud Abouhalima, 1998 US embassy bombings conspirator (and Dratel client) Wadih El-Hage, millennial bomber Ahmed Ressam.

And there are those terrorists of the more homegrown variety: McVeigh's coconspirator Terry Nichols and the 1996 Olympics bomber, Eric Rudolph.

But Spin Ghul is the only one who was tried and convicted for killing US soldiers on the battlefield overseas. His case stands as unique not only at the Florence Supermax but also in modern American history.

For Dave Bitkower and Shreve Ariail, now both in private practice at white-shoe law firms, the Spin Ghul case stands as the pinnacle of their prosecutorial careers. For both men the sentencing was momentous, and not just because it brought to a close seven years of work. Sentencings are their own kind of events, somber and more formal, with the presence of law enforcement supervisors, victims, and witnesses who may not have been there throughout the trial.

Bitkower reflected on that moment not just as the culmination of years of effort, but with amazement. After that 2011 phone call with Ari Mahairas and his first conversation with Shreve, Bitkower knew they'd have to draw an inside straight to get Spin Ghul locked up. They would have to secure immediate assistance from the Italians; have a successful Mirandized interview of a hardened al Qaeda terrorist in a Sicilian prison; figure out just whom he had killed in Afghanistan almost a decade prior; locate sufficient admissible corroborating evidence to satisfy the strictest evidentiary standard in the law; enlist the full support of the US government during a period when skepticism about the use of criminal courts against terrorists was on the rise; and then somehow make all that work before a judge and jury.

And they pulled it off. It was a remarkable investigation, a shining example of law enforcement and American jurisprudence. But was it a template for how terrorists could be prosecuted in criminal court? Surely not every prosecutor will draw an inside straight every time he steps up to the table.

For his part, Judge Cogan was skeptical. Not of Spin Ghul's guilt—in his sentencing, Cogan called Spin Ghul "a person of murderous zeal"—but of the forum for the trial. Cogan never really understood why the case of Spin Ghul had been brought in a civilian court. The judge surely understood the prosecution in US criminal court of foreign terrorists who killed Americans in the US, or even foreign terrorists who killed American civilians abroad—in 2024 he was presiding over the prosecution of a Mauritanian national known as Ibrahim Idress for his role in the November 20, 2015, attack on a Radisson hotel in Mali, where US citizen Anita Ashok Datar was one of twenty innocents killed.

But the battlefield setting for this case always struck him as odd. It seemed like the government was bringing the case to demonstrate how great the US legal system was, as opposed to the trial being a search for truth. After all, they knew the truth. The evidence was overwhelming, and they even had the defendant's confession. The attack on the US servicemembers was the kind of thing that happens in war, and it troubled him for the government to be treating the matter as if it were a drug conspiracy, sending field investigators to track down the fingerprints found on a Quran in Afghanistan.

He understood the larger political context—the status of the military commissions was in disarray, and President Obama had blocked any new detainees from being sent to Gitmo. But it seemed to him that they could have just held Spin Ghul somewhere, in some detention center, until there was a process through which they could proceed, quietly and militarily, with someone who quite obviously was an enemy combatant.

"It just felt like a show trial," the judge told me as I finished writing this book almost six years after the sentencing. "I have a hard time believing there wasn't something else that could have been done."

These officials were, after all, in charge of the US government. And the standards that President Obama had established that he insisted be followed were, after all, the ones that he had established. Why didn't Obama just modify the rules?

He didn't—but then again, despite campaigning to "load [Guantánamo Bay] up with some bad dudes" and signing an executive order in 2018 to keep the detainee center open, President Trump never sent any new terrorist detainees there.

In the meantime, the criminal civilian courts and military commissions have proceeded in parallel worlds. In June 2022, Spin Ghul's former commander in Pakistan, Abd al-Hadi al-Iraqi, a.k.a. "Hadi," in his early sixties, pleaded guilty to war crimes, including attacks that resulted in the 2003–4 deaths of seventeen US and coalition force in Afghanistan. In 2024, a military jury sentenced him to thirty years in prison, but Hadi, now severely disabled with a spinal condition, should be released in 2032 at the latest. "As the commander I take responsibility for what my men did," Hadi told the military commission. "I want you to know I do not have any hate in my heart for anyone. I thought I was doing right. I wasn't. I am sorry."

Whatever one thinks of the debate over trying accused terrorists in military commissions instead of federal criminal courts, two facts are clear. One: the Italians would not have allowed the extradition of Spin Ghul to anything but the US criminal court system. And two: the criminal courts have proven far more efficient. As of the end of 2024, only two cases of suspected terrorists have gone to trial in military commissions, and one of those cases was overturned. There have been nine plea deals. In criminal courts, on the other hand, more than six hundred terrorists have been prosecuted, the overwhelming majority convicted.

It's a perspective reiterated to Shreve after he became deputy general counsel for the CIA, where he was put in charge of the CIA attorneys handling the work of the military commissions. Ten years after he'd left Obama's Guantánamo task force, nothing had changed. The cases were largely stuck at a standstill, the prosecutors rehashing the same arguments from a decade before. Either way, Gold Star family members of those killed in Hadi's attacks were grateful for the continued effort to bring these men to justice via the military commission, though the conviction and sentencing didn't get much news coverage. Indeed,

Hadi's story in 2024 may be most striking in how anachronistic many details of the case may seem. Hadi guided the courtroom through a 360-degree virtual tour of the windowless, six-foot-square, closet-like location where he was held for three months, Quiet Room 4, in a now-shuttered CIA black site in Turkey.

The CIA's black site program is officially over, but the West's fight against terrorism continues. In the early morning of January 1, 2025, a Houston-born US Army veteran named Shamsud-Din Jabbar drove a rented Ford F-150 Lightning into a crowd in New Orleans, exited the vehicle and fired a .308 rifle and Glock handgun into the crowd, killing fourteen innocent people and wounding almost sixty, before police killed him. A flag for the Islamic State was found in the truck. It won't be the last such attack.

Human rights activists argue that Obama's attempt to use criminal courts to try terrorists such as Spin Ghul, and his opposition to the war in Iraq, were mere fig leaves. That these public acts were used to obscure an otherwise consistently militaristic approach to the war on terror, complete with drone strikes that killed innocent civilians and the extrajudicial killing of terrorists including Americans (perhaps most notably New Mexico–born cleric Anwar al-Awlaki, a leader of al Qaeda in the Arabian Peninsula killed by a US drone in 2011). As Tom Junod wrote in 2012, before Obama, "no president has ever waged war by killing enemies one by one, targeting them individually for execution, wherever they are." Now it is standard practice, and the American public has largely seemed to accept what Severino told his men in 2003: we kill them over there so we don't have to kill them over here.

While the differences between Bush and Obama in how to best prosecute the war on terror may have seemed stark at the time, since then US government policy seems to have landed in something of a consensus gray area where Gitmo remains open though it is taking no new terrorist detainees, accused terrorists are tried in both military commissions and criminal courts, though mostly the latter, and the US lethally targets alleged terrorists in many places around the world. Spin Ghul's case was a remarkable piece of law enforcement, but it is also a rarity—one that few in today's national security apparatus and law enforcement community even know about, much less hold up as an example of how these cases can and should be done.

That said, as I finished up this book, there were signs that Spin Ghul's case could serve as a template, even unknowingly.

Referring to the suicide bombing at Abbey Gate in Kabul, Afghanistan, that killed thirteen US servicemembers and more than 150 Afghans, during the chaotic 2021 withdrawal, President Trump, newly reelected, told a joint session of Congress in March 2025 that he was "pleased to announce that we have just apprehended the top terrorist responsible for that atrocity."

Mohammad Sharifullah, known as "Jafar," a member of ISIS-Khorasan, was arrested by the Pakistani Intelligence Service with information provided by the CIA and turned over to the US.

On March 2, 2025, Jafar was interviewed by FBI agents, read his Miranda rights, and ended up before a judge in the Eastern District of Virginia. On CNN on March 12, I asked Sebastian Gorka, the senior director for counterterrorism on the White House's National Security Council, if this would be the new standard—prosecuting in US criminal courts foreign terrorists who commit attacks on US servicemembers in war zones. It was rare—and had only been done once before, with Spin Ghul.

"This man has confessed to us, to our FBI flight team, and the Pakistanis to his involvement as a planner in more than thirty terrorist events," Gorka said. "And how they pay, how they will see justice, that depends upon where they are, what we share with our partners and allies, and the incredible work of our tier one assets and our intelligence community."

The template is worth considering, of course. And though he would surely hate it, this precedent may be Spin Ghul's most lasting legacy.

Because for the families of Jerod Dennis and Ray Losano and the men and women who served with them, the investigation and prosecution of this killer were a comfort, a sign that the US government who sent our brave servicemembers to war did, indeed, care about them. In that act of love, justice found a home.

ACKNOWLEDGMENTS AND SOURCES

The idea for this book began at a paintball birthday party for my son Jack. One of the dads there told me that he knew Dave Roller, a US veteran about whom I wrote in *The Outpost*. Making small talk, I remarked how difficult it was to write the book because the US military is either so bad at keeping records or so reluctant to share them. "Tell me about it," he said, launching into a story that began on the deck of an Italian cruise ship during the Arab Spring in 2011. That man was Dave Bitkower. Soon I was taking him and Shreve to lunch. Then Matt Jacobs was emailing me a Google Drive containing transcripts and evidence from the trial. And it went on from there. I could not have written this book without the help and participation of Jerod Dennis's family, and Ray Losano's, and the Slayers, Raushaunah and Bert and Melody and on and on. I am most appreciative of the help by all the servicemembers who served honorably in Afghanistan and upon whom I imposed by asking for their memories of the most painful day of their lives. Thank you to all those who helped me bring this fascinating history to the page. And thank you for everything all of you do—from the servicemembers to their families, from the defense attorneys to the prosecutors to the judges. I am in immense awe of the work you all do to keep us safe and to safeguard our ideals.

306 ACKNOWLEDGMENTS AND SOURCES

I cannot thank enough Sean deLone with Atria at Simon & Schuster, whose skilled and tough editing I so admire. It is not welcome news when an editor sends back a chapter and tells you to rewrite the whole thing—but it is so vital and exactly what I need. Many thanks and here's to many more projects together. Thank you to Joanna Pinsker, David Brown, Erin Kirby, and the rest of the team at Atria. Many thanks to my incredibly talented writer friend Matt Klam for great suggestions; I am in great debt to fact-checker Lucie Kroening for her excellence and diligence. Thanks to formed DoD officer Matthew Waxman for giving it a read.

My literary agent is Sloan Harris and a more supportive and constructive one a writer couldn't find. And to Taylor Damron, Will Watkins, and Colin Graham at CAA: Thank you!

Lastly, of course, a big thanks to my wife Jennifer, daughter Alice, and son Jack, whose patience, love, laughter, and support I am so lucky to have.

This book is the result of more than three years of work and dozens of interviews. Most of the people mentioned in the book participated in the book. All of the information came from court documents, transcripts, and those interviews, with the exceptions of the citations below:

CHAPTER 1

3 *"... blow themselves up on the subway's 1, 2, and 3 trains"*: John Marzulli, "Zazi, pals planned rush-hour attack on two busiest subway stations," *New York Daily News*, April 12, 2010.

CHAPTER 2

10 footnote *"'Jihad' literally means striving"*: "What is the truth about American Muslims: Questions and Answers," Interfaith Alliance, Religious Freedom Education Project of the First Amendment Center, October 2012.

CHAPTER 3

16 *"thirteen drums of Semtex and TNT"*: Rory Carroll, "Freed Mafia Grass a Marked Man," *The Guardian*, March 14, 2002.

CHAPTER 9

65 *"one former State Department lawyer called it 'the legal equivalent of outer space'"*: Michael Isikoff, "The Gitmo Fallout," *Newsweek*, July 16, 2006.

67 *"'Extraordinary rendition,' which the CIA began during the Clinton administration"*: Jane Mayer, "Outsourcing Torture," *New Yorker*, February 6, 2005.

72 *"suddenly skyrocketed to a billion dollars"*: *New York Daily News* editorial, "Get the Hell Out of Here," January 29, 2010.

72 *"two-tiered security perimeter"*: "Cops Outline Double Security Plan for KSM Trial: NYPD describes perimeter for Sept. 11 case," Associated Press, January 20, 2010.

72 *"New York Democratic senator Chuck Schumer, he of the 2009 local TV headline 'Schumer Not Afraid of Gitmo Goons,'"*: Scott Ross, "Schumer Not Afraid of Gitmo Goons," NBC 4 New York, May 22, 2009.

73 *"he declared it 'obvious'"*: Scott Shane and Benjamin Weiser, "U.S. Drops Plan for a 9/11 Trial in New York City," *New York Times*, January 29, 2010.

74 *"'Oh, don't pay any attention to what I say on the Senate floor. It doesn't mean anything. It's just politics.'"*: John Brennan, *Undaunted: My Fight Against America's Enemies, at Home and Abroad* (Celadon Books, 2020).

CHAPTER 11

87 *"Trahan went to the TOC and learned this report was quite different. John's intel came from a CIA predator drone."*: Drone information

308 ACKNOWLEDGMENTS AND SOURCES

from Craig Whitlock, *The Afghanistan Papers: A Secret History of the War* (Simon & Schuster, 2021).

112 *"Mail bombs were sent to the director of the state tax collection agency . . . "*: Francesco Marone, "A Profile of the Informal Anarchist Federation in Italy," *CTC Sentinel* 7, no. 3 (March 2014).

CHAPTER 14

117 *"Khan knew quite a bit about al Qaeda facilities . . ."*: Senate Select Committee on Intelligence, *Committee Study on the Central Intelligence Agency's Enhanced Interrogation Program*, Declassified version, December 3, 2014.

118 *"Hadi was held in a CIA black site for 170 days, then transferred to Gitmo in April 2007."*: Information about Khan and Hadi from the Senate Select Committee on Intelligence *Committee Study of the Central Intelligence Agency's Detention and Interrogation Program*, Declassified version, December 3, 2014.

119 *"The point, the colonel argued, was that these documents were unfailingly true—'terrorists, criminal, and other adversaries never expected their material to be captured.'"*: Colonel Joseph M. Cox, "DOMEX: The Birth of a New Intelligence Discipline," *Military Intelligence Professional Bulletin* (April–June 2010), https://irp.fas.org/agency/army/mipb/2010_02.pdf.

119 *"Documents recovered from a Japanese plane shot down during the 1941 attack on Pearl Harbor ultimately helped cryptographers break the Imperial Navy operational codes."*: Dr. Greg Bradsher, "The Capture and Exploitation of Japanese Records during World War II," National Archives blog *The Text Message*, October 21, 2021.

120 *"More than three hundred Vietnamese and Americans were trusted with analyzing, translating, and logging photographs, documents, letters, and diaries."*: Texas Tech University, Vietnam Center and Sam

Johnson Vietnam Archive; taken from University of Massachusetts at Boston Joseph P. Healey Library: Combined Document Exploitation Center, Saigon: Captured documents from the Vietnam War, 1966-1973

CHAPTER 17

143 *"Ashafa helped recruit and sponsor"*: "Boko Haram: How We Caught Nigerian Al Qaeda Leader – SSS," *Vanguard*, April 4, 2012.

144 *"al Qaeda members in Pakistan gave him $1,500"*: "Nigeria Wants Secret Trial for al Qaeda Suspect," Reuters, August 9, 2007.

CHAPTER 21

168 *"They sang the hymn 'This Is Holy Ground.'"*: Raymond Bonner, "A NATION CHALLENGED: ISLAMABAD; 2 Americans Killed in Attack on Pakistan Church," *New York Times*, March 18, 2002.

168 *"This is holy ground/We're standing on holy ground"*: "This Is Holy Ground," copyright: 1982 Universal Music, Brentwood Benson Publishing (Admin. by Brentwood-Benson Music Publishing, Inc.), Birdwing Music (Admin. by Capitol CMG Publishing).

173 *"'You're not Muslims!' Abu Zubaydah yelled at his captors."*: Tim McGirk, "Anatomy of a Raid," *Time* magazine, April 8, 2002.

178 *"At the Lahore hospital, a Pakistani doctor took one look at Abu Zubaydah and shook his head pessimistically at Kiriakou, the CIA agent, who met him there."*: John Kiriakou and Michael Ruby, *Reluctant Spy: My Secret Life in the CIA's War on Terror* (Bantam Books, 2010).

CHAPTER 24

188 *"Mena saw five members"*: Tom Hays, "Informant's Pleas Trigger Debate," Associated Press, October 3, 2002.

195 *"A document titled 'The Volume of Crime Scene Investigation—Burglary,' traced to the Qin Dynasty, between 221 and 206 BC, described the first known use of fingerprints as evidence."*: The Fingerprint Sourcebook, US Department of Justice and National Institute of Justice, 2012.

198 *"There was a less destructive chemical, shorthanded as DFO."*: 1,8-Diazafluoren-9-one. Madison Carlin et al., "Quantifying DNA loss in laboratory-created latent prints due to fingerprint processing," *Forensic Science International*, vol. 344, March 2023.

CHAPTER 25

203 *"The modern insanity defense dates back to the afternoon of Friday, January 20, 1843, in the heart of London."*: Court transcripts, Proceedings of the Old Bailey, https://www.oldbaileyonline.org/record/t18430227-874?text=M%27Naughten.

204 *"insanity defenses are extremely rare—raised in fewer than 1 percent of court cases and successfully so only about 25 percent of the time"*: Michael L. Perlin, "The Insanity Defense: Nine Myths That Will Not Go Away," New York Law School, 2017.

CHAPTER 27

218 *"In August 2011, at the United Nations compound in Abuja, a vehicle bomb attack killed twenty-three people, including eleven UN employees, and injured more than eighty."*: Daniel Williams and Eric Guttschuss, et al., "Nigeria: Boko Haram Attacks Likely Crimes Against Humanity," Human Rights Watch, October 11, 2012.

CHAPTER 28

228 *"'Do they not know we have a sentencing in two weeks? We are going to get life now.'"*: Recorded interview with Joshua L. Dratel con-

ducted by Myron A. Farber on March 29, March 31, and April 4, 2011, The Rule of Law Oral History Project, Columbia Center for Oral History, Columbia University, 2011.

CHAPTER 30

242 *"Helms would be relieved from protecting sources and directions given to him, even by a President, if forced to defend himself in a public trial."*: Rowland Evans and Robert Novak, "Prosecuting Richard Helms?" Field Enterprises, retrieved from *Abilene Reporter-News*, Sunday, August 21, 1977.

242 *"Helms escaped by pleading no contest to two misdemeanor charges of giving incomplete information to Congress."*: Nancy Lewis, "'Greymail' Dilemma Hampers Prosecution in Spy Case," Cox Newspapers, retrieved from *Dayton Daily News*, November 6, 1978.

242 *"'with access to military or technological secrets have a broad de facto immunity from prosecution for a variety of crimes.'"*: Greymail Legislation: Hearings Before the Subcommittee on Legislation of the House Permanent Select Committee on Intelligence, 96th Cong., 1st Sess. 4-6 (1979) (statement of Assistant Attorney General Philip Heymann).

CHAPTER 31

251 *"Jacobs started by asking Ghannam about a previous case in which he'd testified . . . "*: Joseph Brean, "Train Plotter Was 'Drug Addicted': Testimony," *National Post*, July 14, 2015.

251 *"'This is an individual who is quite broken, psychologically,' Ghannam told the Canadian court."*: Stephen Engelberg, "Greater Access to Terrorism Data Is Sought for Immigration Agency," *New York Times*, February 6, 1987.

255 Ben Wofford, "The Forgotten Government Plan to Round Up

Muslims," *Politico Magazine*, August 19, 2016; Neil MacFarquhar, "U.S., Stymied 21 Years, Drops Bid to Deport 2 Palestinians," *New York Times*, November 1, 2007.

255 "*Part of the internal memo titled 'Alien Terrorists and Undesirables: A Contingency Plan . . . '*": Ibid.

CHAPTER 33

266 "*The strategy of prosecuting terrorists apprehended abroad*": Andrew McCabe, *The Threat: How the FBI Protects America in the Age of Terror and Trump* (St. Martin's Press, 2019).

266 "*Abu Khaybar—a Sudanese citizen being held by the UAE*": Adam Goldman and Matt Apuzzo, "Administration Delays Prosecuting Qaeda Suspect Once Seen as Candidate for Guantanamo," *New York Times*, January 9, 2018.

AFTERWORD

295 "*A spokesman for Florence Supermax says prisoners also have televisions in addition to a shared dining room and recreation yard.*": Michael Taylor, "The Last Worst Place," *San Francisco Chronicle*, December 28, 1998.

296 "*Every day, Florence Supermax conducts at least five official inmate counts, so Spin Ghul must stand by his bed at various points throughout the day.*": Admission and Orientation Handbook, ADX FLORENCE, COLORADO, A. Ciolli, Complex Warden, updated October 2022.

299 "'*I want you to know I do not have any hate in my heart for anyone. I thought I was doing right. I wasn't. I am sorry.*'": Carol Rosenberg, "Qaeda Commander at Guantánamo Bay Is Sentenced for War Crimes," *New York Times*, June 20, 2024.

299 "*As of the end of 2024,*": Karen J. Greenberg, "The Uncertain Fate of Guantánamo Under Trump: More than 23 years after the 9/11

attacks, here we are in the very same place we've been for endless years—on pause," *The Nation*, January 29, 2025; and interview with Greenberg.

299 *"Hadi guided the courtroom through a 360-degree virtual tour of the windowless, six-foot-square, closet-like location where he was held for three months, Quiet Room 4, in a now-shuttered CIA black site in Turkey."*: Carol Rosenberg, "War Crimes Hearing Gives Public Virtual Look Inside a Secret C.I.A. Prison," *New York Times*, June 17, 2024.

302 *"no president has ever waged war..."*: Tom Junod, "The Lethal Presidency of Barack Obama, *Esquire*, August, 2012.

INDEX

A

Abbey Gate, suicide bombing at, 301
Abdulmutallab, Umar Farouk, 69, 137
Abebe, Hussein, 71
Abidin Muhammad Husayna, Zayn al-, 145
Abouhalima, Mahmud, 296
Abu, mar, 67
Abuja, Nigeria, 143
   Bitkower heading to, 216–17
   flying to, 215–16
   foreign evidence from, 222–24
   meeting with Nigerian government, 218–21
   reviewing Spin Ghul confession before, 217–18
activist, defining, 253–54. *See also* Ghannam, Jess
Adi Ghar Mountains, 49–50
Afghanistan. *See* ambush (on Firebase Shkin); Dennis, Jerod; Losano, Ray
   ambush on Firebase Shkin in, 86–92
   deaths in, 103–11
   Salt Pit in, 226
   Slayers in, 48–55
   wounded soldiers in, 93–102
Afghanistan-Pakistan border, attack on, 32–38

Afghanistan War, 2–3
Agrigento, Italy, trial in
   beginning of proceedings, 20–21
   bringing Spin Ghul into courtroom, 19–20
   debating credibility of story, 32–38
   Italian perception of war in Iraq, 17–19
   Miranda rights, 24–25
   overview, 15–17
   second round of questioning following trial, 77–85
   translation issues, 23–24
   treating Spin Ghul with respect, 21–22
AK-47 (gun), 37, 97, 164, 174
Al Anbar Province, Iraq, 125
ALAT. *See* assistant legal attaché
al-Dujail, Shiite town, 117
al Farouq, training camp, 28–30
"Alien Terrorists and Undesirables: A Contingency Plan," 255
al Qaeda, 114, 217, 281, 290. *See also* Spin Ghul
   and Abu Zubaydah arrest, 170–80
   assessing Spin Ghul role in web of, 272
   beginning retaliation against, 31

316 INDEX

al Qaeda *(cont.)*
  and combatant immunity, 237–40
  hierarchy of, 33
  Kellman meeting potential solider from, 181–86
  modern insanity defense, 203–5
  post-9/11 activity of, 1–2
  ruling on, 263–64
  ruling on terrorist analysis, 259–61
al Qaeda in the Islamic Maghreb (AQIM), 143
al-Shabaab, attack in Africa by, 79
ambush (on Firebase Shkin).
    See Dennis, x; Losano, x
  blood loss during, 96
  calling artillery guys, 100–101
  casualty collection point, 98–99, 103–4
  death of Jerrod Dennis, 107–10
  describing, 273–76
  finding Jerrod Dennis, 104–7
  getting off patrol, 94
  Golden Hour, 99–100
  medic arrival, 93–94
  preparing indirect fire mission, 96–97
  providing cover fire, 101–2
  sharing painful memories of, 271–72
  Simmons focusing on Brown, 95–96
  start of, 86–92
  tactical site exploitation, 110–11
  taking cover, 95
  ten years to day after, 277
  victim witnesses, 124–28
American Airlines Flight 11.
    See September 11, 2001
Angoor Ada, Pakistan, 31, 34, 52, 117–18, 131, 141, 273, 276.
    See also ambush (on Firebase Shkin)
Angor Ada. *See* Afghanistan-Pakistan border, attack on
Antlers, Oklahoma. *See* Dennis, Jerod

Apaches, 37, 48, 88, 274
AQIM. *See* al Qaeda in the Islamic Maghreb
Arab Spring, 6–7
Arab Stories: Bay Area, 253–54
Arab Talk, 254
Ariail, Shreve, 4–5, 113, 134, 206, 265, 274
  at Agrigento, Italy, trial of Spin Ghul, 15–25
  and Bitkower departure, 207–9
  building case, 123–32
  debating credibility of story, 32–38
  forming new team, 112–22
  and Guantanamo Bay, 65–76
  and Hodgson findings, 130–32
  indictment submission, 147–55
  and lack of closing statement, 281–84
  meeting Hodgson, 115–18
  meeting with Dennis family, 231–33
  meeting with Nigerian government, 218–21
  opening arguments, 268–69
  pinnacle of career of, 297–302
  playing catch-up, 6–14
  and proffer process, 187–92
  promotion of, 210
  reviewing Spin Ghul confession, 217
  second round of questioning, 77–85
  United States of America versus John Doe, The, 184–86
  working with Hamdani, 138–40
Armed Forces Day, 124
Ashafa, Mohammed, 221
  arrest of, 144–45
  as final piece of case, 279
  foreign evidence on, 217–24
  meeting, 143–44
assistant legal attaché (ALAT), 220
ASVAB, test, 40–41
Australi, Abu Hamza al-, 276
Australi, Khalid Waleed Hamza al-, 131

Awlaki, Anwar al-, 133, 300
Ayotte, Kelly, 73, 75

B

Baghdad International Airport, 116
Bagley, Nicole, 196–99, 277
Baltimore Sun, 113
Batacla, terrorist attack at, 285–88
Battisti, Gugleimo, 269–70
Belcastro, Victor, 53, 89, 93
Berlusconi, Silvio, 112
Bharara, Preet, 71
Biden, Joe, 157
"Bin Ladin Determined to Strike in US" (Presidential Daily Brief), 171
Bitkower, Dave, 113, 122, 134, 274
   at Agrigento, Italy, trial of Spin Ghul, 15–25
   building case, 123–32
   clerking for Leonard Sand, 150–51
   debating credibility of story, 32–38
   departure from Spin Ghul case, 207–9
   forming new team, 112–22
   and Guantanamo Bay, 65–76
   hearing about Spin Ghul for first time, 1–5
   and Hodgson findings, 130–32
   indictment submission, 147–55
   meeting Hodgson, 115–18
   in new role at DOJ, 216–17
   pinnacle of career of, 297–302
   playing catch-up, 6–14
   primary experiences prosecuting and investigating terrorists, 2–3
   and proffer process, 187–92
   second round of questioning, 77–85
   and sentencing of Spin Ghul, 288–90
   speaking with Trahan, 125–26
   telling Ariail about case, 4–5
   United States of America versus John Doe, The, 184–86
   working with Hamdani, 138–40

Blackstone, William, 183
Blackwell, Lee Marvin, 271
   at Firebase Shkin ambush, 90–98, 274
   recalling Ray Losano, 62–64
Bloomberg, Michael, 72
Blue Devils, 54
Boko Haram, 80, 114, 221
Breaking Bad, 214
Breivik, Anders, 79–80
Brennan, John, 74–75, 152
Breuer, Lanny, 208
Brown, Michiru, 89–90, 211
Bureau of Prisons, 160, 295–96
Burlingame, Debra, 72
Bush, George W., 67, 124–25, 134, 207
   and definition of "activist," 254–55
   differences between Obama and, 300–301
   Guantanamo Bay announcement, 234–36
   pushing back against, 135–36

C

Caddyshack (film), 178
Camacho, Eddie, 54–55, 87, 94, 275
   during Firebase Shkin ambush, 95–99, 101–2, 104
   life after Firebase Shkin ambush, 126–29
   speaking with, 126–29
Camp al-Farouq, 271
Camp Cropper, 116–17
Camp Nine. *See* Maskar 9 (camp)
captured enemy document (CED), 120
Carlson, William "Chief," 121
Carter, Jimmy, 242
CED. *See* captured enemy document
Central Intelligence Agency (CIA), 2, 24, 81, 109
   abducting Hassan Mustafa Osama Nasr, 18–19, 67
   agents, 19, 67, 178

318 INDEX

Central Intelligence Agency (CIA) *(cont.)*
  black site program of, 67, 71, 118, 300
  contractors, 116, 121, 192
  and Ghailani trial, 70–73
  operatives, 152, 177, 201
  presence at Firebase Shkin, 86–87
  taking Abu Zubaydah into custody, 176–80
Checo, Steven, 84, 120–21
Cheney, Dick, 70–71
Cheney, Liz, 72
cherry-picking, 249, 253
Choctaw Nation Reservation.
  See Dennis, Jerod
church bombing, 167–69
CIA. *See* Central Intelligence Agency
CIPA. *See* Classified Information Procedures Act
Civil War, 119
Clarke, Richard, 46
Classified Information Procedures Act (CIPA), 241–43, 249
Clayton, Mikael, 149
Clinton, Bill, 152
Cogan, Brian, 207, 210, 227
  at competency hearing, 250–58
  delivering ruling on competency, 259–61
  hearing about ambush on Firebase Shkin, 273–76
  and lack of closing statement, 281–84
  and sentencing of Spin Ghul, 288–94
  skepticism of, 297–98
combatant immunity, 237–40
Combat Studies Institute, 125
Combined Document Exploitation Center, 119–20
competency, hearing on ruling, 259–61
competency, hearing on.
  See Jacobs, Matt
counter-terrorism detectives, becoming, 1–5. *See also* Ariail, Shreve; Bitkower, Dave
credibility, debating, 32–38
Cropo, Chad, 53
Crossing Jordan. See Bagley, Nicol
cultural competence, lack of, 257
Cyr, David, 271, 290–92
Cyr, David, Jr., 94

D

Datar, Anita Ashok, 298
DeMier, Richard, 256, 260
Dennis, Jane, 39, 40–41, 44–45, 233, 268, 279, 287, 294
Dennis, Jerod, 61, 94, 121–22, 122, 209, 211, 239, 249, 271, 281, 290, 302
  and ambush on Firebase Shkin, 86–92
  autopsy information of, 130
  bringing up in interviews, 129–30
  and building bombing fiasco, 59–64
  as class clown at Firebase Shkin, 56–58
  death of, 107–10
  delivering justice to, 163–66
  early life of, 39–40
  finding, 104–7
  getting shot during, 101–2
  heading to Afghanistan, 46–47
  joining Army, 40–41
  justice for, 283–84
  meeting with family of, 231–33
  rebellion of, 40
  testimony about, 273–76
  and time with Slayers, 48–55
  training for Army, 41–43
  transformation of, 44–46
  urinalysis, 46
  worsening behavior of, 40
Dennis, Jill, 44
Dennis, Renley, 286–88
  addressing Spin Ghul, 292–94
  choosing to speak last, 290–92

Deputies' Committee, 139
DFO, chemical, 198
diamond rattlesnake, sacredness of, 58
Diario–La Prensa, El, 188
Direct Participants in Hostilities, 234
document and media exploitation (DOMEX), 119–21
Doe, John. *See* Spin Ghul
Doherty, Glen, 192
Dolan, Mike, 88
DOMEX, 130–32
DOMEX. *See* document and media exploitation
Donogue, Rich, 148
Dratel, Joshua, 228–30, 242
   opening arguments, 268–69
   and Rae Jaser case, 252–53

E

82nd Airborne, 48, 54, 109, 125, 163–64. *See also* Operation Mongoose; Slayers
El Chapo, 295
Elphick, James, 89
Encyclopedias of Jihad. See *Mossouat al Jiha*
enemy combatants, torturing, 67
enhanced interrogation techniques, 67, 68, 179
   views on, 77–78
Evans, Rowland, 241–42
Excelsior, The, 16, 19, 211, 230, 262–63
   interrogation on, 8–14
Exploitation of Japanese Documents, The, 119
extraordinary rendition, 67

F

Falcone, Giovanni, 16
Faraj. *See* Libi, Abu Faraj al-
FBI. *See* Federal Bureau of Investigation
Federal Bureau of Investigation (FBI), 1–3, 22, 223
   agents, 66, 169, 176, 223, 272, 301
   fly team of, 157
   hostage rescue team of, 157
   interviewing Jafar, 301
   investigations, 170, 172, 175
   Joint Terrorism Task Force of, 15, 114, 130, 157, 162
   labs of, 197, 199, 277
   Latent Print Operations Unit at, 197
   latest tip from, 3–4
   legal attaché, 17, 21
   officials, 69, 128, 172
   and September 11, 2012, case, 192–93
   taking Abu Zubaydah into custody, 170–80
   West Africa team of, 9, 11, 114, 123, 144, 192, 247, 269
Few Good Men, A, 234, 236
Field of Empty Chairs, 232
fingerprints, examination of, 195–99
Firebase Shkin, 121, 130, 132, 209
   ambush on, 84–92
   and building bombing fiasco, 59–64
   confirming Spin Gul presence at, 123–23
   describing ambush on, 273–76
   rocket attack on, 63–64
   sharing painful memories of, 271–72
   Slayers time in, 52–55
   speaking with soldiers from, 161–66
   ten years to day after attack on, 277
   victim witnesses, 124–28
First Chechen War, 26
First Infantry in Vietnam. *See* Dennis, Jerod
504th Parachute Infantry Regiment, 48, 54, 163
Florence Supermax, 295–96
Fort Belvoir, 121
Fort Benning, 44–46, 127
Fort Bragg, 45–46, 127, 128, 290
Fort Gordon, 127
Fort Jackson, 127

Fort Meade, 167
Forward Operating Base Salerno, 100, 108
Frakt, David, 249, 263
   defending Gitmo detainees, 234–37
   familiarizing with Spin Ghul case, 237–40
Franco, Dave, 272–73
   arriving in Pakistan, 169
   signing off on as testifier, 245
   taking Abu Zubaydah into custody, 170–80
friction ridge arrangements, 195–999
friction ridges, 195–99
furrows, 195

G

Gaddafi, Muammar, 7–8
Geneva Conventions, 186
Ghailani, Ahmed Khalfan, trial of.
   See also Guantanamo Bay, 70–75, 245
Ghamdi, Saeed al-, 30
Ghannam, Jess, 248
   competency hearing preparation, 226–28
   conclusions of, 250–58
   defining as activist, 253–54
   direct line between political views and diagnoses, 256–58
   and hearing ruling, 259–61
   and internment camps, 254–55
   meeting with Spin Ghul, 228–30
   professional journey of, 225–26
   and Raed Jaser prosecution, 251–53
Gharbi Mangretay, village, 54
Gitmo. See Guantanamo Bay
Global War on Terror, 158
Go, Marilyn D., 184
Golden Hour, focus on, 99–100.
   See also ambush (on Firebase Shkin)
Gorka, Sebatian, 301

Graf, Victor Keith, 271
   describing ambush on Firebase Shkin, 273–76
   examining Spin Ghul case, 211–14
   recovering Jerod Dennis, 105–7
Graham, Lindsey, 73, 74
Grandi Navi Valoci, 8
Graziano, Tony, 271
Green, Kristen, 167–70
Green, Milton, 167–69
Green, Zachary, 167–69
Green Berets, 7
grenades, 11, 29, 35, 37, 54, 90, 94–95, 97, 121, 125, 168, 238, 274, 280, 291
Grimaldi Lines, 8
Guantánamo Bay, 2, 226, 299
   civilian lawyer at, 229, 234
   damage control regarding failure to convict Ghailani, 74–76
   describing as "legal equivalent of outer space," 65
   Guantanamo Review Task Force, 69
   Hodgson on commission for, 115–18
   ordering Warsame to, 139
   pledging to shut down, 67–70
   setting up detainee center at, 67
   transfer to New York City from, 70–73
Gulbuddin, Hizb-e-Islami, 49
Gulf of Aden, 139

H

Hage, Wadih El-, 149, 230, 242, 296
Haines, Avril, 74
Haleidi, Abu Zubair al-, 28
Hamdan, Salim Ahmed, 235
Hamdani, Alamdar S., 17, 154
   experiences of, 134–37
   United States of America versus John Doe, The, 184–86
   working with, 138–40
Hanson, John, 88

Harun, Ibrahim Adhan. *See* Spin Ghul
Harun, Ibrahim S., 199
Hasnat, Abu al-, 131, 173–74
Hassan Ghul. *See* Khan, Mustafa Hajji Muhammad
Haubner, Robert, 151
Headquarters and Headquarters Company (HHC), 125
Helms, Richard, 241–42
Henry Fingerprint Classification System, 196
Heymann, Philip, 242
HHC. *See* Headquarters and Headquarters Company
Hicks, David, 30
HIG. *See* Gulbuddin, Hizb-e-Islami
Hodge, Michael, 46, 61
Hodgson, Jim
  background of, 115–18
  presenting findings, 130
Holder, Eric, 72, 76, 133, 139, 148
Humvees, 87–91, 98–99, 104–5
Hussein, Saddam, 116–17
Hutus, 151–52
Huvelle, Ellen Judith, 152

I

Iljazi, Sussana, 244–45
Immigration and Naturalization Service, 255
indictment. *See* Spin Ghul
  evaluating, 152–54
  handing down, 154–55
  and Rwandan precedent, 150–52
  submitting, 147–50
International Criminal Court, 200
International Criminal Tribunal for Rwanda, 79
International Executive Committee of Al-Awda, 254
interviews
  difficulty of, 129–30
  with victim witnesses, 124–29

Iraqi, Abdul Hadi al-, 29, 31, 69, 83, 118, 299
  and credibility of Spin Ghul story, 32–38
Iraq War, 2–3
Irish Times, 84
Islamabad, Pakistan
  arresting Abu Zabaydah in, 170–80
  death of Greens in, 167–69
Islamabad, Pakistan. *See* Pakistan
Ismail, Somali interpreter, 9–11

J

Jabbar, Shamsud-Din, 300
Jacobs, Matt, 265, 279
  and "activist" definition, 253–54
  bringing up internment camps, 254–55
  dealing with foreign evidence, 222–24
  examining Spin Ghul case, 211–14
  flying to Nigeria, 215–16
  and hearing ruling, 259–61
  meeting with Dennis family, 231–33
  opening arguments, 268–69
  opening attack of, 251–53
  preparations, 250–51
  and sentencing of Spin Ghul, 288–90
  suggesting direct line between political views and diagnoses, 256–58
Jafar. *See* Sharifullah, Mohammad
Jaish-e-Muhammad (al Qaeda affiliate), 171
JAMA, 260
Jaser, Raed, 251–53
Jawad, Mohamed, 236
jihad, desire for
  collapse of USSR, 26–27
  joining al Qaeda, 27–28
  time at al Farouq training camp, 28–30
  tune at Maskar 9, 30–31

jihadists, 145, 153
Jihad of Annoyance. *See* Spin Ghul
Joint Readiness Training Center Army, 91
Joint Terrorism Task Force (JTTF), 15, 114, 130, 157, 162
Jolie, Angelina, 7–8
Jordan, 142
Journal of the American Medical Association, 255
JTTF. *See* Joint Terrorism Task Force
Junod, Tom, 300

K

Kabir, Abdul. *See* Williams, Kobie Diallo
Kaczynski, Ted, 295
Kalashnikov rifles, 29, 34–37
Kandahar Province, Afghanistan. *See* Slayers
Kaplan, Lewis A., 71
Kaster, Joe, 138, 148, 243, 265, 268–69
Kaziu, Betim, 185
Keenan, Jennifer, 179–80
  signing off on as testifier, 245
Keep America Safe, group, 72
Kellman, Susan
  at competency hearing, 250–58
  and lack of closing statement, 281–84
  meeting Spin Ghul, 184–86
  opening arguments, 268–69
  overview of, 181–84
  potential modern insanity defense for Spin Ghul, 200–206
  and proffer process, 187–92
  and Rae Jaser case, 252–53
  and sentencing of Spin Ghul, 288–90
Kelly, Ray, 72
Kent, Andy, 89, 93
Kerry, John, 254–5
Khadr, Omar Ahmed Said, 235–36

Khalid, Abu, 276
Khan, Mustafa Hajji Muhammad, 117–18
Khattala, Ahmed Abu, 193
Khaybar, Abu, 266
Kiriakou, John, 176–79
known fingerprints, 196
Kohlmann, Evan, 271–72
Korean War, 113
Korman, Edward R., 200–202, 204, 207, 210, 226
KSM. *See* Mohammed, Khalid Sheik
Kunstler, William, 182–83
Kurosawa, Akira, 273, 278
Kuwaiti, Khallad al-, 29

L

LaCroix, Bert, 115, 121, 123, 197
  arrest of Spin Ghul, 156–60
  finding fingerprint, 277
  forgetting Quran, 192–93
  and proffer process, 187–92
  speaking with Camacho, 126–28
  speaking with Drew Nathan, 161–63
  speaking with Dwane McKnight, 128–29, 163–66
  working with Hamdani, 138–40
Laden, Osama bin, 4, 27–28, 131, 142, 144, 172, 269
Lagos, Nigeria, 80, 130, 141–43, 158, 217, 278
Lahore, Pakistan, 123, 132, 142, 144, 172, 178–79, 217, 272
Lampedusa, Italy
  Angelina Jolie in, 7–8
  escalation in, 12–14
  involvement in Arab Spring, 6–7
  Spin Ghul in, 8–12
Landstuhl Regional Medical Center, 110, 124
Legal Aid Society, 184–86
legal attaché (LEGAT), 17, 169, 220, 224

LEGAT. *See* legal attaché
Leiris, Antoine, 285–88, 293
Leiris, Melvil, 285–88
Levin, Carl, 73
Libi, Abu Faraj al-, 29, 69
Libya, 6–7, 10–12, 24, 145, 191–92, 202, 211, 217
Lindh, John Walker, 30
Lonergan, Roger, 56
Losada, Bobby, 266
  and proffer process, 187–92
  seeing demonstrative madness, 193–94
Losano, Ray, 62, 87, 92, 94, 121, 122, 209, 239, 249, 281, 290, 302
  autopsy information of, 130
  death of, 103–4
  delivering justice to, 163–66
  meeting with family of, 232
  testimony about, 273–76
Lynch, Lorenzo, Jr., 122
Lynch, Loretta, 8, 122, 134, 212

M

Maersk Alabama, 114
Mahairas, Ari, 1–2, 80, 297
Mahir, liaison, 27–28
Main Justice, 138–40, 150, 208
malinger, term, 206
maneuver unit, 59
Manhattan Correctional Center (MCC), 182, 193
Maradone, connection, 144
Martins, Mark, 134, 149–50
Maskar 9 (camp), 30–31
Masri, Abu Hamza al-, 296
Masri, Khabab al-, 27
Mauritani, Abu Hafs al-, 141
MCC. *See* Manhattan Correctional Center
McCabe, Andrew, 266
McDonough, Denis, 74

McGuine, Barbara Jean, 167–70
McKnight, Dwayne. *See also* Slayers, 55, 92, 126, 271
  Muhammad and LaCroix speaking with, 129–29
  second examination of Quran of, 278
  speaking with about prosecution, 163–66
McVeigh, Timothy, 231–33, 295
Medical Center for Federal Prisoners, 226
Medicolegal Investigator Office, 121
Mena, John, 188
Meters, Matthew, 92
Military Commission Convening Authority, 237
military commissions, ruling on, 235
Military Intelligence Professional Bulletin, 119
military policemen (MPs), 87, 91
Miller, Marshall, 147–48, 150
Miller, Mel, 182
Miller, Susan, 151
Mills, Mark, 205–6, 256, 260
MLAT. *See* mutual legal assistance treaty
M'Naghten, Daniel, 203–5
modern insanity defense, 203–5
Mohajiri, Al-, 29
Mohammed, Khalid Sheik, 70
Monaco, Lisa, 73, 75, 148
  indictment evaluation, 152–54
  and indictment submission, 147–50
Morgese, Francesco, 6–8, 16, 216, 269
Morocco, 142
Mossouat al Jihad (Encyclopedias of Jihad), 142
motions, filing, 248–49. *See* Spin Ghul
Moussaoui, Zacarias, 296
MPs. *See* military policemen
Mueller, Christopher, 121
Muhammad, Noor, 131

324 INDEX

Muhammad, Raushaunah, 113–15, 123, 154
   arrest of Spin Ghul, 156–60
   confirming battle, 123–24
   and proffer process, 187–92
   and sentencing of Spin Ghul, 288–90
   speaking with Camacho, 126–28
   speaking with McKnight, 128–29
   working with Hamdani, 138–40
Muhammed, Noor Uthman, 131, 256
Mullaney, Mike, 138
Murphy, John, 139
Muslim Americans, 135, 255
Muslims, 2, 29, 82, 135–36, 142, 173, 218, 247, 257, 266
mutual legal assistance treaty (MLAT), 17, 222
Muyal-Leiris, Hélène, 285–87

N

Nader, Raph, 254
Nahan, Drew, 161–63
Nami, Ahmed al-, 30
Nardini, Bill, 15–16, 112
Nasr, Hassan Mustafa Osama. *See* Omar, Abu
Nathan, Drew, 50–51. *See also* Slayers
National Security Agency, 113
National Security Agency (NSA), 2, 244
Nelson, Jane. *See* Dennis, Jerod
Newman, David, 150
New York Times, 182
New York v. Quarles, 75
Nichols, Terry, 231–33, 296
Nickerson, Eugene, 182222
Niger, 12, 14, 24, 27, 65, 142–43, 189, 201, 210–11
Nigeria, 142
9/11 Commission, 149
Novak, Robert, 241–42
NSA. *See* National Security Agency

O

Obama, Barack, 2, 76, 81, 148, 154, 298
   differences between Bush and, 300–301
   and Ghailani transfer, 70–73
   indictment evaluation, 152–54
   planning to shut down Gitmo, 68–70
   policy changes ushered in by, 66–67
   running for president, 67–68
   vetoing $662 billion spending package, 133–34
Odeh, Mohammed Saddiq, 30
OGAs. *See* Other Government Agencies
Okafor, Chiedu, 253
Omar, Mullah, 144
O'Neill, Evan, 121
Operation Iraqi Freedom, 116
Operation Mongoose
   feeling like joke, 51–52
   flying to Adi Ghar Mountains, 49–50
   troops involved in, 48–49
Organized Crime and Gang section, DOJ, 216
Other Government Agencies (OGAs), 244
'Owhali, Mohamed Rashed Daoud al-, 30, 151

P

Paciorek, Greg, 19, 20, 22, 80, 211–12, 223, 268–69, 273, 279, 289
Pakistan. *See* ambush (on Firebase Shkin); Spin Ghul
Pakistan-Afghanistan border, attack on, 32–38. *See also* Firebase Shkin
Paktika Province, Afghanistan. *See* Firebase Shkin
Palermo, Sicily, 15–18, 216
Pealr Harbor, attack on, 119
Pearl, Daniel, 170
Petty, Nathan, 105–7
PIka. *See* PK light machine gun

Pizza Connection prosecution, 184
PK light machine gun (Pika), 29
pocket litter, DOMEX and, 131
political capital, obtaining, 130–32.
    See also Hodgson, Jim; Spin Ghul
political micromanagement, 133
Presentence Investigation Report, 289
Presidential Daily Brief, 171
Principals' Committee, 150
prisoners of war, minimal standard treatment of, 66–7
proffer process, Spin Ghul and, 187–92
Protestant International Church, 168, 170

Q

Qin Dynasty, 195
Quantico, 192–93, 197
Quaran, 164–66
Quarles, Benjamin, 75
Quran, 129, 142, 192, 281, 298
    Bagley examining, 197–99
    presenting at trial, 277
    searching for copy of, 201–2
    second examination on, 278

R

Rabia, Hamza
    communicating with Spin Ghul, 245–48
    working with Spin Ghul, 142–46, 217, 218, 245
racial profiling, 135
Rafah, Gaza, 254
Raiders of the Lost Ark (film), 118
Ramses the Fifth. *See also* credibility, debating; Spin Ghul
    reference to, 33–34, 38
    translating talk of, 82–85
Rashomon, 273
Ray, Jonathan, 45, 61, 87
Reed, Konrad, 59–61, 62, 90, 93, 97, 271, 281

rehearsal of concept (ROC), 156
Reid, Richard, 170
Reimann, Christopher, 272–73
    arriving in Pakistan, 169
    signing off on as testifier, 245
    taking Abu Zubaydah into custody, 170–80
Ressam, Ahmed, 171, 296
Roberts, 17–18
ROC. *See* rehearsal of concept
Rosado, Ivan, 211, 223
Rosi, Riccardo, 269–70
Ross, John, 265
    and proffer process, 187–92
    seeing demonstrative madness, 193–94
Rudolph, Eric, 296
Rumsfeld, Donald, 83, 124
Rwandan precedent, George Toscas and, 150–52

S

Sacconi, Maurizio, 112–13
Saipov, Sayfullo, 296
Salafis Group for Combat and Preaching, 221
Salafist Group for Prayer and Combat, 143, 144
Salman, Abdul Rehman Hussain, 131
SAM-7, missile, 34
Sand, Leonard, 150
San Francisco Chronicle, 295–96
Saudi Arabia, 16, 21, 24, 26–27, 142, 152, 155, 171, 190, 210, 244, 273, 282, 288
Schmidt, Sam, 228
Schumer, Chuck, 72–73
Second Chechen War, 26
Secrets of the Medellín Cartel (Unanue), 188
Securities and Exchange Commission, 208
Senate Armed Services Committee, 73

326 INDEX

September 11, 2001, 2, 28, 67
Setzer, John, 89, 93, 98–99, 101–2, 104–5, 108, 110, 121, 275
Severino, Brian, 50, 57, 163, 271, 273, 276–78, 290–91, 300
   during Firebase Shkin ambush, 99–100, 105, 107–8
   and failed urinalysis results, 46
   in McKnight memory, 16364
   photograph of, 127–28
   speaking against Spin Ghul, 290–92
Shabaab, al-, 79, 138–39
Sha'ban, Basim, 145–46
Shafiq, Haji Farooq Abu Hamza, 131
Shahzad, Faisal, 296
Sharia, Ansar al-, 192–93
Sharifullah, Mohammad, 301
Shehri, Wail al-, 30
Shehri, Waleed al-, 30
Shkin, village. *See* ambush (on Firebase Shkin)
Silence of the Lambs (film), 194
Simmons, David "Doc," 50–51. *See also* Slayers
Simmons, Doc, 50–51, 89, 93–96, 98–100, 103–4, 110, 271. 276
Slayers. *See also* ambush (on Firebase Shkin)
   and building bombing fiasco, 59–64
   flying to Adi Ghar Mountains, 49–50
   joining, 48–49
   moving up to Firebase Shkin, 52–55
   Operation Mongoose feeling like joke, 51–52
Smith, Martha, 41
Smith, Sean, 192
South Asian Bar Association, 137
Soviet Union (USSR), 25–26
Specialist Ray. *See* Ray, Jonathan
Spin Ghul, 113, 122, 180
   aftermath of trial of, 295–302
   Agrigento, Italy, trial of, 15–25
   arrest of, 156–60
   assessing role in Al Qaeda web, 272
   beginning of Brooklyn trial of, 243–44
   Bitkower departing case of, 207–9
   building case against, 77–85, 123–32
   charges against, 280–81
   closing arguments for trial of, 270–73
   and combatant immunity, 237–40
   communicating with Hamza Rabia, 245–48
   debating credibility of story of, 32–38
   defending, 248–49
   demonstrative madness of, 193–94
   describing ambush on Firebase Shkin, 273–76
   desire for jihad, 26–31
   end of cooperation with, 187–92
   evaluating indictment against, 152–54
   evaluating psychology for, 225–30
   examining fingerprints of, 195–99
   final verdict against, 283–84
   finding defendant for, 181–86
   forming new team for working on case of, 112–22
   hearing on competency of, 250–58
   Hodgson investigating, 119–21
   Hodgson path to team investigating, 115–18
   Hodgson presenting findings on, 130–32
   imprisonment of, 295–96
   Italian authorities holding in custody, 1–5
   lack of closing statement in trial of, 281–84
   in Lampedusa, Italy, 8–12
   last day as free man, 141–46
   meeting Dennis family regarding, 231–33
   playing catch-up regarding, 6–14
   plot to replicate US embassy bombings, 278–79

potential modern insanity defense for, 200–206
ruling on competency of, 259–61
and Rwandan precedent, 150–52
second questioning, 82–85
sentencing, 288–94
submitting indictment against, 147–55
Star Wars: A New Hope, 223
Stern, David, 201, 225, 228, 257, 281
   opening arguments, 268–69
   overview of, 184–86
   and Rae Jaser case, 252–53
   and sentencing of Spin Ghul, 288–90
Stevens, J. Christopher, 192
Suleiman, Abid, 27
Suleiman, Mohammed Ashafa, 143
Suri, Abdul Bara al-, 29
Survivor Tree, 232

T

tactical operations center (TOC), 62, 86–87, 278. *See also* ambush (on Firebase Shkin)
tactical site exploitation (TSE), 110–11
Taif City, Saudi Arabia. *See* jihad, desire for
Tamim, Abu, 23, 131, 277.
   See also Spin Ghul
Task Force Panther, 54
Tatro, Daniel, 53
tea, memories triggered by, 191–92
Tenet, George, 152, 177
10th Mountain Division, 164
terrorism prosecution. *See* Spin Ghul; trial (of Spin Ghul)
Terrorist Analysis Group, 197
Thapar, Amul, 137
3rd Platoon, 48–50, 54–55, 87.
   See also Slayers
Thorne, David Hoadley, 150
Tombstone, 62–63, 90–92
Torbet, James, 92

Torture Papers: The Legal Road to Abu Ghraib, The (Dratel), 229
Toscas, George, 138, 148, 267
   and Rwandan precedent, 150–52
Trahan, Gregory "Scott," 46, 51, 53, 61, 84, 281
   at Firebase Shkin ambush, 86–90
   life after battle, 124–25
Transcorp Hilton, 218
trial (of Spin Ghul)
   aftermath of, 295–302
   closing arguments, 270–73
   competency hearing, 251–58
   describing ambush on Firebase Shkin, 273–76
   discussing charges, 280–81
   final verdict, 283–84
   Government Exhibit 280, 276–77
   Government Exhibit 17T, 269
   lack of closing statement, 281–84
   last pieces of case, 278–79
   opening arguments, 268–69
   sentencing, 288–94
   setting stage for, 261–62
   stakes of, 263–64
   start of, 265–67
   storytelling tradition in, 262–63
   trimming fat, 270
   witnesses at, 269–70
trials, reality of, 209–10
true mental illness, diagnosing, 203–4
Trump, Donald, 266–67
Tsarnaev, Dzhokhar, 296
TSE. *See* tactical site exploitation

U

Unanue, Manuel de Dios, 188
United States, 23–24, 71, 74, 133, 184, 201–2, 255, 260, 280, 290
   consistency with interests of, 68
   establishing Combined Document Exploitation Center, 119–20
   Obama giving speech in Cairo, 2

United States (cont.)
   Spin Ghul trial in. *See* trial
     (of Spin Ghul)
United States of America versus John Doe, The, 184–86
University of Houston Law School, 134
University of Texas–Austin, 134
Urduni, Hamza al-, 34–35
US Army Criminal Investigation Division, 271
US Campaign for the Academic and Cultural Boycott of Israel, 254
US embassy, deaths in, 167–69
US Justice Department, 15, 17, 20, 67, 78, 137–38, 208, 216, 243
USS *Boxer*, 139
USS *Cole*, 29, 280
USS *Mertz*, 165
USSR. *See* Soviet Union

V

Valentino, Pellegrini, 13
victim witnesses, 124–28.
    See also Camacho, Eddi; Trahan, Gregory "Scott"
Vietnam War, 119–20
Violent Crimes and Terrorism Section, Eastern District, 1
"Volume of Crime Scene Investigation—Burglary, The," 195

W

Walid, Abu, 131–32, 276–77
Wall Street Journal, 170
Walter Reed National Military Medical Center, 124–26
War Crimes Investigation Team, Army CID, 116
Warsame, Ahmed Abdulkadir, 139
wasiyya, leaving behind, 29
Waziristan, Pakistan, 31, 34, 38, 52, 63, 66, 84, 114, 117, 123, 132, 142, 256, 272

Weinstein, Jason, 208
Wells, Melody, 265, 279
   on day of closing arguments, 270–73
   dealing with foreign evidence, 222–24
   discussing charges, 280–81
   examining Spin Ghul case, 211–14
   flying to Nigeria, 215–16
   meeting with Dennis family, 231–33
   opening arguments, 268–69
   presenting latent prints, 276–78
   and storytelling, 262–63
West Africa team. *See* Iljazi, Sussana; LaCroix, Bert; Muhammad, Raushaunah
West Africa team (FBI), 9, 11, 114, 123, 144, 192, 247, 269
Williams, Kobie Diallo, 136–37
Wolfe, Tom, 22
Woods, Tyrone, 192
World War II, 119
Wormsley, Bruce, 167–69

X

Xanax, 204

Y

Yahoo!, 143
Yemen, 142
Yemeni, Abdul Fida al-, 28
Yemeni, Usaid al-, 28
Yousef, Ramzi, 296
You Will Not Have My Hate (Leiris), 286–87

Z

Zammuto, Stefano, 15
Zaria Road, Kano, verifying details on, 278–79
Zawahiri, Ayman al-, 4
Zazi, Najibullah, 138
Zubaydah, Abu, 152–53
   prelude to arrest of, 167–69
   taking into custody, 170–80